THE BOOK OF UMBANDA

THE GRAND COMPENDIUM

Copyright© 2024 by David Barreto
All rights reserved.

THE BOOK OF
UMBANDA

THE GRAND
COMPENDIUM

First edition: New York, 2024

ISBN 978-1-9162111-1-7

Cover and design by David Barreto

www.davidbarreto.net

No part of this book may be reproduced or used in any form or by any means, including electronic or mechanical methods such as photocopying, recording, or as a downloadable file, without the prior written permission of the author.

Table of Contents

Preface..viii

Introduction...12

Spiritualism and Spiritism.......................................16

The Foundation of Umbanda...................................28

Principles and Philosophies.....................................40
Spiritual Progress: Cause and Effect, and Reincarnation............42

Branches of Umbanda..46
Outside the Umbanda Umbrella....................................55

God and the Pantheon..60
West African Mythology: The Creation.........................65
From Yorubaland to The New World............................69
Orishas According to Umbanda....................................72
Head-Orisha..78
Worship and Cult..84

Orishas: Attributes and Stories...............................88
Oshala...89
Logunan..95
Oshun..97
Oshumare..102
Oshossi..107
Oba..111
Shango...114
Egunita..120

Ogun	124
Yansa	129
Obaluaye	134
Nana	141
Yemanja	146
Omulu	152
Ibeji	156
Logunede	160
Ossain	166
Eshu	170
Other Orishas	176

Classes of Spirits....................................178
The Two Polarities	180
Class and Phalanx	182
Old Blacks	185
Mestizos	187
Children	189
Auxiliary Classes	192
Eshus and Pombagiras	192
Bohemians	199
Sailors	201
Witches	203
Gypsies	205
Orient	209
Cowboys	211
Legions and Peoples	213

Obsessors, Dragons, and Cocoons..............218

The Temple's Layout and its Tools................222
The Altar	222
Tools of Umbanda	224
Cigar, Cigarettes, and Pipes	225
Beverages and Alcohol	226
Candles	227
Herbal Baths and Smudging	228
Bead Necklace	230
Crystals and Sacred Stones	231
Ritual Chalk and Sketched Points	233
Occasional Items	235

Mediumship and Channeling..................................**236**
The Medium's Spiritual Guide...238

Chants..**240**

The Services..**244**
Festivities...247

Offerings...**248**

Glossary..**256**

Bibliography...**261**
Further Readings..264

Credits...**265**

Preface

This work encompasses both the official history and the underlying factors that have shaped Umbanda into the religion it represents. Conducted as a comprehensive investigation, the research involves the author's personal participation in services and an extensive review of the most esteemed literature in the field. Therefore, this compendium is positioned as an authentic, credible, albeit impartial resource regarding Umbanda. Meticulously, this work examines both the visible proceedings in the temples and those known exclusively to the mediums engaged in the rituals. Over the course of many years, if not decades, the author has diligently compiled information and organized it in a manner that allows readers to experience the postulated historical narrative as if they had physically witnessed the events or actively participated in a religious service.

Within this compendium, the author delves into Umbanda as a rich tapestry of spirituality, philosophy, and esotericism. Characterized by both spiritual and mystical elements, as well as scientific and pragmatic aspects, this New World religion reflects a modern interpretation of "religare," prioritizing simplicity over complexity and humility over exaggerated intellectualism.

Within this compendium, the majority of terms, including names of entities and intricately characterized nomenclatures rooted in Umbanda, have been translated into English. The translations provided in this work adhere to precise and apt analogies, even though some words may have originated from slang, dead languages, or unknown sources. Despite this work being research-based, Umbanda, as a religion, will not be confined hereupon to perpetually being labeled a "Brazilian religion" but is simply a modern religion, and hence translated core terms are to be common.

The terminology employed in this reference work reflects the traditional and contemporaneous reality of Umbanda in Brazil. While some terms and names may sound archaic, prejudiced, or offensive to an unprepared reader, it is crucial to emphasize that the followers, as well as all spirits working in Umbanda, presenting themselves through mediumistic channeling, autonomously chose their names. For instance, 'Old Black' is how wise spirits, predominantly enslaved in their past lives, identify themselves. This nomenclature is not indicative of them believing they are old or black; rather, this attire allows them to present an extremely humble archetype, with no intention of appearing powerful or important, despite being the religion's most sublime and evolved spirits. Overall, this work aims to provide English-speaking readers with the true translation of the term, one that makes sense and does not always refer to something intrinsically local to any region. When a religion is introduced into academic fields, it often appears to remain exclusively local, as if it is an eternal fragment of a specific culture or as owned solely by a particular ethnicity. This cannot be sustained in the case of Umbanda, as it draws from European, African, and South American sources equally.

Umbanda not only represents a blend of European, Amerindian, and African cults and beliefs but also serves as a platform for spirits presenting themselves as an array of nationalities, each conveying their unique messages. The deities, as observed in Umbanda, do not adhere to a specific religion and should not be understood as the property of a particular region or a specific group of people. Consequently, this compendium treats Umbanda and all its roots as originating from planet Earth, transcending geographical limitations tied to Europe, Africa, or Brazil.

Throughout the 20th century, Umbanda was unjustly labeled as pagan and often associated with a Satanic cult. Although this unfounded concept has more recently dissipated amidst the waning prejudices of Brazil's Christian orthodoxy, Umbanda remains largely unfamiliar to the global populace, particularly to students of universalist, spiritualist, or esoteric schools outside of Brazil and its sphere of influence. Therefore, the arrangement of this volume endeavors to unveil the history, practices, and secret understandings of Umbanda to the rest of the world, with a particular focus on the English-speaking audience. By doing so, it aspires to establish this modern religion as an essential read for those seeking universalist knowledge.

The principal aim of this work is to function as a comprehensive reference for scholars and students. However, the content is designed to be equally accessible and advantageous for individuals with an interest in spiritualist or esoteric studies.

Thus, the reader is invited to immerse themselves in what is undeniably the most comprehensive work on Umbanda in the English language.

In essence, this compendium seeks not only to present Umbanda from the perspective of academically or researched universalist niches but also serves as a foundational work intended to disseminate the cult, should the reader opt to incorporate Umbanda into their faith.

Introduction

Officially established in 1908, Umbanda finds its origins in various cults of earlier centuries. It is an amalgamation of European Spiritism and Catholicism, native Brazilian shamanism, and slave circles, along with minor influences from modern paganism, Hindu practices, and Buddhist teachings, distinguishing Umbanda as, quite possibly, the world's most diverse and inclusive religion.

The rise of Umbanda aligns with a universal pattern observed in the emergence of religions worldwide: guiding and regenerating local populations burdened with significant karmic debts. While not asserting superiority over materialistic sciences, Umbanda recognizes the need for religion to assist certain spirits, upon becoming religious on Earth, to endeavor in the fields of faith and belief, as there are valuable lessons to be learned in those areas. In other cases, religion would serve some spirits in comprehending universal laws before they are introduced to complex scientific and philosophical concepts, which remain elusive to many populations based on their stages of consciousness.

Spiritual progress, as understood in spiritualist, theosophic, hermetic, yogic, and Umbandist philosophy, emphasizes the continuous evolution of the spirit through Earthly reincarnations. Within this framework, religion would play a pivotal role in preparing spirits at their specific levels of consciousness, providing a foundation where universalist understandings and holistic sciences may appear less tangible than the mythologies embraced by these spirits.

Religions and cults born in different parts of the world, including India, the Middle East, China, and Brazil (in the case of Umbanda), serve as catalysts for local populations in need of spiritual guidance.

Despite debates over the potential harm of certain religions, seldom does a religion emerge in countries where populations do not require profound lessons in the fields of faith or belief. Such countries are viewed as "hospital nations," where religion plays a role akin to first aid, presenting itself as a solution that arises in proximity to the problem.

Within this context, it is believed that Brazil carries the weight of numerous karmic wounds, primarily stemming from its history of slavery. Numerous individuals who experienced enslavement were later reincarnated as white individuals, while others preferred to seek retribution against past oppressors from beyond. Additionally, spirits from other parts of the world saw the era of slavery as an opportunity to emancipate themselves from roles as slave owners, malicious merchants, and exploitative criminals.

It is also believed that most individuals associated with the Inquisition in Europe were born in Brazil, seeking redemption within the realm of religion and faith after having committed deceptive wrongs in that field. Furthermore, it is said that thousands discovered an affinity within this context, leading them to be born among groups of mediums working in Umbanda and Spiritism.

In the context of karma over a specific country, it is more adequate to group those individuals and not the land where the karma was created. This means that if countless karmic accounts were produced in Russia, it is possible that the population bearing akin karmic debts may reincarnate together, to expiate their karma together, regardless of the locations where they undergo such a scheme. Therefore, thousands of individuals who created karma in Russia, for example, may reincarnate as a group in America. Thus, the karma does not belong to Russia but to those individuals who were temporarily allocated in Russia and are now in American land.

Umbanda's teachings are heavily based on spiritual channeling, meaning that the tenets are passed from spirits to medium individuals. Along these lines, and according to certain spirits who have conveyed their messages through spiritual channeling, one of the primary purposes for the establishment of Umbanda was to counteract practices associated with lower magic and vengeance. The religion aimed to address individuals who, in their past lives, employed magic for malevolent purposes or were still seeking revenge from the spiritual planes.

Brazil accounts for the highest number of Spiritism followers in the world, despite the origin of Spiritism being in France. Xavier (1938) conveys in a psychographic work that the 'evangelist tree' was passed from France, where Spiritism was supposed to have flourished, to Brazil. This phenomenon is attributed to a spiritual exchange, where the debtor spirits of France began reincarnating in Brazil, contributing to the alleviation of France's collective karma so that the European nation could fulfill its purposes in the fields of politics, arts, and science. In turn, Brazil assumed the main roles of a nation-hospital with Spiritism, and later Umbanda. In such a context, spiritual entities, particularly the spiritual guides of each nation, transcend geopolitical boundaries, recognizing humans not as French, Brazilian, or Japanese individuals but as incarnate beings in need of assistance, thus guiding them where physical life would best be served.

As the world advances, a lesser number of religions are expected to emerge, paving the way for a world society where all aligns with science founded on moral principles, altruism, and the acknowledgment that everyone is a spiritual entity. Umbanda, primarily born to assist spirits in shedding arrogance and selfishness, stands as a simple and humble school guiding these spirits toward an understanding of these principles, which were initially introduced by Spiritism.

The emergence of Spiritism, in the mid-1850s, has undeniably been one of the main factors for Umbanda to be officially founded half a century later. Spiritism shares numerous similarities with Umbanda, from rooted beliefs to the essence of the services, where spiritual channeling, energetic cleansing, and spiritual healings are performed.

As Spiritism found fertile ground to flourish in Brazil, the former slave circles, where ritualistic music and trance were observed, further gave Umbanda its nature. Several of these circles, prior to the emergence of Umbanda as it is, displayed the cult of Orishas—the archetypal manifestations of God on Earth—the cult of spirits, including that of ancestors, and other ritualistic traits such as Offerings, which are prevalent in religions all around the world, play a crucial role in Umbanda. The Orishas, an extremely important part of Umbanda, gained notoriety for the nature Umbanda adopted, shaped by Spiritism into a precise and organized system of beliefs.

The cult of Orishas, as observed in the slave circles or even those of Yorubaland in West Africa, served to influence Umbanda in its primitive days (albeit those circles typically lacked the hierarchical association of spiritual workers and element-based division seen later on in Umbanda).

Notably, Umbanda drew significant influences from native Brazilian shamanism, where these teachings were primarily transmitted through the spirits who channeled and passed on their knowledge.

Drawing from the wellsprings of numerous cultures, Umbanda is portrayed as a ritualistic religion. As an urban form of spirituality—dramatically reflected in the spirits that manifest—it coexists and often blends alongside Spiritism, pagan, new age, and even Catholic circles in Brazil's major cities. This phenomenon mirrors the contemporary tolerance, acceptance, and interest that society holds towards diverse faiths. However, the apparent mysticism depicted in Umbanda, encompassing ritual regalia, objects, and dramatization of spiritual channeling sessions, is deeply rooted in pragmatic reasons, to be fully explored in the forthcoming chapters.

Spiritualism and Spiritism

Umbanda is a religion that originated in Brazil during the early 20th century, incorporating diverse cultural and religious influences such as European, African, and Indigenous traditions. Its primary foundation, however, is rooted in Spiritism, a movement that emerged in France during the 19th century. To gain a comprehensive understanding of the history and evolution of Umbanda, it is essential to explore the historical context and beliefs of Spiritism, which played a pivotal role in forming the base for Umbanda. Spiritism, considered a philosophical and spiritual doctrine, has provided Umbanda with the essential elements to thrive; the origins of Spiritism, however, can be traced back to a school of thought known as Spiritualism.

At the core of Spiritualism is the belief that one's consciousness survives physical death and that communication between different planes is possible. These beliefs led Spiritualists to a third conviction: that spirits can provide valuable knowledge about ethical and moral issues, as well as insights into the nature of God, creation, and the afterlife. The afterlife and the so-called "spirit world", however, may often be poorly described among Spiritualists due to the lack of canonical texts or formal organization.

As spirits and the living can communicate, it is natural that mediumship is not only broadly accepted in the movement but also exercised in every spiritualist temple. Paranormal abilities and other supernatural phenomena are typically subjects of interest too. Most Spiritualists also refer to the notion of spirit guides, which refers to specific spirits commonly contacted for guidance.

Spiritualist concepts were initially introduced during the 1840s. However, it was not until the late 1880s that these ideas evolved into a well-established movement grounded in the belief of life after death, communication with spirits, reincarnation, and the existence of a higher power commonly referred to as God. The origins of Spiritualism can be traced back to the events of 1848, when the Fox sisters made claims of contacting the spirit of a murdered peddler who had been allegedly buried beneath their home (Weisberg, 2005). The domicile in question, located in Hydesville, New York, has since become the site of a significant historical event. The Foxes, comprised of John Fox, his wife Margaret, and their three daughters, Margaretta, Catherine, and Leah, found themselves residing in the aforementioned abode while their farm was under construction. According to the family, shortly after moving in, they began hearing inexplicable noises such as footsteps and knocking sounds. Despite John Fox's attempts to uncover the source of the commotion, he could not find any rational explanation. On March 31st, Catherine Fox noticed that a knocking sound was responding to her father's knocks. Intrigued, she initiated communication with the unseen spirit. After successfully requesting the spirit to clap twice and hearing it respond from within a wall, Margaretta Fox began to ask specific questions, to which the spirit provided accurate answers. Via the rapping sounds, the supposed spirit had also claimed to be called Charles Rosna. The phenomenon amazed the family and spurred them to invite skeptical neighbors to observe the events. According to the narrative, the neighbors witnessed the spirit accurately answering their questions, and the news of the remarkable incident quickly spread. Years later, as indicated by Doyle (1926), neighbors dug up the cellar and indeed found bones, despite the fact that no evidence of the existence of Charles Rosna has ever been found.

It is noteworthy that prior to the arrival of the Fox family, the previous owners of the Hydesville house, the Weekmans, also claimed they had been terrorized by the spooky sounds (Cadwallader, 1917), as their maid, Jane Lape, stated that she had actually seen the apparition of a man in the house. Prior to the Weekmans, Mr. and Mrs. Bell were the owners, and, according to their housekeeper, Lucretia Pulver, they had indeed accommodated a traveling salesman between the years 1833 and 1844 that resembled the man of Jane's description. Nevertheless, factual evidence of such a peddler residing in the house was never made known.

Image 1: The Fox sisters, 1884

This purported encounter with the spirit world drew the attention of the Fox sisters' neighbors, as more and more people would witness the occurrences. Thus, the girls' reputation rapidly spread, and they started holding public appearances in the theaters to demonstrate the conversations with spirits, where the spirits would allegedly knock and make other noises to communicate. The sisters became celebrity mediums in New York, but they were also popular in neighboring areas. Despite their notoriety, numerous people have regarded the Fox sisters' claims with skepticism. In fact, some historians have suggested that the story was simply a fabrication created to attract attention and gain fame. It is also likely that the older sister, Leah Fox, demanded the younger girls portray séances under her tutelage, as she was probably interested in promulgating an opportunistic movement (Stuart 2005). In the late 1880s, even Margaretta and Catherine Fox themselves confessed that the contact with the spirits was a hoax, whereby they publicly demonstrated their fraudulent knocking and rapping mechanisms (Davenport, 2013, originally published in 1888). However, they refuted their own claims shortly after, but their reputation was already discredited. All three sisters died in the early 1890s.

The Fox sisters' performances in various theaters across New York sparked a movement that sought to establish communication with spirits as a public activity. However, the growth of Spiritualism in the mid-19th century can also be attributed to various other social and cultural factors, including the emergence of women's rights, as discussed by Braude (2001), and the rise of groups with an interest in the occult and supernatural. As argued by Carroll (1997), the people in the region of New York had acquired a more lenient view of God compared to the beliefs of other parts of the United States. For instance, for those in the northeastern United States in the late 19th century, God would not condemn unbaptized infants to eternal damnation in Hell. Thus, this region appeared to be a fertile place for Spiritualism and its debates.

Despite the possibility that the Fox sisters may have engaged in fraudulent practices, their demonstrations generated such significant interest in the salons and theaters of New York that these spectacles eventually spread to Europe, particularly Paris. However, the communication practices in Paris progressed to focus on conversation around a table, while in America, the phenomenon remained centered on demonstrations of levitating tables and their noises. Notwithstanding, throughout the 19th century, Andrew Jackson Davis, a clairvoyant and author from Blooming Grove, New York, was one of the first Americans to introduce early spiritualist ideas to the country. According to purported accounts, Davis made prescient declarations in his publication "The Penetralia: Being Harmonial, Answers to Important Questions" in 1856, wherein he professedly foresaw the emergence of advancements and technological innovations through the aid of clairvoyance. The ideas and practices of Davis exhibited similarities to the theories espoused by Franz Mesmer in the late 18th century, who believed in animal magnetism—a force that flowed through all living beings and could be manipulated to cure illness and induce trance-like states. Davis also found inspiration in the works of Emmanuel Swedenborg, a Swedish scientist and theologian who claimed to have had spiritual experiences that allowed him to communicate with angels and the spirits of the dead. Swedenborg's 1758 book, "Heaven and Hell," presented testimonies of his experiences and provided explanations of the nature of different heavens and hells, as well as other information related to the spiritual realm. Davis later developed a belief system called the "Harmonial Philosophy," which is based on the idea that all things in the universe are interconnected and that there is a fundamental unity underlying all existence. This philosophy draws on various esoteric traditions and emphasizes practices such as meditation, self-improvement, mesmerism, faith healing, and clairvoyance. In 1847, he dictated a book called "The Principles of Nature, Her Divine Revelations, and a Voice to Mankind" while in a trance state, where he claimed Swedenborg spoke to him, conveying information in anticipation of the rise of Spiritualism. He further predicted that society as a whole would eagerly welcome the era in which the innermost thoughts of individuals would be revealed and spiritual interaction would be initiated. Subsequently, Davis believed that his forecast was realized a year later when the Fox sisters claimed to have communicated with a spirit in their house. The aforementioned book became a seminal work of reference in the imminent Spiritualist movement.

After learning about the events in Rochester, Davis extended an invitation to the Fox sisters to come to his residence in New York City to demonstrate their mediumistic abilities. Supposedly, a collaboration with the sisters and their spectral manifestations would significantly enhance his reputation, elevating him from a relatively unknown prophet to a prominent figurehead within the burgeoning Spiritualist movement. The sisters and Davis embarked on regional tours together. As the curiosity for the claimed phenomena grew, so did the interest of those willing to experience a religious reform, whereas Spiritualism would offer them more control over their own destinies, which was the opposite idea of predestination offered by Calvinism.

The partnership between the Fox sisters and Andrew Jackson Davis eventually ended on a sour note after their confessions of fraud. Nevertheless, Davis continued to defend the legitimacy of his own spiritual experiences and philosophical beliefs, while distancing himself from the sisters and their debunked claims.

Image 2: Table turning in a Parisian salon, 1853

In the latter half of the 19th century, the popularity of séances and tours conducted by mediums was widespread. The salons of Paris and London were especially sought-after venues for displaying the alleged supernatural phenomena, including the levitation of tables and communication with spirits. In Britain, by 1853, invitations to tea among the prosperous and fashionable often included table-turning. Notable members of the club included Charles Dickens and William Crookes (Brock, 2008). As Spiritualism gained momentum there, the Ghost Club was established in London in 1862 with the primary objective of discussing the existence of ghosts and purported paranormal activities. A significant number of scientists who explored the phenomenon of spiritualism were receptive to its tenets, such as esteemed evolutionary biologist Alfred Russel Wallace and physicist Oliver Lodge. Nobel laureate Pierre Curie was also a proponent of spiritualism, while his wife Marie Curie held a more skeptical view. In the United States, the renowned New York City physician John Franklin Gray was also a prominent spiritualist.

Although Spiritualism gained momentum in various parts of the world, its lack of clear texts or structures made it vulnerable to exploitation by charlatans. Regrettably, throughout history, there have been instances where individuals pretending to be magicians or mediums have staged fake séances to gain fame and fortune. To investigate claims related to communication with spirits and expose fraudulent practices, the Society for Psychical Research was established in London in 1882. Professional magicians such as John Nevil Maskelyne were also instrumental in revealing the tricks employed by fraudulent mediums. Despite these efforts, séances remained popular, continuing to draw large crowds, with spirits purportedly providing insight on a range of topics. However, these practices faced criticism from some religious authorities, who categorized them as potentially influenced by demonic forces, further raising concerns about their validity.

While the popularity of Spiritualism dwindled in America and Britain due to a lack of clear structure and foundational principles, it continued to thrive in France. In fact, it was in Paris that the first systematic body of study and texts on communicating with spirits were established, leading to the development of a consistent philosophical doctrine behind the séance frenzy. The doctrine was formulated by Allan Kardec, who was initially skeptical of the movement but later became one of its strongest advocates.

Allan Kardec (1804–1869), whose real name was Hippolyte Léon Denizard Rivail, came from a family with a Catholic-oriented background in the legal and advocacy fields. His interest in science and philosophy led him to study at the School of Pestalozzi in Switzerland, where he became one of the most distinguished disciples of Pestalozzi's method, which had a significant impact on education reform in France and Germany. Rivail began teaching his peers at the age of fourteen and had graduated in science and literature by the age of eighteen. Upon returning to France, he published in 1828 a plan for the improvement of public education in Paris (Rivail, 1828), became a member of the Royal Academy of Natural Sciences, and authored several works on education. As a pedagogue, Rivail fought for greater democratization of public education and offered free courses in various subjects, including chemistry, physics, comparative anatomy, and astronomy, between 1835 and 1840. He also wrote a manual on arithmetic during this time, and his expertise included teaching chemistry, mathematics, physics, physiology, rhetoric, and French.

Rivail was a member of several academic societies, including the Historical Institute of Paris and the Royal Academy of Arras, which awarded him a prize in 1831 for his essay on the system of studies that aligned with the needs of the time. In 1832, he married Amélie Gabrielle Boudet. Later, he translated various works on education and morals, particularly those of François Fénelon, into German. He was also proficient in English, Dutch, Italian, and Spanish (Duncan, 1987).

Rivail initially learned about the phenomenon of "turning-tables" through a friend who was a magnetizer and follower of Franz Mesmer. Before witnessing the alleged séances in person, Rivail attributed the movement of tables to so-called animal magnetism, with which he was familiar. According to Vartier (1971), Rivail's curiosity was piqued in May 1855 when he began attending séances and witnessing real-time communication with spirits. During these séances, spirits would answer questions mostly through taps or by pointing in the direction of letters to spell out words (Cuchet, 2012). The answers provided by the alleged spirits were convincing, which led Rivail to question Michael Faraday's theory of ideomotor phenomena, where unconscious muscular reactions reflect as a response to suggestions and are the supposed cause of answers given over a table (Faraday, 1853).

Intrigued by the mysterious movements and sounds of tables, Rivail started investigating another, even more intriguing phenomenon: the writing baskets. A pencil inserted into the bottom of a basket, with the tip facing downward, "answered" questions posed by guests on sheets of paper. In one of these sessions, in 1856, the basket turned towards Rivail, as the pencil wrote an enigmatic message: "You are the worker who rebuilds what was demolished" (Maior 2013). This was a cue for Rivail to begin organizing what would become The Spirits' Book. During this period, he also became aware of meetings where spirits would write through mediums, a phenomenon called psychography. After noticing strong grounds for knowledge in those answers, Rivail became convinced that the responses from the tables were due to the intervention of the supposed spirits, leading the educator to devote his life to the study of the intelligent principles behind séance phenomena.

Subsequently, Rivail endeavored to formulate the first book that attempted to bring philosophical and scientific grounds to the existence of spirits and their empirical works on the séances. He requested and cataged several answers from private séances where he would ask the same questions to different spirits channeled by different mediums. These séances were carried out via channeling and psychograhy, not by tables and its mechanical noises. While collecting the answers, Rivail observed that the spirits would answer questions in the language they were asked and would each have a particular and unique handwriting. He noticed that the rates of similarity of answers were remarkably high on questions that would cover topics such as God, life after death, the creation of the universe, reincarnation, the constitution of spirits, moral principles, the past, present, and future of humanity, mediumship, and so on.

Caroline and Julie Boudin, along with Ermmance Defaux, were the primary mediums for Rivial's work. During this time, the pen name "Allan Kardec" was chosen because an entity channeled by the sisters revealed that this was Hippolyte's name when they lived together in a past life among Celtic druids in what is now France.

On a certain day, Kardec's "familiar spirit" informed him through the girls that there was something wrong on the 33rd line of the chapter he had written the night before. Kardec immediately checked it, and he had no doubts that the familiar spirit was mentoring and guiding his work, which was being analyzed line by line by higher spirituality.

The answers from the Boudin sisters were compared to the responses of more than 10 other French mediums (Abadde, 2015), and Ruth Céline Japhet, also a medium, thoroughly reviewed the entire work. Kardec naturally revised the book as well and found no discrepancies or contradictions between the answers channeled by the girls and the responses from mediums in over 15 countries, which he had additionally requested. This left him thoroughly convinced about the veracity of the answers.

As a compiled work, meticulously arranged by the pedagogue mind of Kardec, The Spirits' Book consists of over a thousand questions heavily influenced by his scientific thinking, where its answers are remarkably complex and shaped by philosophy, something atypical for the spiritualist literature of those times. The book was published on April 18, 1857, at the Palais Royal in Paris and was the first in a series of five books edited by the educator on similar themes. In 1861, Kardec published The Book of Mediums, which expounds upon the practical implications of his earlier work. Subsequently, he augmented the spiritist doctrine by offering a novel interpretation of primitive Christianity, incorporating it with ethical and societal codes of morality. This culminated in the publications of The Gospel According to Spiritism (1864), Heaven and Hell (1865), and Genesis According to Spiritism (1868).

The Spirits' Book was the first official canonical literature on the phenomena of spirits that, for decades, had been an amalgamation of curiosity, mystery, and fraud among Spiritualists.

Spiritism appeared to have developed a strong foundation, something that Spiritualism lacked. In The Spirits' Books, Kardec coined the term "Spiritism," thus distancing it from Spiritualism and therefore founding a new doctrine based on the works of the spirits under the three concepts of religion, science, and philosophy.

The book enjoyed widespread success not only in France but also abroad. Riding on the wave of this success, Kardec founded the Parisian Society of Spiritist Studies in 1858. The same year also saw the launch of the Spiritist Magazine, which published quarterly. The speed at which Spiritism spread through society was remarkable, particularly for a doctrinal movement. As a result, Kardec realized that the growing number of mediums and heated debates could lead to chaos, and he embarked on journeys to unify followers in different provinces. As Aubrée (1990) explains, Kardec established small groups everywhere that were aimed at becoming "serious" spiritualist centers by excluding those who were merely attracted to sensationalism.

In 1862, spiritists in Lyon boasted a following of 30,000 individuals, and in that year, Kardec traveled to major French cities to disseminate his teachings. Apart from emphasizing universalist studies, the movement placed great importance on charity. With the growth of Spiritism, there was a shift towards social work and philanthropy, with the movement organizing relief funds and advocating for causes related to social justice. The Spiritist Magazine also supported women's suffrage, the abolition of slavery, the elimination of the death penalty, internationalism, and pacifism. Despite being criticized by detractors, Kardec tirelessly promoted his cause until his passing in 1869. By then, spiritualism had gained over half a million followers in France alone, with numerous Spiritist centers established in various European cities and beyond.

By the late 1800s, the movement began to slow down in France due to the Church's adoption of the cult of purgatory and the rise of neo-rationalism, and in 1917, the Vatican officially forbade Catholics from participating in spiritualist sessions (Lachapelle, 2011). The movement splintered into different currents, with some becoming more rationalist and evolving into parapsychology. The stagnation of Spiritism in France was also due to fraud, tensions with other movements, and rejection by the scientific community. Furthermore, Theosophy and its teachings gained popularity, leading some groups of students to favor it over Spiritism. On November 17, 1875, Helena Blavatsky founded the Theosophical Society in New York City and released Theosophy's first book, The Secret Doctrine, in 1888. By the early 1900s, Spiritism seemed to have flattened in Europe, but it continued to have an impact in other parts of the world, especially in Brazil.

Prior to the release of The Spirits' Book in Brazil, there was a select group interested in "animal magnetism," also known as "mesmerism." The study of mesmerism gained popularity, especially in Rio de Janeiro, the capital of the Empire, where wealthy scholars and some nobility eagerly financed research. Spiritualist séances, communication with spirits using spinning tables, and other forms of spiritualist manifestations were already somewhat popular before the establishment of Spiritism in Brazil. Although Spiritualism, as a social movement, did not gain ground in Brazil, these manifestations were already common in the 1840s and 1850s.

During the second half of the 1850s, while France was under the reign of Napoleon III, a significant number of French citizens sought asylum in Rio de Janeiro, bringing with them robust ideas of Spiritism in the form of books, magazines, and the concept of Spiritist séances. As asserted by Hessen (2016), the séances in Rio were conducted among a select group of French students. As a result, Spiritist sessions officially began to take place in the city.

While the Spiritist Magazine was already popular in various countries, such as France, Britain, and the USA, it became distinctly sensational in Brazil. In 1863, Allan Kardec commented that in Brazil, Spiritism was achieving notable popularity. *"We note with satisfaction that the spiritist idea is making significant progress in Rio de Janeiro, where it has numerous dedicated and devoted representatives."*

Image 3: Brazilian stamp depicting Kardec, 1957

In 1860, the first spiritist book was published in Brazil, and in 1873, the Spiritist Society of Studies Group Confucius was founded in Rio, becoming the nation's first official center for Spiritism studies. They translated all of Kardec's works into Portuguese and replicated his books for distribution. Consequently, many spiritist societies and temples were erected across the empire.

In 1877, a division occurred within the Spiritism movement in Rio, with one faction primarily focused on scientific Spiritism studies and the other more inclined toward esoteric Spiritism. Both groups comprised members of the elite or were affiliated with the royalty, enabling the new religion to gain ground without significant intervention from the church. Moreover, society appeared to be more receptive to these new ideas than what they initially faced in Western Europe and the US.

The Brazilian Federation of Spiritism was founded in 1884, establishing a notable presence in the country. With numerous spiritist centers across Brazil, Spiritism gained recognition among the majority of the population. In these spiritist centers, practices formerly known as "mesmerism" or "magnetism" persisted as characteristic healing support in meetings, now referred to as "passes." During these passes, healing energy is transmitted from the medium to the visitor with the assistance of a friendly spirit. In addition to passes, spiritist sessions involved readings around a table, channeled messages for those seeking aid, the study of Kardec's books and other spiritist literature, talks, and training in mediumship development, among other activities.

After Brazil became a republic in 1889, the country lacked a clear constitution, and the government associated the practice of Spiritism with fraudulent magic and pagan healing, leading to the repression of spiritist gatherings. However, as presidents changed, and respected academics lobbied for its freedom, Spiritism gained more acceptance from the state over time. By the end of the 19th century, several Spiritist magazines were distributed nationwide, and associations were formed in several capital cities. Despite still facing mild repudiation from the government and marginalization from the psychiatric community, Spiritism continued to gain popularity, and many doctors, scientists, and scholars converted to it. Although a small part of society still marginalized it, their opposition was unsuccessful as Spiritism became more widespread over the years. Around the turn of the century, Spiritist centers could be found in every city in Brazil, attended not only by those interested in the doctrine but also by the general population seeking answers and support where they could not find it from doctors or churches. With the increasing acceptance, principles of Spiritism, such as reincarnation and communication with spirits, became part of Brazil's cultural tapestry, even though the vast majority of people identified as Christians.

The Foundation of Umbanda

During the initial years of the 20th century, Spiritism had already gained significant recognition in Brazil as a means of assessing health conditions and emotional problems that traditional medical practitioners or priests were unable to address. The people, predominantly of the Catholic faith, began to consider Spiritism a congenial institution. Due to Spiritism being a doctrine rather than a competing religion, individuals from any religious background could visit a spiritist center without any significant obligation. It is notable that Spiritism is a self-proclaimed doctrine, distinct from any established religion. However, it is apparent that this distinction was made to prevent potential conflicts with the church and non-secular national constitutions, both in France during the times of Kardec, and years later in Brazil.

Towards the close of 1908, Zelio Fernandino de Moraes, a 17-year-old youth preparing to embark on a naval career, began to experience peculiar seizures. According to Veiga (2021), during one of these episodes, Zelio suffered from an enigmatic paralysis that confounded medical professionals, defying their attempts at treatment. Astonishingly, he declared, "*Tomorrow, I will be healed*," and the subsequent day witnessed his departure from the hospital, apparently cured. The abrupt onset of these episodes took his family by surprise. During these episodes, Zelio would adopt the persona of an elderly gentleman, articulating incoherent and disjointed statements, as if channeling the words of an individual from a bygone era. Notably, he exhibited an unexpected familiarity with various subjects related to nature, despite lacking any formal education in these areas. On certain occasions, he displayed behavior reminiscent of a feline, causing consternation among his close acquaintances.

After several days of observation, the family's psychiatrist, who coincidentally was Zelio's uncle, recommended seeking the guidance of a priest as the young man's condition, perceived as "madness," did not align with any recognized psychiatric ailment. The psychiatrist was of the belief that Zelio might be possessed by evil spirits. Subsequently, another uncle of Zelio, a priest, attempted to intervene through exorcisms, but these efforts proved ineffective. Meanwhile, the occurrences described as "seizures" persisted and grew in frequency.

Faced with the ongoing challenges, Zelio's mother decided to consult a local folk healer. Channeling the spirit of an ex-slave, the healer revealed that Zelio possessed mediumistic abilities and advised that he should utilize this gift to assist others through charitable endeavors. Zelio's father, a Navy general and an avid reader of Spiritism literature, became intrigued by his son's condition. After confiding in one of his lieutenants, a close friend, the lieutenant suggested that "this was a matter of Spiritism" and recommended taking Zelio to the Spiritist Federation of Niteroi.

On November 15th, young Zelio was invited to attend a Spiritist service, where mediums engaged in activities such as reading excerpts from Kardec's books, offering prayers, and channeling spirits for counseling. According to the his family members, Zelio took a seat at the table, but at the commencement of the service, he was overcome by a strange force that hindered the exercise of his will. In defiance of the customary rule that attendees should remain at the table until the service concluded, Zelio stood up and proclaimed, "*There is something missing here.*" He then exited the room, strolled to the garden, and returned with a white rose, which he placed on the table, asserting that "*the service was now complete*" and could proceed.

Upon Zelio's placement of the flower on the table, some of the mediums began channeling the spirits of black slaves and native Brazilians, causing a disturbance in demeanor contrary to the then-accepted spiritualist norm. However, when the service resumed, the center's director sternly admonished that those were spirits of 'low spiritual development' and insisted they depart. The spirit channeling through Zelio persisted.

A heated dialogue ensued, and those responsible for the service sought to indoctrinate and ward off the unknown spirit, who developed a compelling argument. The spirit questioned the present mediums, asking why they would not allow the spirits of blacks and indigenous people in without even having the decency to listen to their messages. "*Is it because of our social backgrounds and color?*" questioned the spirit. Intrigued, the director of the service asked who he was and his name. The spirit simply answered that he was an indigenous Brazilian. Nevertheless, the director, being a clairvoyant medium, challenged the entity, asking, "*Why are you saying you are an indigenous man and speaking in this way if I can see your clerical robes?*" The spirit responded that what the medium was seeing were fragments of one of his past lives when he was an Italian priest called Gabriel Malagrida, a missionary priest in Brazil sentenced to death by the Portuguese church in 1761 after accusations of heresy. "*But in my last physical existence,*" continued the spirit, "*God granted me the privilege of being born as a native Brazilian.*" Subsequently, the spirit emphatically declared: "*If you want a name, let it be this: I am the Mestizo[1] of the Seven Crossroads. Because for me,*" the spirit

Image 4: Jesuit missionary Gabriel Malagrida, circa 1760s-1770s

---

1 The term "mestizo" in this work is commonly used to refer to individuals of Native American and European background in the Americas, despite connoting a generalized ethnic term. In Brazilian Portuguese, the equivalent term is *caboclo*, meaning the child of parents of different ethnicities, one being indigenous and the other white.

Adherents and entities of primitive Umbanda have employed words and designations that may seem outdated or peculiar today but are retained out of respect for how the spirits described themselves to a simpler audience. An example is the term "Old Blacks," used to denote wise spirits of individuals who were enslaved in previous lives. These terms were coined by the spirits themselves, reflecting their lack of ostentation in conveying elevated spiritual status. Furthermore, these labels and terms are explicit and legitimate translations from Brazilian Portuguese.

This work will henceforth refer to the spirits of Caboclos as "Mestizos," symbolizing their embodiment of Amerindian essence within a life intertwined with modern and colonized influences.

raised his tone, *"there will be no closed paths."* And he asserted: *"If you believe that the spirits of blacks and native peoples are of low spirituality, then I must inform you that tomorrow, on the 16th of November, I will be at the house of my medium* [Zelio] *at 8 p.m., to commence a service in which these brothers can deliver their messages and fulfill the mission that has been entrusted to them by the Spiritual Plane."*

The director verified the spirit's identity as described and continued the conversation, albeit with some reluctance to welcome such a spirit into the center. The spirit stated that they were bringing a new religion, one that would promote harmony in families and equality among people, both the living and the departed. Seven Crossroads emphasized that all spirits would have the opportunity to work and assist others. However, the director argued that there were already too many religions in existence. Despite this, the spirit affirmed that *"God, in his infinite mercy, has established in death the great universal equalizer. Rich or poor, powerful or humble, all become equal in death. But you, prejudiced men, are not happy with establishing differences among the living. You seek to apply the same approach to the dead."* This was a clear reference to the fact that some Spiritist directors were categorizing spirits based on their past lives' status and race rather than the messages they had to convey.

Immediately prior to departing from service, the spirit issued a solemn warning: *"This realm of transgressions shall once again be eradicated by suffering, due to the insatiable ambition of mankind and the flagrant disregard for divine laws. A deluge of blood shall engulf Europe soon, and when humanity deems it insufficient, a subsequent and even greater deluge shall encompass the world. With the mere implementation of a single instrument of warfare, countless lives shall be extinguished."* It is apparent that the Mestizo spirit was foretelling the occurrence of World War I, World War II, and the atomic bomb, albeit no individuals present at the time possessed the capacity to comprehend these prophecies, which were realized in the following decades.

On the following day, members of the Spiritist Federation, along with Zelio's closest relatives, friends, neighbors, and a multitude of strangers and dissidents from other spiritist groups, had already assembled at his family home at 8:00 p.m., as scheduled, to validate the authenticity of the previous day's revelation. Zelio, a 17-year-old boy with no prior experience as a medium, was uncertain how to proceed during the initial service. However, the force that had possessed him the previous day left him with no uncertainty that he was to execute everything the entity had commanded. Though Zelio was not cognizant of being a medium, he was lucid during the communication in the previous day and therefore comprehended that the spirit Mestizo Seven Crossroads had indicated to him the most crucial aspect of his existence: the mission of inaugurating a new religion.

During the first Umbanda service, Zelio used the settings of spiritist centers as a point of reference, and the initial gathering took place around his family's dining table. While seated around the table, the Mestizo spirit promptly channeled through Zelio, and shortly after, he stood up to heal a disabled person who was present. This demonstration, reminiscent of a biblical passage, mirrored Jesus' approach of demonstrating the validity of his teachings through small "miracles" and healings, drawing greater attention to the emerging movement. Those in attendance who witnessed the healing were astounded and spread the news across the region. Following his channeling, the Mestizo spirit answered the queries of the present mediums in Latin and German before providing the foundations of the cult and proceeding to the practical portion of the service.

Image 5: Zelio de Moraes, 1939

The day after the first Umbanda service, a true pilgrimage formed on Zelio's street, with the sick, blind, and hopeless coming to seek a cure, as many claimed to have been cured of their illnesses or relieved of their pain on the previous day. And mediums, who had been considered mentally ill and confined to asylums, had the opportunity to show their abilities.

After giving passes to the audience, Seven Crossroads returned to the table, announcing that he would need to depart as another entity wanted to manifest, that is, be channeled. As the Mestizo left, another Father Tony introduced himself. A former slave, Father Tony, spoke humbly and delivered messages of simplicity. Thereupon, Father Tony would be a fundamental figure for sustaining charity and humility as Umbanda's motto. Both Mestizo Seven Crossroads and Father Tony brought significant ancestral knowledge to Umbanda, which, while heavily based on theoretical Spiritism, started incorporating significant elements of indigenous[2] shamanism and African[3] cult practices in its tapestry. Assisted by another spirit, Mestizo Orisha Mallet, an entity experienced in dismantling low magic spells, Seven Crossroads worked tirelessly to clarify and establish Umbanda as a religion.

Under the guidance of Seven Crossroads, Zelio founded, in that same year, the first Umbanda tent, named Spiritist Tent Our Lady of Sorrows (Kloppenburg, 1991). During his regular sessions, Mestizo Seven Crossroads established the norms of worship, refining the foundations of what would become a religion grounded in the principles of Spiritism, yet receptive to the influences of other groups of spirits that would collaborate with it. During the inaugural Umbanda sessions, participants would engage in reverential prayer, perform acts of worship towards specific Orishas and divinities, and proceed to invoke enlightened spirits, who would utilize the mediums as a mediumistic conduit for communication. Upon establishing contact, these spirits would engage in ceremonial cleansing and magnetizing the assembly via "passes," in addition to providing personalized consultations replete with guidance, counsel, and blessings.

Umbanda quickly gathered its own and most notorious characteristics as the days and years went by. This was made possible through the joining of several separatist mediums from spiritist centers and, especially, the addition of a multitude of direct descendants of slaves with mediumistic practices. Along with Father Tony's daily introduction of Orishas as facets of God manifest as *ashe*, or divine energy, the swarming of adherents of "Macumba" circles gave Umbanda its most crucial Afro-Brazilian elements.

Prior to the emergence of Umbanda, the religious practices of slave communities were known as Calundu (Bastide, 1978, originally published in 1960). Calundu originated from the percussion circles

---

[2] Incorporation of indigenous elements entails, among other things, the integration of traditional herbs in the preparation of baths, the utilization of smudging techniques, and cleansing rituals.

[3] The integration of African elements encompasses various practices, including the utilization of percussion to achieve a trance state (which was not present in Zelio's initial tent), the recitation of ancestral mantras, the veneration of Orishas as manifestations of the divine, and rituals with offerings to the spirits.

where slaves would gather during their free time to dance and play drums in a ritual trance for channeling spirits. Despite their efforts to disguise their ritual practices as pure recreation, they were still persecuted by the colonizers. Calundu was a syncretic movement that combined African beliefs, indigenous rites, and Catholicism. According to Cossard (2006), over time it bifurcated into Cabula and Candomblé: Cabula retained its influences from Catholicism and indigenous practices, while Candomblé maintained only African beliefs, uniting all the cults of the major Orishas as one cult. As more slaves from different parts of Africa arrived, Candomblé eventually became more prominent than Cabula, causing the latter to gradually fade away. However, with the emergence of Umbanda, aspects of Cabula appeared to have been unintentionally revived. While Cabula has ceased to exist, Popular Macumba emerged among slaves as an unofficial movement that incorporated diverse religious beliefs, such as European witchcraft, the Book of Saint Cyprian, gypsy tenets, Hebrew teachings, and others. Macumba circles, which were named after a musical instrument used in the cult, became so popular that even decades later, Umbanda was sometimes interchangeably referred to as Macumba, despite its occasional pejorative hue. Although Cabula and Macumba are not included in the theoretical structure provided by Spiritism, they can be seen as precursors to Umbanda. Despite the original form of Umbanda, established by Zelio, was initially similar to Spiritist practices, the modern iteration of Umbanda is considered by some to be more akin to Cabula than any other religious tradition. This has led to speculation that Umbanda is merely a rebranded version of Cabula. Nevertheless, since its inception in 1908, Umbanda has naturally incorporated diverse influences from various sects, rather than attempting to emulate Macumba circles.

    The use of the term "spiritist" in the name of the initial Umbanda tents was indicative of the connection between Umbanda and Spiritism. Both religions shared similar principles, such as communication with spirits via channeling, the law of spiritual progress, and the use of mediumistic passes to assist the community. During this time, Umbanda had more in common with Spiritism than Spiritism had with its predecessor, Spiritualism, making the term "spiritist" a justifiable designation. It is also important to note that Seven Crossroads referred to these establishments as "tents" instead of "temples" or "centers" because he felt that those terms had a connotation of superiority or grandeur. By using the term "tent," it conveyed a sense of simplicity and accessibility.

Along with the term "spiritist," the name of a Catholic saint would also appear in the tents' names. There are two primary reasons for this. Firstly, prior to the abolition of slavery, only Christian faiths were permitted to be practiced, even in the slaves' quarters, which were often separate from their owners' main house. As many African slaves and their descendants traditionally worshiped African deities that were not related to the Abrahamic God, Jesus Christ, or any of the Catholic saints, they were firmly prohibited from doing so by their white slaveholders. Furthermore, practicing any faith other than Christianity was a criminal offense in Brazil until the empire became a secular republic in 1889.

The church repeatedly suppressed any religious manifestation by the slaves. However, for the elite, allowing the slaves to express religiosity, albeit Catholic, could help maintain old rivalries and antagonisms among different groups of African slaves, therefore preventing uprisings or mass escapes. As such, in some regions, slaves were typically baptized and compelled to profess the Catholic religion as soon as they arrived in their owners' homes. The elite also made sure that most of the slaves brought to Brazil during the colonization period were from various regions in Africa, where they had different languages and cultures. Often, ships from different parts of Africa would dock at a single city in Brazil to ensure that the enslaved would not understand one another, thereby preventing rebellions.

Allowed to only worship Christian deities, the slaves began to compare and associate the qualities of the Catholic saints to those of their traditional African divinities. It became clear that a few aspects were invariably shared between European and African narratives, stories, and myths. As simple as it may sound, the slaves viewed it as just a matter of appearance and names that separated the two, which allowed them to worship their own sacred entities, using Christian religious imagery and names as camouflage. Statues of Catholic saints were given to the slaves, as it was believed that they were interested in repenting and finally being enthusiastic about their indoctrination to Christianity. The slaves prayed, knelt, and spoke to the Catholic idols, calling them by their European names while keeping in their hearts the idea of another deity. Moreover, they would hide their sacred stones associated with the African deities behind, under, or inside the statues, allowing worship via an ancestral agent to proceed more legitimately. Although most slave owners and priests were aware that the slaves were possibly worshiping another deity dressed as a Catholic saint, it was still a better scenario than the open worship of African deities. Thus, the prospect of sacrilege was widely dismissed, and the slaves also began to celebrate their deities's special days simultaneously with the Catholic saints' festivities to avoid drawing attention to their cult. Even though the decriminalization of religions other than Catholicism only occurred in the late 19th century in Brazil, Candomblé[4] centers were inaugurated in the north-east regions before official permission was granted. To avoid persecution, these centers were named after Catholic saints as well. Syncretism, or the blending of beliefs, originated with slaves, was carried on in Candomblé, and is still prevalent in many Umbanda centers, especially with regard to the existence and importance of Jesus. In contrast, the use of Christian saints is less significant in Candomblé centers or absent altogether.

In addition to the aforementioned reasons for naming the first seven Umbandist centers after Catholic saints, another contributing factor was the worship of Orishas. Orishas are deities that can be viewed as representations of God [more on this topic is to be profoundly discussed in the upcoming chapters]. Their introduction to Umbanda was initially made by Father Tony at Zelio's place, but further developed with the addition of adherents of Afro-movements, who would bring their rites and customs with them. Thus, each tent, or center, is dedicated to a specific Orisha, who is the tent's "patron", thus wielding spiritual influence over it.

The main point of worship at an Umbandist center is the house Orisha, and the temple is run in accordance with the qualities of that Orisha. The spiritual essence of the center's priest is typically determined by an Orisha, which, through a series of rituals and spiritual consultations, is revealed as the Orisha influencing their crown chakra—the main part of the soul—throughout their lifetime. The patron Orisha, known as the priest's 'head-Orisha,' remains consistent and serves as the primary influence for the temple's spirit

---

[4] An Afro-Brazilian religion that united the cult of multiple Orishas within a single tradition.

leader. This spirit is responsible for the founding and works of the temple, as exemplified by Seven Crossroads, who served as the spirit leader of the first Umbanda tents and was also one of Zelio's spirit guides.

From the Spiritist Tent Our Lady of Sorrows, Seven Crossroads selected mediums who founded other seven Umbandist tents. These tents were designated to spread Umbanda, and each was associated with a specific Orisha who served as the patrons of the center and exercised spiritual influence over it. The tents and their corresponding patrons, the Orishas, were:

Spiritist Tent Our Lady of the Rosary, which had Yemanja, the Orisha of the oceans and families, as its patron;

Spiritist Tent Our Lady of the Conception, which had Oshun, the Orisha of love and beauty, as its patron;

Spiritist Tent Our Lady Saint Barbara, which had Yansa, the Orisha of winds and lightning, as its patron;

Spiritist Tent Saint Peter, which had Shango, the Orisha of justice and the mountains, as its patron;

Spiritist Tent Oshala, which had no syncretism in its name. However, Oshala is associated with Jesus;

Spiritist Tent Saint George, which had Ogun, the Orisha of battles and technology, as its patron;

Spiritist Tent Saint Jerome, which is also syncretized with Shango.

In the first half of the 20th century, numerous Umbanda centers emerged following the founding of the first seven tents. While the early Umbanda centers were initially referred to as "tents", the subsequent generation of them were more often called centers, temples, and yards. The Umbanda centers are usually associated with the term 'yards' due to their humble and nature-based beginnings. This also recalls the primitive religious spaces of Afro-Brazilian rites, where unpaved sheds were used to facilitate the connection with the earth. As the religion gained acceptance in communities across the country, the term "spiritist" also became less common in those centers less identified with Spiritism.

During Umbanda's early years, the spirits that primarily presented themselves were the Mestizos (implicitly native Brazilians), the Old Blacks, and the Children, symbolizing strength and simplicity, wisdom and humility, and innocence and happiness, respectively. These three groups of spirits are the foundational entities of Umbanda. Additional groups of spirits that appeared later in the religion are linked to specific spiritual assignments, primarily for balancing the trinity on a different energetic polarity.

According to tradition, before Seven Crossroads adopted the name "umbanda" for the new religion, the initial reference to it was "allabanda," a term believed to be associated with Allah, meaning "next to God." The appellation is said to have been chosen by Seven Crossroads as a tribute to the spirit Orisha Mallet, who was also a collaborator of Zelio. Legend has it that in a previous existence, Orisha Mallet was a Malay Muslim. However, after the first "Spiritism of Umbanda Congress" in 1941, it was officially declared that the term "umbanda" originated from the Sanskrit words *aum* (essence of the universe; unlimited) and *bhanda* (restraint; confinement), translated as "the limit in the unlimited" (Smith, 2004). It is worth noting that the term "aumbanda" may have subsequently been misconstrued as "umbanda." This could be due to the fact that, in Portuguese, the definite article "the" translates to "a," leading individuals to assume that the initial "a" in "aumbanda" was the article "a," resulting in the removal of the prefix and adoption of the name "umbanda." Notwithstanding, some legitimately argue that "Umbanda" derives from the Quimbunda language of Angola and means "magic" or "art of healing," and this claim appears to be the one most accepted by scholars. Nevertheless, others refute this claim, stating that it differs from the origins described by the Mestizo Seven Crossroads, a founding figure of the religion.

Umbanda was founded on the principles of compassion and simplicity, providing a welcoming environment not only for varied benevolent spirits but also for those who were marginalized due to their social and ethnic roots. From its inception, Umbanda emphasized the strict avoidance of rituals that aimed to interfere with somebody else's free will, cause harm to others, charge for spiritual services, or engage in animal sacrifices, all of which were acceptable in other Afro-religious circles that ultimately influenced Umbanda's development.

During Zelio's lifetime, more than 10,000 Umbanda temples were established (Reis, 2011). Fernandino de Moraes devoted 66 years of his life to the advancement and cultivation of Umbanda until his passing in 1975.

Principles and Philosophies

The principles of Umbanda are firmly grounded in the values of charity, humility, and freedom. These fundamental premises underscore the importance of putting others before oneself and cultivating a spirit of selflessness. In the context of Umbanda, charity is the manifestation of compassion among all spirits, regardless of whether they are incarnated or discarnate. By helping others, one can refine their emotions and overcome negative feelings. The principle of charity also emphasizes the importance of avoiding egocentric and selfish behavior and instead giving freely without expecting anything in return. The spirits portraying themselves as native peoples, or mestizos, for example, view the abundance they promote as having enough to share with others, and not as a means of accumulating wealth for oneself.

Humility is another hallmark of Umbanda that emphasizes the fundamental equality of all spirits, irrespective of their material circumstances or social status. It acknowledges that everyone originates from the same creative source and is on a similar journey of spiritual progress, albeit at different stages. The distinctions one makes between individuals are ultimately superficial and have no bearing on the true essence of the spirit. While Umbanda recognizes the existence of hierarchies, these are based solely on merit, and no individual is considered superior to another. Even the most lofty beings within Umbanda, the Old Blacks, reveal themselves as once-marginalized victims of slavery, distancing themselves from any pompous presentation based on their spiritual relevance.

Furthermore, the principle of freedom is of paramount importance in Umbanda as it underscores the significance of individual agency and free will, both for incarnated and disembodied spirits. Although universal laws of cause and effect do govern the consequences of one's actions, Umbanda's notion of freedom is focused on religious and cult freedom, as well as the liberty of working spirits from various cultures to utilize Umbanda as a platform to aid others. Children spirits serve as a clear embodiment of the spirit of freedom and acceptance within Umbanda as they endeavor to alleviate difficulties, cultivate joy amid distress, and propagate innocence in the face of malice.

In addition to the aforementioned principles, Umbanda subscribes to fundamental beliefs shared with Spiritism, such as the existence of a single God, the immortality of the spirit, communication between different planes, reincarnation, and the plurality of inhabited worlds.

As a monotheistic religion, Umbanda also recognizes the concept of Orishas. Orishas can be understood as various depictions of God reflected as divine energy, strongly present in nature. It is important to note that Umbandists view the Orishas not as minor deities or semi-gods but rather as different aspects of the same God. This God is usually referred to as Olorum or Zambi, similar to how other cultures refer to God as Yahveh in Judaism or Allah in Islam. However, the term "God" is invariably favored among Umbandists, while Olorum and Zambi are commonly used for specific reasons or emphasis.

The concept of the immortality of the spirit is central to Umbanda's belief system. The spirit is not seen as a temporary aspect but rather as an eternal being that undergoes constant evolution. As eternal beings that persist beyond physical death, communication with them is possible through the mediation of sensitive individuals. Along these lines, direct assistance from spirits is also a practiced aspect.

Regarding reincarnation, it is viewed as a process that enables the spirit to continue learning and expanding. While the philosophy maintains that spirits are not obligated to reincarnate indefinitely, it emphasizes that it is the most common path for human spirits to propel their spiritual evolution. Thus, reincarnation is considered a means for both humans and animals to gain experience and knowledge. Animals, exempt from accruing karma, journey solely based on acquiring experiences. In contrast, humans not only accumulate experiences but also confront emotional imbalances and strive to evolve through love.

Similarly, the entities working within Umbanda are in constant evolution, and some may choose to reincarnate on Earth to fulfill specific missions. In this context, reincarnation in other realms is more likely for Umbanda's spiritual triad—Mestizos, Old Blacks, and Children—where incarnated life is not necessarily limited to the third dimension of the physical universe.

The ideas presented by Spiritism, which posits that moral principles encompass a set of divine laws governing an individual's moral aspects, including their relationship with themselves and others, serve as inspiration for principles and philosophies embraced by Umbanda. These principles are characterized by balance within the universe rather than prudishness and have existed since before the dawn of humanity. Adhering to these laws is deemed essential for spiritual progress. While often referred to as 'divine laws,' it is crucial to note that God did not deliberately establish or implement them in these doctrines. Instead, sage spirits passed on information from higher hierarchical entities throughout the histories of Spiritism and Umbanda.

According to Spiritism, a divine principle is eternal, immutable, perfect, and equal for all. Furthermore, it is inscribed in the conscience of humanity and has been revealed at all times, progressively becoming clearer and aligning with the progress of human consciousness. Although Spiritist principles deeply influence Umbanda, they are not considered the foundations of the religion; rather, they are seen as ideas compatible with the universal laws approached by Umbanda's working spirits, particularly in the early days of its foundation in the early 20th century. Additionally, as a plural religious expression, Umbanda has unofficially incorporated theosophic and hermetic principles, despite a seemingly closer alignment with Spiritism in more recent decades.

Spiritual Progress: Cause and Effect, and Reincarnation

Without canonical texts to deliberately allow access to people of all kinds, many of the beliefs of Umbanda are somewhat fluid, adapting to what each temple and priest deems appropriate, although significant discrepancies are almost nonexistent. Therefore, it seems that the philosophy encountered in Spiritism is heavily adopted, either accidentally or purposefully, especially in the case of Kardecist Umbanda, Traditional and Popular Umbanda, and other modern varieties of Umbanda.

Generally, in the Umbanda belief system, the philosophy of spiritual evolution, commonly known as spiritual progress, also finds its roots in Spiritism. This philosophy is based on the transmission of information from more advanced entities to mediums and is grounded in the principles of the Kardecist Pentateuch[5]. The creation of the spirit, which occurs gradually, is driven by the divine expansion through Its creations. As a detached aspect of the divine, the spirit accumulates experiences and wisdom until it ultimately returns to the divine realm as a divine fragment.

Given that the creation of a spirit takes place over a prolonged period, its initial stages may be considered rudimentary and elementary in nature. Across millennia, this divine spark migrates from one vessel to another, adapting to each stage of evolutionary development. It transitions from dimension to dimension, from kingdom to kingdom, until eventually reaching the humanoid kingdoms in the third dimension, where it can perceive itself as human, endowed with a humanoid form and a moderately expanded consciousness. Just as physical bodies did not arise in the manner depicted in the Adam and Eve mythology, neither were spirits created in their current form. Instead, both the spirit and the physical body had their origins in a simple and primitive state.

As part of the process of spiritual evolution, progress is understood to involve a shift from primitive animal instincts towards

---

5   The Spirits' Book, The Mediums' Book, The Gospel According to Spiritism, Heaven and Hell, and The Genesis According to Spiritism.

intellectual and fraternal principles. It is worth noting that human consciousness has already achieved a certain level of advancement, with ideals and intellect surpassing the basic survival traits of ancestral hominids, who were primarily concerned with eating, reproduction, and self-preservation. However, the physical manifestation of life through reincarnations continues until instincts are replaced with benevolence and wisdom.

In the context of humanity's spiritual evolution, progress is synonymous with the eradication of negative thoughts and emotions. This involves replacing resentment with tolerance, anger with compassion, and selfishness with generosity. The concept of "karma," a Sanskrit term meaning "action" or "duty," proposes necessary activity to reduce the imbalance of virtues generated in the past. Karma does not necessarily involve suffering or pain but rather an involuntary action or life event aimed at correcting one's spiritual disharmony. Unlike animals, which act solely or mostly on physiological instincts, human beings are capable of harboring malice and evil feelings throughout their lives. Thus, it is believed that once an individual has purged most of their karma through experiences, their evolutionary process changes. They move from evolution via atonement to evolution via regeneration. Evolution via regeneration occurs when the individual no longer needs to suffer, atone, or perform actions to repair past wrongs. In this fashion, regeneration is associated with acts of charity and a broad intellect, whereby the spirit ceases to accrue karma and begins to expand consciousness.

The evolution of the spirit is not always necessarily linked to the concepts of reincarnation or karma. When contemplating the evolution of the spirits that inhabit the bodies of human beings, reincarnation can be viewed as a means of spiritual education. Through temporarily forgetting their past experiences, spirits have the opportunity to face recurring challenges from a fresh perspective and make better choices in a suitable manner. Moreover, reincarnation allows for the reconciliation of spirits who may have disagreed and ended their previous lives holding harmful emotions towards one another. The new experience in the physical realm, shrouded in forgetfulness, provides them with a chance to interact again, leading to a better understanding, tolerance, and forgiveness of one another. Although past hurt may resurface in a current life, the relationship between individuals may be different, and so the old emotion will be assimilated differently. Former enemies in battle may now be siblings, and once emotionally bound together by the bonds of kinship, they are more likely to forgive one another because the love they share may lessen the pain from their previous existence. Thus, where there is love, there is forgiveness.

It is important to note that evolution is an ongoing process, not only for the energy inhabiting stones or for archangels but also for God itself. The working entities of Umbanda are also evolving, and various groups of spirits continue to eradicate their karma through spiritual work. While these spirits are typically more evolved than most incarnate humans, they are still learning to love unconditionally and to understand existence from a divine perspective.

Branches of Umbanda

Although Umbanda has established principles and even dogmas, it lacks a codification that would ensure its constancy and immutability, as is the case, for example, with Hinduism and the various forms of Christianity. These religions possess sacred texts and established norms that prescribe the behavior of their adherents and dictate the maintenance of the religion in an unchanging manner, regardless of the nation, language, or culture in which they are adopted. Churches, synagogues, mosques, and Buddhist and Hindu temples, whatever their location, are meant to be franchises of the same system or a faithful reproduction of the original churches or temples. These religions change little over decades, with significant modifications occurring only over the course of centuries. Based on scriptures or a set of written codes, it is the responsibility of the followers, but especially of hierarchical leaders, to adapt to the regulations, norms, and formalities of the religious practices and their surroundings.

In contrast to many other religions, and as previously stated, Umbanda does not have a codified set of norms or sacred texts that prescribe its practice. This can be attributed to the freedom and flexibility that Umbanda offers both to its practitioners and the spirits that work within it. More than just a religion, Umbanda is a spiritual practice that adapts to the needs of individuals, mediums, and spiritual entities. As a result, this lack of standardization has resulted in the creation of various branches of Umbanda, not all of which can be considered truly representative of the original practice. While the absence of a fixed authority or set of rules allows for other religions to blend their rites and beliefs with Umbanda, it also leads to the misuse of the term "umbanda" by those who seek to gain recognition or spread their influence.

Another reason why Umbanda has developed into different variants is due to the fact that each center is led by a different priest or caretaker. As such, each umbanda practiced there inevitably reflects the unique characteristics and preferences of a single individual. A priest who favors a more esoteric approach will incorporate these values into their sessions and rites, while a priest with roots in Spiritism will naturally adopt a more Kardecist perspective in their liturgy. Another with a deeper understanding of Afro-Brazilian culture, on the other hand, may incorporate more ancestral elements into their practice, thus distancing the temple from a Euro-Brazilian influence.

Although there are variations in the practice, the majority of religions that adopt the term "umbanda" can be considered legitimate expressions of that faith. The original Umbanda, also known as "Traditional Umbanda" or "White Umbanda" (a reference to the Spiritist tables clothed in white, not to an ethnicity), serves as the foundation for all other forms of Umbanda. However, it is worth noting that the Umbanda founded in 1908 is not necessarily the most widely practiced variant of the religion. The denomination of an Umbanda center under any branch of Umbanda does not necessarily reflect how its adherents identify themselves. Rather, it is a label assigned by the temple's founders and caretakers.

Traditional Umbanda is characterized by several features inherited from Spiritism. In terms of ritualistic practice, this variety is among the simplest of the various classes. The religion employs syncretized images, bead necklaces, smudging, candles, sigils, and basic offerings. Occasionally, chants and mantras are recited, but percussion is not frequently used in Traditional Umbanda. It is noteworthy that the religion is deeply rooted in Spiritism, and therefore, the books authored by Allan Kardec are often employed as doctrinal references.

In Traditional Umbanda services, the proceedings typically begin with an initial prayer, often of a Christian nature, followed by the channeling of spirits. In public sessions, the audience may receive cleansing passes and advice from the spirits channeled by the mediums. The sessions usually end after the spirits depart, which occurs when the channeling ceases, followed by a closing prayer. Private sessions, on the other hand, are attended only by the center's workers and mediums, typically used for mediumship development and worship of an Orisha. Worship often takes the form of seeking guidance and divine strength rather than veneration. In these private sessions, simple rituals may also be carried out, such as the energetic disinfecting of objects or the mediums themselves.

The religion venerates the most widely worshiped Orishas, including Oshala, Oshun, Shango, Yemanja, Ogun, Oshossi, Yansa (Oya), and Obaluaye. These deities work in conjunction with fundamental entities such as Mestizos, Old Blacks, and occasionally Children. In contrast, other groups of spirits, such as Cowboys, Gypsies, Bohemians, Sailors, Eshus, and Pombagiras, are rarely incorporated into Traditional Umbanda rituals.

Within their temples, a minimalist aesthetic is commonly observed, featuring an altar adorned in white with flowers and imagery of the saints, particularly Jesus. While candles are frequently used, their use is not universal. The ritualistic consumption of cigars and alcoholic beverages is a rarity, if not altogether avoided. Additionally, those who work within these centers, including the mediums, typically wear a uniform consisting solely of white garments, accompanied only by bead necklaces. These necklaces serve to protect and channel the energies of the Orishas and other entities with which they collaborate.

Popular Umbanda, also known as Crossed Umbanda or Mystical Umbanda, is a widely practiced and popular branch of Umbanda in Brazil and around the world. It is one of the oldest and most prevalent types of Umbanda, with approximately nine out of every ten Umbanda centers in Brazil identifying as Popular Umbanda. Of all the religious expressions that fall under the "umbanda" term, Popular Umbanda is the variant that bears the closest resemblance to Cabula (Macumba circles).

In Popular Umbanda, a variety of rituals and prayers are performed during the services. These rituals are typically performed while the spirits are channeling and may include traced sigils on the floor, names written on papers, and other tools employed for benevolent spells, like the use of flowers, herbs, and smoke for cleansing and harmony. In all sessions, visitors receive guidance from the entities that are being channeled, and energetic passes may be given as well. In the case of celebrations for an Orisha's day, the temple worships the Orisha by chanting their mantras and giving offerings, especially for the channeling entities that work under the influence of that particular Orisha. Upon being channeled, the entities usually express themselves in the vocalized salutations that are typical of each of them, and the clothing or colors that their mediums wear before channeling also reflect the nature of the spirits to be channeled. While channeling, the mediums may also dance to the sound of percussioned mantras, but this is done as a form of cleansing and energizing for the mediums and visitors rather than for fun or frivolity.

In this variant, there is a syncretization of Orishas with Catholic saints, although the combination of statues of Orishas as their African personifications is also common. Moreover, they worship several more Orishas than Traditional Umbanda does, such as Nana, Oshumare, Oba, and Ibeji, in addition to those worshiped in Traditional Umbanda. They also occasionally worship Orishas Eshu, Ossain, and Logunede.

The groups of spirits, also known as "phalanx," who come to work in the Umbanda centers are diverse and include Mestizos, Old Blacks, Children, Cowboys, Sailors, Mermaids, Gypsies, Eshus and Pombagiras, Bohemians, and even legions of Pirates and Witches.

Ritualistic tools, such as tridents, bows, daggers, vines, crowns, indigenous headdresses, and capes, are also seen. Additionally, the use of flowers on altars, colored candles, drinks, cigars, incense, and crystals is common. The regalia of the mediums varies according to the spirit guides they are to channel, although white is the preferred color during the sessions.

Seven Rays Umbanda is another aspect of Umbanda that can sometimes be mistaken for either Popular Umbanda or Sacred Umbanda, especially due to its reinterpretation of the Orishas in a more universalist manner. Ney Nery introduced this particular form of Umbanda in the early 1970s when he presented the foundational knowledge of the 7 divine rays in one of his books. In Seven Rays Umbanda, the Orishas are classified into seven "divine rays" as manifestations of God. Within these 7 divine rays, there are 12

Orishas: Oshala; Ogun and Ibeji; Shango and Yansa; Oshun and Oshumare; Oshossi and Ossain; Yemanja and Nana; and Omulu.

The division of Orishas into seven main groups, or seven main Orishas, has been adopted since the early decades of Umbanda by various Umbanda researchers. In 1925, Leal de Souza introduced the seven groups of Orishas, whereby they were divided into different frequencies, despite such nomenclature not necessarily being utilized back then. Throughout the decades, many other authors, invariably priests of Umbanda, also introduced seven groups or seven main Orishas, all based on how their temples and their spirit guides informed them. These several "seven main Orishas" usually maintained Oshala, Yemanja, Ogun, Shango, but occasionally had other Orishas such as Oshun and Omulu absent or replaced.

The 'seven rays' may have also been influenced by Theosophical thought, where the Seven Rays are described as the energy channels through which the energy of the Logos, or supreme creator, flows in the solar system. In the Seven Rays described by Theosophical references[6], seven masters command each of these rays. The similarities between that school and Umbanda, with its seven main domains where each Orisha commands, are noteworthy. Nonetheless, it is crucial to highlight that the Orishas are considered energies, whereas the masters proposed by Theosophists are entities akin to archangels, considered the most elevated beings in the solar system. A similar division is also found in the Old Testament, where seven main angels represent traits of God. Nevertheless, the influence from Theosophy or biblical angels in Umbanda Seven Rays is debatable.

Practitioners of Seven Rays Umbanda work with a diverse range of groups and phalanxes of spirits, such as Eshus and Pombagiras, Mestizos, Old Blacks, Children, Gypsies, and others, similar to Popular and Sacred Umbanda. They also employ various ritual instruments such as swords, arrow and bows, tridents, and axes. Candles, incense burners, herbs and flowers, drinks, sigil boards, and sacred images are also commonly used in their rituals. Additionally, they engage in percussion, chanting, and elaborate offerings to the deities. During ceremonies, it is typical to see practitioners wearing clothing associated with the specific classes of entities they are working with, although white attire is often preferred. The same

---

6 Helena Blavatsky's "The Secret Doctrine" (1888) and C. W. Leadbeater's "The Masters and the Path" (1925).

preference for white can be observed in the altars and overall ambiance of the center.

Sacred Umbanda is a branch of Umbanda that gained significant influence in the 1990s under the leadership of priest Rubens Saraceni. This variant of Umbanda is characterized by a universalist approach that draws upon a wide range of philosophical and spiritual traditions, including Hermeticism and Rosicrucian beliefs. Of greater significance, Sacred Umbanda incorporates a range of symbolic correlations that have been adapted to the cult of the Orishas, which govern the "divine thrones" occupied by these deities that are all facets of God. Esoteric and Shamanic practices are also present in this form of Umbanda. Although it incorporates a variety of influences, Sacred Umbanda recognizes the fundamental role that Spiritism, Yoruba, and Amerindian traditions played in shaping the religion.

In terms of rituals, worship, and spiritual practices, Sacred Umbanda shares many similarities with Popular Umbanda, making it difficult to distinguish between the two. In fact, many contemporary Umbanda centers combine elements of both. However, Sacred Umbanda is known for its distinct focus on rituals involving Orishas, including petitions, benevolent incantations, and a variety of rites using the elements of nature.

In Sacred Umbanda, the entities that are channeled and evoked by its practitioners are similar to those found in Popular Umbanda. Additionally, the religion recognizes 14 main Orishas, which are divided into 7 masculine and 7 feminine polarities, reflecting the *yin* and *yang* principles.

Altars are usually adorned with candles, crystals, flowers, bead necklaces, idols, and drinks, while ritualistic herbal baths and specific colors for clothing and crystals are also addressed accordingly. The mediums may also mimic the appearance of the entities before channeling, thereby choosing the tools, such as capes, to better portray the spirit during service.

Eclectic Umbanda is a variant that bears a remarkable resemblance to Traditional Umbanda and given the similarities, the former is often regarded as a direct subtype of the latter. Eclectic Umbanda established its principles and foundation around the 1940s, and in 1976, a compilation of maxims titled "Fundamentals of the Eclectic Doctrine" was published by Master Yokaanam, the spiritual leader of the Eclectic Spirituality.

Within this practice, the Orishas are frequently syncretized with Catholic saints, resulting in a significant departure from their African roots. The rites, or services, closely resemble those of Traditional Umbanda, where words of wisdom, particularly directed towards Jesus, are commonly expressed. Mediums channel spirits, convey messages, and perform passes. They also work with traditional spirit groups such as Mestizos, Old Blacks, and Children.

The Orishas consist of seven main deities, apart from the primary one, predominantly through syncretic personification: Jesus, who serves as the principal symbol; St. John the Baptist; St. Custodian; Saint Catherine; St. Sebastian; St. George; St. Hieronymus; and St. Lazarus. Within the centers, it is not uncommon to find Christian crosses, depictions of Jesus, and images of Catholic saints.

Unlike other forms of Umbanda, percussion instruments, bead necklaces, alcoholic beverages, and cigars are seldom, if not entirely avoided. In rituals, however, candles, smokers, flowers, and other tools of natural origin are utilized.

The leaders of Eclectic Umbanda are referred to as clerics, emphasizing their focus on Jesus and his teachings. The attire of the mediums typically consists of traditional white clothing, which stands out in contrast to the vibrant garments commonly worn in other forms of Umbanda. Often, the priests may adopt the appearance of devout Franciscans.

Esoteric Umbanda, also known as Aumbhanda or Initiatory Umbanda, is a type of Umbanda that draws heavily on the influences of esoteric schools, including Theosophy, Jewish Kabbalah, European paganism, yoga, numerology, and astrology. Woodrow Wilson Silva founded this branch of Umbanda and established its principles in a book published in 1956. In this branch of Umbanda, initiation is usually required. A sort of Umbanda guru, usually called a master, teaches and decides with their pupils whether they are ready to receive certain information and be able to perform certain spiritual works.

Within Esoteric Umbanda, the Orishas are somewhat distanced from their African origins and have adapted to a contemporary reality where the divine is not tied to culture or ethnicity. It is worth noting that across all forms of Umbanda, the Orishas are interpreted differently when compared to traditional African cults and Candomblé. While they retain their names and essence, their mythologies and liturgical practices are perceived with a more universalist and modern view rather than through the lens of ancestral or worldly characteristics.

Its mediums work with a range of spirit groups, especially Mestizos, Old Blacks, and Children. The spirits of Eshus and Pombagiras are also present. This branch of Umbanda is grounded in the concept of trinities, which permeate various aspects of its belief system. Within the cult, the Orishas are categorized into three distinct groups, as are the classes of spirits they collaborate with. These classes symbolize strength, wisdom, and purity, aligning with the Yogic principles of *mantra*, *tantra*, and *yantra*. The methods employed in this branch are deeply intertwined with the notion of "threes," extending across diverse realms. For instance, from a cosmic perspective, the concept of the 'big bang' encompasses light, sound, and movement, while the divisions of realms manifest as endless, timeless, and dimensionless, as well as finite, timed, and spatial.

Esoteric Umbanda also places particular emphasis on the number seven, correlating the seven vibrations of Orishas to other systems that adopt or reveal seven categories. Symbols and sigils hold significant importance within their practice, serving as potent representations of its core elements.

Esoteric Umbanda is one of the branches most connected to nature, not only in their rites but also in their philosophy, where elementals of nature and nature spirits play a significant role in their practices and beliefs. During services, the mediums may wear mostly white or bright-colored clothing and utilize natural necklaces and ritualistic instruments such as flowers, candles, drinks, crystals, smokers, and boards marked with symbols. Unlike in other forms of Umbanda, drumming is not present in these centers, though chants and mantras are invariably adopted.

Jurema Umbanda places central importance on the reverence for the sacred Jurema tree (*mimosa tenuiflora*), symbolizing the ancestral essence of humanity. While different variations of Umbanda may lean more towards a Spiritist doctrine, esoteric, or have stronger Yoruba influences, Jurema places a broader emphasis on the indigenous Brazilian roots of Umbanda. Occasionally referred to as 'catimbó,' derived from the Tupi language for "smoke," this form of Umbanda incorporates Catholic prayers in a syncretic manner and includes the imagery of Christian saints. It is important to note that in Jurema Umbanda, the Jurema tree itself is of utmost importance but is not worshipped; rather, it is seen as a bridge facilitating a connection with the spiritual realms. Followers of Jurema Umbanda may partake in a tea made from the bark of this plant, among others, which can induce alleged expanded states of consciousness. This practice enables contact with the divine, ancestral spirits, and nature spirits, also known as "enchanted beings," which constitute a fundamental concept in the belief system. Among the spirits revered, channeled, and celebrated in Jurema Umbanda, Mestizos hold a prominent position. Additionally, Old Blacks, Eshus, Pombagiras, Bohemians, and others are also part of their ritual practices.

Jurema Umbanda draws heavily from shamanic traditions, incorporating herb-based baths, smudging, and other rituals that tap into the power and assistance of nature. Rattles, drums, pipes, candles, and other natural tools are commonly employed to facilitate trance states and spiritual experiences.

Jurema Umbanda is characterized by its adaptability, as it does not discriminate among deities or practices while maintaining a strong emphasis on traditional shamanic practices involving the use of herbs. However, despite its distinct practices, Jurema Umbanda remains firmly rooted in the core principles of Umbanda, thus legitimately categorizing it as a form of Umbanda.

As part of their spiritual journey, adherents of Jurema Umbanda often undergo a baptism where they receive the symbolic seed of Jurema, signifying their role as disseminators of the tree's energies. In Jurema Umbanda centers, one may observe similarities to Popular Umbanda, and followers may wear white or various other colors and garments typical of Umbanda practices.

Outside the Umbanda Umbrella

Numerous religions share qualities with Umbanda, and some have adopted the term "Umbanda" to broaden their reach and expand their following. Others have adapted their rituals and sessions, thus diversifying their religious possibilities. However, it is essential to acknowledge that a religion can be entirely transformed if its core principles are ignored or adulterated.

For example, Christianity diverged from the principle of the coming of an almighty, vengeful messiah in Judaism by presenting a forgiving and humble man who accepted his crucifixion. Consequently, Christianity is recognized as a new religion distinct from Judaism. Similarly, the principles of papal authority and the veneration of saints, beatified figures who lived in obedience to God's will and are now in heaven, are not acknowledged in Protestantism, resulting in the creation of a new religion rather than a new version of Catholicism.

Umbanda is not a version of Spiritism, as several principles of Spiritism were ignored, such as the lack of a doctrinal text, and adulterated with the inclusion of deity worship. Along these lines, although several religions may appear to be similar to Umbanda, an analysis should be conducted to determine whether the principles of Umbanda have been ignored or adulterated. If the principles are preserved, even with certain elements added or removed, it may still be considered Umbanda. However, if there is an alteration or removal of essential principles, it is not Umbanda but a religion heavily influenced by it, similar to how Christianity was influenced by Judaism and Protestantism was influenced by Catholicism.

> The principles of Umbanda do not include animal sacrifices, rituals aimed at harming others, or charging for spiritual work in the temples. Furthermore, the religion places a strong emphasis on the worship of god-mediating deities, the Orishas. Any deviation from these conventions would categorize the religion in question as an entirely different one, rather than a type of Umbanda. It is important to respect and value all religions, but this assessment is based on their relationship with Umbanda.
>
> As examples, there are certain religions that include the term "umbanda" in their nomenclature, such as "Umbanda Omoloko," "Umbanda of Souls," and "Umbandomblé," as well as those commonly referred to as "traced umbandas." These religions have an Afro- or African-inspired nature and have incorporated certain elements of Umbanda, or those shared with Umbanda, but they are distinct from Umbanda and cannot be accurately characterized as such based on the aforementioned absent principles. Overall, these religions may occasionally be referred to as "Umbanda of Nation" due to the influence of the West African nations from which the cult of Orishas and the cult of ancestors originated.

Kardecist Umbanda, which is essentially Kardecist Spiritism with influences from Umbanda, serves as an example of a religion strongly impacted by Umbandist practices. However, due to the abandonment of many Umbandist principles, it is not considered true Umbanda.

Kardecist Umbanda does not involve the cult of Orishas, nor does it incorporate groups of spiritual entities such as Gypsies or Bohemians in its rituals. Typical features of Umbandist ceremonies, such as the use of smokers, offerings, or candles, are not observed in this branch of Spiritism. Kardecist Umbanda is rooted in the teachings of Spiritist books, particularly those written by Allan Kardec. Nevertheless, this variant of Spiritism accepts in its sessions the presence of spirits identifying themselves as Mestizos, Old Blacks, and others.

A comparison is often made between White Umbanda and Kardecist Umbanda, given their shared absence of Orishas and the use of a table as the focal point for channeling instead of a dedicated open space.

Quimbanda, also spelled Kimbanda, perhaps represents the most widely recognized cult associated with or perceived as a form of Umbanda. Quimbanda amalgamates elements of Macumba, or old Cabula, and European esotericism. The association between Umbanda and Quimbanda may have emerged in early Umbanda when the mediums, subsequent to ceasing the channeling of Mestizo spirits and Old Blacks, began to channel Eshus and Pombagiras. This shift during the service was often referred to as "going Quimbanda."

Quimbanda is heavily rooted in the worship of spirits such as Eshus and Pombagiras, as well as the Orisha Eshu, albeit in a contemporary, urban, and Westernized adaptation of the Yoruba cult. Aligned with magic and a focus on worldly matters, Quimbanda embodies the Left Polarity of spirits, many of whom operate within the realm of Umbanda. Entities such as Old Blacks, Mestizos, and Children of Umbanda are considered representatives of the Right Polarity, whereas Eshus, Pombagiras, and occasionally Bohemians are associated with the Left Polarity. Together, they create a balance of energies, with the Right Polarity emanating the light of God and the Left Polarity absorbing and dispelling the darkness of evil.

In Quimbanda, Eshus and Pombagiras are the only classes of spirits with platforms, and their work primarily focuses on the densest aspects of reality. Quimbanda heavily relies on magic, incantations, and rituals, which are employed for personal benefits such as health, prosperity, and passion, as well as for less virtuous purposes like revenge-driven curses. Within Quimbanda, it is believed that Eshus and Pombagiras possess a neutral stance concerning good and evil, responding to offerings and requests accordingly. In contrast, Umbanda holds the belief that such spirits solely serve the light of God, strictly prohibiting them from engaging in actions that contribute to the misfortunes of individuals. Therefore, those who claim to be working as Eshus and Pombagiras in such a manner are not understood to be authentic manifestations of these spirits but rather Kiumbas[7] disguised as Eshus.

Quimbanda temples differ noticeably from Umbanda centers, characterized by prominent black and red colors and the presence of idols resembling Christian demons. Although these entities are believed to adopt the appearance of demonic beings, it is believed that they do so to command respect in the lower realms, where the spirits of malevolent individuals are governed by fear. Quimbandists do not identify themselves as Umbandists, although certain rituals within Umbanda may involve the participation of Eshus and Pombagiras. Despite distinctions between Umbanda and Quimbanda, some individuals may perceive both as part of the same religious tradition. In addition to the absence of core principles such as charity and humility, Quimbanda may involve animal sacrifices—a practice found in Candomblé and other cults but not in any form of Umbanda. As a result, only traces of Quimbanda can be observed within Umbanda, albeit in a contrasting aspect.

---

7   Kiumbas are spirits of ordinary people who engage in reciprocal exchanges of favors and offerings. Typically driven by malicious intentions, they may masquerade as Eshus and Pombagiras within Quimbanda temples.

God and The Pantheon

The Supreme God, traditionally observed but rarely, if ever, spoken of in Umbanda, has three manifestations: Olodumare as the Creator; Olorun[8] as the ruler of the heavens; and Olofin as the conduit between Heaven and Earth. These distinct manifestations are more closely associated with the myths in which each of these names was employed than with an actual separation of their qualities. [This resembles what is observed in the Hindu pantheon with Brahman, Vishnu, and Shiva.]

In Umbanda, Olorun is considered the one and only God who created and sustains all that exists. While Umbandists believe that God's essence is divine, it is widely acknowledged that It manifests in both spiritual and physical forms through Its creations. That is, for humans, God is perceived to have both spiritual and physical manifestations, and these aspects are often classified into multiple and distinct entities.

The idea of the Judaeo-Christian God, for instance, is primarily rooted in the portrayal of an elderly man with a white beard and hair sitting on a throne. However, the First Testament explicitly states that "no one can see God's face" (Exodus 33:20), while the Second Testament asserts that "God's appearance is indescribable" (John 4:24), which are deemed the most accurate accounts. Nonetheless, the books of Ezekiel (1:26–28) and Revelation (1:14–16), from both Testaments, appear to delve into the personification or clairvoyant vision of what the alleged prophets believed was God. In Ezekiel

---

8 For didactic purposes, this work will employ "Olorun" more often than "Olodumare" or "Olofin," as it appears to be the term more widely used in Umbanda second to "God."

1:26–28, the passage describes a figure like that of a man sitting on a throne of sapphire, while in Revelation 1:14–16, God is revealed as having hair as white as snow. Perhaps these passages were not a vision of God but of another deity, but if not, they were likely attempts to personify God to better convey His power through a throne and His wisdom through a certain age group. Notwithstanding, while Judaeo-Christian schools depict a purely monotheistic system with one God, Yoruba and later Umbanda schools metaphorically describe their only God's appearance as different traits embodied by distinct entities. Along these lines, it can be suggested that the Greek and Roman pantheons, which represent a single god as various deities, are examples of this idea of how a variety of gods create and sustain creation, despite those cultures' theological view defending empirical polytheism as opposed to a supreme god represented by other gods.

Your text is well-written, but I've made a slight refinement for clarity:

As a classification system for the divine, it is commonly believed that the Orishas, synonymous with God expressed on Earth, can be further segmented into distinct frequencies, much like radio frequencies (purely for didactic purposes). Each frequency, or each god, carries a unique characteristic of creation and sustenance, akin to the vibration scale of musical octaves or the various streams of light in a rainbow. For example, the color red, associated with the longest wavelength, represents the slowest oscillation of light within matter and, on a metaphysical level, governs attributes such as physical strength, determination, conquest, and impulse. That color hence acquires an archetype, being violet its opposite.

Based on the analogy, the archetypal holograms of these frequencies, often personified as deities, are responsible for shaping all that is related to the mentioned qualities, ranging from physical atoms to solar systems and other multiverses. The derivations of the main facets of God into frequencies go beyond just two or three aspects; they extend into various others. In this fashion, each Orisha possesses one or more attributes based on the frequencies they represent, or on which wavelength they are analogous to. Consider that each Orisha is part of the same God, and, akin to colors and their wavelengths, each deity has a different vibratory signature.

Viewing God as a field benefits in comprehending how It subdivides into distinct divine frequencies within the physical universe. Consequently, God, and by extension the Orishas in Umbanda, can be likened[9] to a field that permeates all space-time. This concept can also be perceived as an amalgamation of diverse waves at varying frequencies interpenetrating each other. Each frequency composing God possesses a unique amplitude, which organizes them into vibrational groups that can be analogous to the Orishas. Thus, every Orisha represents a facet of God, with their manifestations occurring at different frequencies. This is analogous to how light, seemingly uniform as a white or colorless ray, is actually dispersed into a spectrum of colors, as observed in a rainbow.

God creates and sustains Its creations consistently; however, Its creations are diverse. Therefore, each creation emerges from specific vibrations and is sustained by precise and corresponding frequencies.

All in all, an Orisha is a specific personality of God on Earth, allowing It to be accessed and understood more effectively. God is "wholeness," thus the Orishas are divisions of the whole.

In terms of frequency, the Greek god Ares personifies the initial category and is comparable to Hanuman in Hinduism, Montu in ancient Egypt, Tyr in Scandinavian mythology, Huitzilopochtli in Aztec mythology, Hachiman in Shintoism, Camalus in Celtic mythology, and Ogun in Umbanda. While many of these deities have been associated with warfare, their metaphorical significance lies in representing the physical strength and courage associated with that divine frequency itself.

Characteristics such as 'war' and 'beauty,' or tools like swords and scepters, served as straightforward ways to convey the deity's intended symbolism, but natural occurrences such as rain, sunshine, or lightning ultimately determined the essence of that specific divine being. In ancient times, many cultures attributed thunder to the wrath of a deity, which is why the term "god of thunder" was commonly used. However, this belief is not entirely founded in the religion's theology. Rather, such gods symbolize the aspects of God that are represented through the powerful and awe-inspiring phenomenon of thunder, such as order and strength. Along these lines, thunder symbolically conveys an aspect of the divine related to rigor. These

---

9 Also for didactic purposes only.

characteristics are deeply rooted in the collective unconscious, as evidenced by the fact that thunder is often perceived as a sound that imposes its authority, causing fear and temporarily paralyzing those who hear it. Over time, the association melted into religious dogma and misinformation, where devotees started to literally link gods with their mundane or natural world, thus forgetting that that was a result of associative metaphors.

Throughout the history of theist religions, various divine frequencies were personified and incorporated into the image and dominion of certain gods, based on interpretations of nature's characteristics. Concurrently, the absence of written communication in ancient times necessitated the dissemination of religion through myths, fostering emotional understanding and easy recall. When mythology portrays a god of war carrying a sword, guarding gates, wearing red clothes, and triumphing over all challenges and opponents, the worshiper I able to imagine the image of that god and attune to its qualities. By entering into a mental state correlated with the archetype of that particular god, the worshiper may feel closer and more intimate, psychologically embodying the god's traits, or at least, as per what they have learned about that god.

It is unlikely that people of several millennia ago would have comprehended the concept of a singular God expressed in diverse manners, much like some might not have understood that a rainbow is composed of apparently transparent and colorless light. Thus, it was easier to represent similar characteristics in a god with a human appearance, enabling religious foundations to be passed on without intrinsic complications.

The correlation among gods and divinities across various cultures reveals a consistent presence of shared characteristics, albeit manifested through different names and attire. These parallel divinities convey analogous messages, resonances, and distinctive qualities as perceived by the mediums, shamans, and prophets of each respective culture.

The following comparison is grounded in the fundamental features of gods, deities, and divine figures. It is essential to note that, while the cult of a particular god in one religion may be the central focus of their pantheon, its association or correlation with a god from another culture, which may have a minor cult, occurs due to variations in the preferences of each religion, region, and era of religious dissemination. These variations are based on the specific needs and priorities of the local population.

For instance, a community facing constant invasions, where battles are crucial for their survival, is likely to prioritize a god of war as their primary deity. In contrast, a population heavily dependent on rain for their crops will probably emphasize a deity associated with rain and harvest as their paramount figure. In the context of Umbanda, for instance, Ogun embodies qualities of battle, assertiveness, and strength among the Orishas. However, despite his popularity, he is not considered the most prominent or powerful Orisha in the religion. Conversely, for the Aztecs, the deity that can be paralleled with Ogun in terms of similarities in personality assumes the utmost importance.

As an illustration of deities and gods from diverse cultures, which can be compared to some extent based on their attributes, follows:

Scandinavian	Shinto	Yoruba	Greek	Aztec	Celtic	Hindu	Egyptian
Rán	Izanami	Nana	Hecate	Mictēcacihuātl	Cailleach	Kali	Isis
Freyja	Kichijoten	Oshun	Aphrodite	Xochiquetzal	Branwen	Lakshmi	Hathor
Tyr	Hachiman	Ogun	Ares	Huitzilopochtli	Camalus	Hanuman	Montu
Skadi	Fūjin	Oya	Artemis	Itzpapalotl	Nemain	Durga	Bast
Frigg	Benzaiten	Yemoja	Athena	Chalchiuhtlicue	Rosmerta	Saraswati	Bastet
Loki	Ame-no-Uzume	Eshu	Hermes	Ehecatl	Nantosuelta	Shiva	Set
Ullr	Inari Ōkami	Inle	Dynisius	Patecatl	Cernunnos	Banka-Mundi	Tote
Odin	Amaterasu	Obatala	Pistis	Quetzalcoatl	Brigid	Brahma	Ra
Hel	Izanagi	Omulu	Hades				Anubis
Heimdallr	Kuninotokotachi	Oshunmare	Attis		Artio		Kebechet
Eir	Ōkuninushi	Osanyin	Asclepius	Ixtlilton	Diancecht		
Thor	Takemikazuchi	Shango	Zeus		Taranis	Indra	Ma'at
Njord	Ryūjin	Olokun	Poseidon				
Braggi	Tenjin	Ewa	Apollo	Xochipilli	Caer Ibormeith		Qetesh
Yggdrasil	Jurōjin	Iroko	Cronos			Kala	
Balder		Logunede	Eros / Adonis		Aengus	Krishna	
		Aje Shaluga	Plutus		Nehalennia		
		Ibeji	Pollux and Castor				Bes
	Jizo	Obaluaye		Mictlāntēcutli	Airmed	Shitala Devi	Osiris
		Oba	Atalanta		Flidais	Banka-Mundi	Pakhet

West African Mythology: The Creation

According to Yoruba mythology[10], Olorun (Olódùmarè)—the supreme God—sent the Orishas to Earth to aid in His creation and impart knowledge to humanity.

In one of the most widely disseminated mythologies regarding creation, Olorun, the divine creator, embarked on the task of shaping the Earth. Upon its creation, the planet was a chaotic sphere engulfed in fire, volcanic eruptions, and smoke. However, Olorun's vision extended beyond the tumultuous landscape, desiring firm ground, flowing water, and, most importantly, the capacity to sustain life. To fulfill this grand design, Olorun chose his son, Obatala, to descend to Earth and give it form. Equipped with a celestial bag containing the essential elements for creation, a chicken for cultivating the soil, and a lizard to propagate life, Obatala commenced his sacred mission.

This legend says that the Orishas have always existed and that they all inhabited *orun*, or the heavens, before their incarnation on Earth. However, other legends suggest that certain Orishas, such as Shango (Sàngó), were once humans and later became Orishas, while others, like Oshossi (Ọ̀ṣọ́ọ̀sì), were Orishas that incarnated and later returned to orun. However, most myths agree that Obatala (Ọbàtálá; 'Oshala' in Umbanda) and Odudua (Odùduwà) only came to Earth to participate in the creation of the world, subsequently returning to the divine planes.

Before setting foot on Earth, Obatala sought guidance from the oracle Orunmila, an Orisha revered for wisdom. Orunmila advised Obatala to make an offering to Orisha Eshu, a crucial step to ensure a smooth journey and successful creation. However, as Obatala

---

10 Umbanda, as a practice, typically does not integrate the myths or African symbology linked to the narratives of Orishas. Nevertheless, for the purpose of fostering a more comprehensive understanding, this work endeavors to explore the mythological origins of these entities.

descended, he encountered Eshu but neglected to make the prescribed offering.

In response to this oversight, Eshu, the mischievous messenger of the Orishas, enacted a consequence: Obatala would face thirst during his earthly journey. But undeterred, Obatala pressed on and, miraculously, discovered a palm tree. Drawing wine from its trunk, he quenched his thirst, inadvertently becoming drunk and eventually succumbing to a deep slumber.

Meanwhile, Obatala's sister, Odudua, a figure often misconstrued as male, had made a prior offering to Eshu. Observing the events that unfolded with him, Odudua seized the opportunity to take the bag of creation from her inebriated brother. With the divine artifacts in her possession, Odudua ascended to the heavens and recounted the story to their father, Olorun.

Acknowledging the turn of events, Olorun granted Odudua permission to complete the creation of the world. Bestowing upon her a chicken, a lizard, and a pigeon, Olorun entrusted Odudua with the responsibility of fashioning the Earth into a harmonious and life-sustaining realm.

Odudua descended to Earth, opened the bag of creation, and scattered a handful of earth, which the chicken scratched at, spreading life and expanding the land.

Upon awakening from his drunken stupor, Obatala returned to heaven and informed his father that everything had already been created by someone else. Olorun, disappointed, punished Obatala for failing in his mission, forbidding him from ever drinking wine again.

This myth also serves to remind those worshiping Orishas to always offer Eshu before they start any ritual or any worship of other Orishas, as Eshu is the communicating energy between planes and thus the one who conveys all to and from other planes. Furthermore, it contains a hint to never offer Obatala alcoholic drinks, whom can only receive in his offerings water and juices—for vibratory reasons that this book will dive into deeper in the next chapters.

Another well-known myth about the origins of Earth and humans states that Olorun lived in the heavens with the Orishas, but He wished for them to have their own home and kingdom. Thereupon, Olorun created Earth, or *àiyé*. The first Orisha sent to Earth was

Odudua, followed by Obatala, who was sent to help spread life. On his mission, Obatala asked all the other Orishas to assist him in choosing where they would like to reside on Earth. Obara[11] chose the paths; Ogun chose the minerals; Oshun chose the freshwater; Yemoja, the rivers and seawaters; Oya, the winds; Shango, the mountaintops and the lava of the volcanoes; Oshossi, the forests and woodlands; Obaluaye, the drylands; and Nana, the swamps and mud.

Afterwards, Obatala decided to create humanity, seeking the assistance of the Orishas for that. He attempted to create humans from freshwater and seawater, but it slipped from his grasp. He tried making humans from air, but they had no form. Then he tried to create them from stones and minerals, but they were too rigid. He also tried making them from green leaves, but they would not bond together. Finally, Orisha Nana brought him mud, which contained the essence of all the Orishas, and with it, Obatala was finally able to create humans. Pleased, he then blew the breath of life into them.

Obatala was content with his creation and decided to make all humans unique, and just as each Orisha has a distinct personality, each human would resemble an Orisha in their temperament: some would be calm like himself, or sweet like Oshun, or brave like Ogun, or patient like Nana, or agile like Oya, or fair like Shango, or communicative like Obara, or nurturing like Yemoja, or diligent like Oshossi, and so on.

According to Yoruba theology, it is held that the entirety of the Orishas trace their origins back to the four primary deities initially created by Olorun. These deities are:

Ọbàtálá, Ọrúnmìlà, Odùduwà, and Olóòkun. Ọbatala symbolizes the embodiment of the divine breath of life, signifying the essence of air itself. This deity serves as a representation of the vital force that animates all living beings.

Ọ̀rúnmìlà is recognized as the witness of creation and, consequently, the observer of the choices individuals make throughout their lives. This deity embodies the transformative power of fire, illustrating the profound influence of personal decisions on one's existence.

---

11 Obara is the name by which the Orisha Eshu is known in some religious circles. In the Caribbean and in the United States, Eshu is known as *Elegbara, Bara, Elegba,* or *Eleggua*, depending on the cult.

Odùduwà embodies the divinization of Earth and the process of its creation. As the representative of the earth, this deity symbolizes the fertile ground from which all life springs forth.

Olóòkun, known as the mother of the seas, but occasionally observed as masculine, epitomizes the unity of all things and all individuals. This deity stands as a symbol of the unifying element of water, representing the interconnectedness and harmonious coexistence of everything.

The distinctive embodiments of air, fire, earth, and water by the primary Orishas contribute to a better comprehension of Yoruba cosmology, illuminating the intricate interplay between the divine and human experiences. Consequently, it becomes apparent that certain Orishas, namely Yemoja and Oshun, trace their origins back to Olokun, the Orisha representing water. Similarly, Shango find his roots in Orunmila, the Orisha associated with fire. Orishas representing air, such as Oya (Yansa) and Ogun, can be traced back to Obatala (Oshala). And finally, Orishas embodying earth, such as Oshossi and Obaluaye, derive their existence from Odudua. Nonetheless, it is important to note that an Orisha can have multiple origins or affiliations. For instance, Shango, known for embodying the element of fire, also has earth in his lineage, descending from both Orunmila and Odudua.

From Yorubaland to The New World

Scholars have varying views on the timeline of the origins of the Ifá[12] philosophy, which preceded the cult of Orisha in West Africa. Ifá is a philosophical and oracular tool that is used to communicate with the knowledge of Orunmila—the Orisha of wisdom and divination—and receive messages through signs, poems, and stories based on *odù*. Each odù reveals a particular essence and represents different situations, actions, and consequences in life. Orunmila is a prominent figure in Yoruba mythology and is known for his encounter with the trickster Orisha, Eshu. According to the myth, Orunmila descended from heaven into the world of humans with a divination tray filled with sixteen sacred palm nuts. Eshu, a mischievous and unpredictable deity, played a trick on Orunmila by offering him a choice between a long life filled with poverty or a short life filled with wealth. Orunmila wisely chose a long life and, thus, was able to accumulate great wisdom and knowledge. In the context of Ifá, it is believed that Eshu is the intermediary who provides the necessary energy to the oracle, enabling communication between *orun* (heaven) and *aiye* (earth).

Ifá is regarded as the source of answers to the questions that humans seek, and it all starts with Orunmila. The oracle employs *erindinlogun* (cowrie shells) and *obi* (kola nuts) to convey messages, which are predetermined by the calculations based on how these

---

12 Smith (2013) highlighted that Ifá holds a mathematical analogy with the Real Clifford Algebra Cl(8), and the 16 Orishas of each *odù* mirror the 8+8 Spinors of Cl(8). Continuing, the author asserts that, as human migrations from Africa to India unfolded via the Arabian Sea, ideas from Ifá found expression in the Sanskrit Rig Veda and were encoded within the game *Pachisi*. These concepts were also encoded in the Great Pyramid. Around 500 B.C.E., Indian Vedic Pachisi transformed into Tarot, and by 1300 C.E., Tarot, along with certain aspects of Ifá, had reached Mallorca. There, Ramon Llull used these ideas to organize the D4 and D8 Lie Algebras that are part of the Ifá Clifford Algebra Cl(8) and its tensor square Cl(8)xCl(8) = Cl(16). The work establishes that Ifá, originating in Ancient Africa, disseminated globally, mirroring the spread of humanity itself. Descendant systems, including the 128-element Shinto Divination, the 64-element I Ching, and the 16-element Ilm Al Raml, may all stem from the comprehensive 256-element Ifá framework.

items fall on the tray. Although Ifá is occasionally used as a name for Orunmila, it is important to note that Ifá is not an Orisha, a religion, or a sect. Instead, it can be understood as a system, similar to astrology, that aims to guide regardless of one's religion. Along these lines, practitioners of Ifá are those who worship Orunmila and hence utilize that tool.

Akintoye (2010) posits that Ifá dates back to the 4th to 8th centuries B.C.E., originating from the Neolithic proto-Benue-Kwa populations who expanded with the use of iron tools. It is also observed that by the 8th century C.E., Ilé-Ifẹ̀, one of the earliest and most powerful kingdoms in Africa, had already been established, and the proto-Yoruboid, who developed from the earlier populations, had a variety of practices inherited from their proto-Benue-Kwa ancestors. These included cultivating a variety of vegetables and fruits, iron smelting, and particularly the use of the 16-point divination system.

As the various *odù* of Ifá were associated with various Orishas due to the similarities between the messages and what the Orishas represented, over time, the direct worship of Orishas became more prominent and developed into a separate cult.

As the cult of Orisha originated in West African nations such as today Nigeria and Benin, the significance and roles of the Orishas differed across these regions and among their neighboring tribes. Some tribes observed the Orishas as manifestations of God, while others viewed these deities as symbols of legendary and often mythical martyrs who, after death, gained the power to rule their tribes on behalf of God. These perspectives were also shared by other ancient West African nations, such as the Dahomey, Odinani, and Ekpe.

According to the Yoruba people and their understanding of the Orishas (then spelled *òrìṣà*), these entities possess the ability to reflect some of the manifestations of Olodumare, the Supreme God.

The Yoruba Orishas, often improperly translated as "idols" and sometimes as "deities" or "gods," are typically depicted and venerated as intermediaries between humanity and the supernatural. Within Yorubaland, these Orishas were esteemed for their mastery over specific aspects of nature. However, it is important to note that not all Orishas were considered primordial deities; some were perceived more like ancient heroes and sages. As Olumide (1948) suggests, those belonging to the latter category were better described as "dema" deities.

Certain òrìṣà were originally linked to ancestor worship. This included warriors, kings, and the founders of cities, who were honored even after their passing and eventually integrated into the pantheon of Yoruba deities. Rather than being perceived as having passed away, these ancestors were viewed as having 'disappeared' and transitioned into òrìṣà. As noted by Brandon (2009), some historically-based Orishas were primarily worshiped within their respective families or the cities of their origin, while others gained reverence across wider geographical regions.

Before the onset of the transatlantic slave trade to the Americas, the West African nations where the worship of Orishas was evolving did not adhere to a pantheon cult of Orishas. Instead, each nation, which can be described as a 'city,' primarily revered a single Orisha. This meant that, for example, if Ṣàngó was the patron Orisha in the West African city of Oyó, then Ṣàngó and no other Orisha would preside over it, as all its inhabitants would only worship Ṣàngó as their primary deity. However, upon their forced relocation to regions such as Brazil, the United States, Haiti, and other New World colonies, many of these African tribes from various regions were amalgamated, leading to the emergence of cults centered around multiple Orishas, with Candomblé being one of the prominent examples.

In the early 16th century, enslaved people were taken to Brazil from regions where the Yoruba and Nkisi[13] cults held sway, and they carried with them the concept of various Orishas. These Orishas had been patrons of their native lands, and their worship gained prominence among the enslaved population in the New World. In Candomblé, a Brazilian religion that amalgamated the worship of various Orishas from different West African nations, incorporating elements from local worship practices, the concept of each Orisha presiding over a specific city ceased to exist. This transformation occurred primarily because the religion was established by enslaved individuals and former slaves hailing from diverse parts of Africa, each part with their own patron Orisha. Furthermore, all the Orishas

---

13 The Nkisi are analogous to the Orishas in the Central African region, specifically in the Congo and Angola. The term 'nkisi' can have multiple meanings, such as spirit, healing, and amulet.

revered in Candomblé underwent slight adaptations to fit the Brazilian style of worship. While there was initial syncretism for safety reasons, it eventually led to a unique Brazilian perspective on Orisha worship. This approach made each Orisha's conception less redundant and less contradictory compared to their counterparts in Africa, where certain cities and tribes were often at odds with one another and, consequently, with their respective patron Orishas. In most cases, however, the animosity in Yorubaland was rooted more in the *itans*, or Yoruba myths, than in actual rivalries among the Orishas.

Nevertheless, it is crucial to emphasize that there are significant distinctions between the cult of Orishas in Candomblé and that in Umbanda, and even more so between the Yoruba perspective and that of Umbanda. While the original names and primary characteristics were, to some extent, retained, their interpretation within the religion and the methods and motivations behind their worship differed significantly. Additionally, the belief in a supreme God and the role of the Orishas as intermediaries between "above" (God) and "below" (humans) are non-negotiable aspects of Umbanda. However, the human qualities attributed to the Orishas have largely remained unchanged, although their less favorable qualities are absent in Umbanda, as other traits are observed in a more metaphorical sense.

In Umbanda, the perception of an Orisha is that they not only mediate between God and Earth but also represent facets of the Supreme God. Furthermore, the view of an Orisha as a spirit is entirely absent, as is the possibility that some of them may have incarnated as individuals at a certain point in history.

Umbanda's approach to Orisha worship differs from other religious traditions where deities occupy a more prominent role. The substitution of Orishas with phalanxes, or groups of spirits operating under the auspices of those Orishas, is inherent in the practice. Consequently, appeals to Oshossi, for instance, involve interaction with Mestizo spirits, while appeals to Oshala find resonance with the Old Blacks as a point of access. Similarly, invoking the spirits of Eshus and Pombagiras, aligned with the class of spirits associated with Orisha Eshu, is the customary approach in contrast to summoning that Orisha directly.

Orishas According to Umbanda

Umbanda, as a cohesive religion, exhibits a unified framework, yet it diverges into distinct branches that revere, acknowledge, or contemplate a varying number of Orishas—ranging from 7 to 11, and occasionally even more. Therefore, the present study compiles a comprehensive number of Orishas, presented in no particular hierarchy, nevertheless, it commences with Oshala, often regarded as the patriarch of all Orishas, and culminates with Eshu, epitomizing the absolute counterpoint to Oshala in terms of spiritual frequency within the divine realm reflected on Earth.

Establishing a parallel between the Seven Domains of Orishas, present in various branches of Umbanda, the Seven Rays delineated in occultist schools[14], the Seven Archangels of God depicted in Christian literature[15], and an esoteric planetary association, one can discern a potential influence on some of the proposed classifications of the Orishas and their seven domains from other philosophical traditions. This observation adds an intriguing layer to this subject. However, it is equally plausible that no external influence was exerted, and the alignment with seven expressions of the Orishas merely reflects the inherent harmony found in the seven branches of diverse philosophies.

The items in the following comparison table may not precisely align with one another due to variations in angelic classifications or differences in hierarchical orders proposed by diverse schools. Nevertheless, this work will adhere to the conventions of the most traditional schools within each philosophy. Consequently, there may be occasional discrepancies in the compatibility of the items.

---

14 H.P. Blavatsky, (1888). The Secret Doctrine; C. W. Leadbeater, (1925). *The Masters and the Path.*
15 Pseudo-Dionysius the Areopagite, (5th-6th C.E.). *Corpus*: Divine Names.

Domains of Orishas (Umbanda)	Seven Rays (Theosophy)	Seven Archangels of God (Christian)	Planetary association
Faith	First Ray – will	Michael – fortress	Mars
Knowledge	Second Ray – mind	Gabriel – consciousness	Mercury
Justice	Third Ray – magnetic forces	Raphael – healing	Sun
Generation	Fourth Ray – physical development	Jophiel – beauty	Moon
Evolution	Fifth Ray – material substances	Uriel – wisdom	Jupiter
Love	Sixth Ray – devotion	Camael – compassion	Venus
Law	Seventh Ray – ceremony	Zadkiel – mercy	Saturn

Umbanda is a monotheistic religion where the Orishas can occasionally be understood as divine intermediary deities to God. Along these lines, they facilitate a connection with God, rather than being separate entities or considered lesser than a supreme God.

In Umbanda's tenets, God primarily expresses Itself through seven main attributes: faith, knowledge, law, love, justice, evolution, and generation. From these attributes, other distinct qualities emerge. For instance, patience and peace derive from faith, work and art stem from knowledge, vitality and courage are born of law, beauty and desire emanate from love, justice leads to prosperity and purification, evolution transforms into healing and change, and generation conceives principles and family.

The idea of Orishas was introduced to Umbanda by Orisha Mallet[16] and Father Tony, who envisioned bridging God with the various groups of spirits that were going to work in Umbanda, based on the divine energy influencing them. Moreover, the concept of Orishas helped reconcile the idea of a single God displaying different

---

16 Orisha Mallet is a spirit who chose to take his name in honor of the Orishas, but he is not considered an Orisha himself.

characteristics, much like facets of human personality. While God is considered perfect, it is implicitly believed that humans cannot fully comprehend It. Therefore, they rely on reflections of God's attributes through other deities to gain glimpses of its vastness. For example, Yemanja, the Orisha of maternity, family, the mind, and generation, represents a facet of the Supreme God expressed in the world as these divine concepts: maternity, family, the mind, and generation.

In Umbanda, the personality traits of the Orishas have evolved to become more magnanimous and benevolent. Mundane traits that once served to exemplify their essence, as seen in the Yoruba religion, have weakened, and their rivalries, as portrayed in myths, have disappeared. For instance, explosive behavior, envy, or grumpiness, which are typically depicted in the myths of Ogun, Oshun, and Nana, have been replaced with explanations of how those under the guidance of these Orishas may behave when not spiritually aligned with the Orisha's teachings.

Image 6: Statue of Yemanja, Brazil

Unlike Yoruba cults and their immediate derivatives, Umbanda does not emphasize specific dogmas based on the characteristics of the Orisha, such as avoiding certain foods, habits, or dressing codes that are discordant with that Orisha. However, these notions are still considered legitimate efforts to prevent devotees from encountering conflicting energies that might impede their connection with their Orisha.

One of the most significant differences between Yoruba cults and Umbanda lies in their rituals. In Yoruba and its offshoots, such as Candomblé, mediums can channel the Orishas through deep trance, where they wear regalia to emulate the Orisha, dance and manifest the Orisha's *ashe*—its divine energy. On the other hand, in Umbanda, Orishas are perceived as archetypal energies directly linked to God, making direct channeling impossible, as it would mean channeling God Itself. Instead, in Umbanda, Orishas can influence spiritual entities who can be channeled since they are spirits like incarnated humans are.

As archetypes of God, the Orishas are associated with the beliefs of those who worship them, creating an 'agregore,' or shared thought-form. It is still possible that individuals may have clairvoyant visions of an Orisha, serving as catalysts for their spiritual growth. These visions may appear in astral projections or, during wakefulness, be the visions of spirits who work under the influence of that Orisha, whereby they emulate their divine supporter. In this manner, it is common for spirits working under the guidance of an Orisha to encounter them and receive their blessings or initiations. The manifested image of an Orisha may even be accessible to a psychic if circumstances warrant. Although considered facets of the divine, the Orishas have indeed engendered a spiritual impression shaped by human beliefs and personification ideas. Their essence remains unaltered, but they harmonize with the faith of their devotees, even if adorned with distinctive imagery, thus acquiring different personifications in various cultures. The energy of God and consequently that of the Orisha is intelligent and can take various forms to suit different situations or be made visible. Therefore, what an individual perceives as an Orisha may be a manifestation of divine energy that has taken on a particular form. This potentiality is applicable to the vast majority of multiple gods in numerous other religions around the world.

Another major difference between the two philosophies is the use of language. In Yoruba and other closely related religions, ancestral terms are employed for tools, foods, and especially chants with percussion, which are mostly sung in Yoruba languages. In Umbanda, Yoruba terms are absent, and chants with percussion are solely sung in Portuguese[17].

In Umbanda, the Orishas are regarded as natural forces that embody the presence of God on Earth. Among them, Oshun, for

---

17 Umbanda chants are conducted in Portuguese as it is the most spoken language of Brazil, which also has a small number of German and Italian speakers. However, if Umbanda is to be practiced in regions outside Brazil, chants can be adapted to the local languages. Chants in Umbanda are essential for helping mediums attain a focused state conducive to trance induction and channeling. In a later part of this work dedicated to chant analysis, examples of chants translated into English will be provided.

instance, is the Orisha associated with rivers, love, prosperity, and beauty. Accordingly, the rivers and waterfalls are the natural sites where Oshun's energy is most abundantly found. Thus, by worshiping near a river or waterfall, devotees believe they can connect with Oshun's divine frequencies of love, beauty, and abundance, which include qualities such as maternal and self-love, self-worth, and material prosperity. Additionally, the spirits who operate under the guidance of Oshun not only embody these qualities but also aid humanity in matters related to love and self-esteem. These attributes belong to an array of deities, as opposed to a singular god that would possess all aspects simultaneously, a characteristic found in most monotheistic religions. In Abrahamic religions, God is singular: omnipotent, meaning all-powerful; omniscient, meaning all-knowing; and omnipresent, meaning God is everywhere at all times. However, a more refined assumption of monotheism is that God possesses all divine characteristics without the need for other gods to represent contrasting properties.

Using the already posited analogy of rainbows, light, as perceived from the Sun, is typically recognized as white or simply 'transparent bright.' However, a rainbow dissects the spectrum, displaying an array of colors within the same flow of light. As is known, contrasting colors are found within the same flash, such as blue and orange, or yellow and violet. All colors in the visible spectrum travel at the same speed. Nevertheless, when light passes through raindrops, the behavior of different colors changes. They appear to shift from all moving at the speed of light to a speed proportional to their unique wavelength, with red moving slower and violet moving faster. Thus, light can be perceived as a spectrum of colors, and each color can be approached differently based on its wavelength. All wavelengths still represent the same light. However, when perceived separately, it becomes easier to understand why light appears white or even colorless.

Applying the example of the rainbow to the Greek pantheon, where each god was associated with a specific quality, it can be assumed that they may have represented variations of the source god, which is singular: Ares as the god of war, representing a physical and aggressive aspect; Apollo as the god of the arts, representing an intellectual aspect; Hermes as the messenger god, representing trade, communication, and exchange; Zeus as the god of thunder, representing order, justice, and laws; and Aphrodite as the goddess of love and beauty, representing passion. In a similar vein, numerous other religions and mythologies throughout history have used a pantheon as a means of accessing the singular God. Ancient Egyptians, Aztecs, Scandinavians, Celts, and Hindus all had and still have polytheism in common. However, the reasons for believing in a pantheon versus just one god were precisely this variety of attributes, which needed to be passed in a less confusion manner. Accepting different gods to portray distinct qualities served to facilitate the understanding of God, as it was almost inconceivable to encompass somewhat contradictory aspects as part of the same god, such as motherhood and combat, or beauty and death. In this context, the Orishas could have emerged in any other geographic location worldwide, irrespective of local depictions in terms of clothing, appearance, and names. This phenomenon is observable in numerous mythologies, pantheons, and religions, all of which could have seen their gods or deities emerge elsewhere. As an example, one might propose that the Kami in Japanese Shintoism shares remarkable similarities with the Orishas, along with other pantheons and religions mentioned earlier.

Head-Orisha

Practitioners of Yoruba traditions believe that daily life depends on proper alignment and understanding of the *ori*. Ori literally means "head," but in spiritual matters, it refers to a portion of the soul (the crown chakra, or *Sahasrara* in Hindu and Yogic traditions) that determines one's personal destiny. *Ori* encompasses the person's intuitive destiny, or the path they are meant to follow in life. In like manner, *orisha* means "lord of the head" and refers to the deities who select one's ori to guide them through life. As the crown chakra represents the principal center of the incarnated soul, the governing Orisha can be understood as the essence that the soul seeks to express throughout its incarnation. It is believed that each individual has a head-Orisha, symbolically alluding to the crown chakra being endowed with a vibratory aspect resonant with a specific facet of God.

Also known as the 'front Orisha,' the head-Orisha refers to the Orisha that emerges with greater strength than any other in one's spiritual path. This Orisha holds authority over an individual's head, and one is advised to cultivate proximity with that deity. Accordingly, as the Orisha selects the individual based on one's needs, they spiritually influence their protégé's life, employing their characteristics in one's journey and personality to foster personal growth.

The selection of an Orisha for their proteges is based on the experiences that the spirit is destined to undergo in earthly life, determined by personal karma, and the challenges the individual has chosen or been advised to face. The 'selection,' simply put, is more about the natural affinity between the individual and the frequency of the Orisha. Therefore, it is unlikely to involve the Orishas personally selecting a protegee.

The identification of an individual's head-Orishas in Umbanda is typically accomplished through mediumship and clairvoyant analysis conducted by the priest of their Umbanda center. In this process, the priest performs a series of rituals and offerings to all the revered Orishas in the temple. If the altar associated with a specific Orisha emits an energetic glow or transmits other forms of non-physical information, it is assumed that that Orisha is the individual's head-Orisha. Additionally, the revelation of one's Orishas may also come through communication from their spirit guide or worker spirit. Another, although less common, method of identification in the Umbanda tradition involves using a divination board and cowrie shells. In this technique, a mathematical, albeit esoteric, counting method determines the specific Orisha. This divination oracle, simply called 'cowries,' is not an integral part of Umbanda sectarism; however, some priests, particularly those influenced by Afro-traditions, may use it. This divination tool is derived from the systems of Ifá.

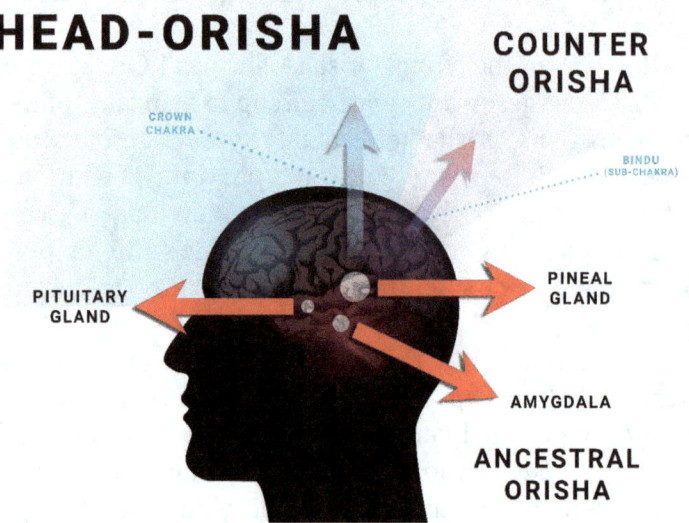

Upon discovering their Orishas, individuals typically embark on a journey of reverence toward their designated master. This usually involves establishing a personal altar, engaging in regular meditation, and performing small rituals at locations associated with the Orisha's places of strength. It is believed that by establishing this connection with their Orishas, devotees experience a sudden beneficial transformation in their lives. Embracing this presence allows one to nurture their essence within themselves and enhance the qualities necessary for personal growth and transformation. Consequently, when a person is aligned with their head-Orisha, it is inevitable that they will be at their best in terms of spiritual needs. Furthermore, entities most closely associated with that Orisha's domain are the ones who predominantly accompany the individual, particularly in the case of mediums. The concept of the head-Orisha, embodying the predominant divine quality within an individual's spiritual framework, does not solely determine behavior or appearance. Rather, it represents the culmination of past actions and behaviors, unfolding as a guiding divine frequency that necessitates cultivation during one's lifetime to foster spiritual growth. Accordingly, the alleged traits characteristic of a particular Orisha that may be present in an individual signify a spiritual imperative to rectify negative traits and enhance positive attributes. These traits are understood to stem from the reason that the Orisha has chosen that individual. In accordance with the belief that all individuals, irrespective of their religious or spiritual beliefs, possess a head-Orisha, it is also believed that each person has a corresponding counter-Orisha whose influence serves to balance that of the head-Orisha. The counter-Orisha imparts reasonable traits of an opposite vibration to their protege, albeit in a minor form. Regarding head-Orisha and counter-Orisha, it is invariably understood that if the former is a 'universal' Orisha, the latter shall be a 'cosmic' Orisha. Universal Orishas encompass those deities that radiate divine light within their respective domains, mainly to one's rational mind, whereas Cosmic Orishas act on draining and consuming the deviated emotions of individuals. As an example, Oshun, being a Universal Orisha, acts on the expansion of love, self-worth, and prosperity. On the other hand, Oshumare, a Cosmic Orisha and the opposing vibration to Oshun in the domain of 'Love,' serves to restrict and restrain that which degrades love, self-worth, and prosperity. In essence, while Oshun expands love in one's life, Oshumare curtails animosity and indifference. Similarly, if Oshala, as a Universal Orisha, expands faith within one's life, Logunan, a Cosmic Orisha, and the opposing vibration to Oshala in the domain of 'Faith,' is believed to diminish mistrust and illusions. Likewise, when Ogun, a Universal Orisha, fortifies courage and determination, Yansa, a Cosmic Orisha, lessens fear and insecurities. One's head-Orisha and counter-Orisha are rarely both representatives of the same domain, meaning that it is seldom, if not almost impossible, to find Oshun and Oshumare as head- and counter-Orisha; or Ogun and Yansa; or Oshala and Logunan, and so on. Typically, the individual will have either a universal or cosmic Orisha of a certain domain as their head-Orisha. Their counter-Orisha will usually belong to another domain, and the polarity will be opposite (cosmic or universal). In summary, if one's head-Orisha is Yansa, a cosmic Orisha, their counter-Orisha should be a universal Orisha. In this scenario, Oshossi would be a suitable counter-Orisha due to its universal nature, while Oshumare, representing cosmic vibration, would not be fitting for this role. Furthermore, the Orishas are classified not only based on their vibratory schemes as Universal or Cosmic deities but also as male and female polarities. These gender classifications, rooted in mythology, hint at the presence of polarities within a vibratory scheme. Consequently, it is not possible to have Yemanja as the head-Orisha and Yansa as the counter-Orisha, or to have Ogun as the head-Orisha and Omulu as the counter-Orisha.

Throne / Domain	Universal Orishas	Cosmic Orishas
Faith	Oshala	Logunan
Knowledge	Oshossi	Oba
Law	Ogun	Yansa
Justice	Shango	Egunita
Love	Oshun	Oshumare
Generation	Yemanja	Omulu
Evolution	Obaluaye	Nana

The Orishas exhibit personalities strikingly akin to those of humans. However, while they embody the pinnacle of human virtues, encompassing boundless love, optimism, relentless personal effort, and profound compassion, they do not mirror the darker aspects of humanity. Instead, when individuals are in their negative aspects of personality, they are believed to be deviating from divine principles associated with their Orisha. For instance, if an individual's head is governed by Ogun—the Orisha of iron, battles, and law—and they conduct themselves uprightly, virtuously, and in alignment with the tenets of the divine, it is said that they embody the positive attributes of Ogun, including resolute determination, courage, indomitable willpower, and adherence to righteousness. However, if an individual employs the shared qualities of Ogun in nefarious pursuits, such as utilizing personal influence to dominate others, harnessing their above-average vitality to engage in conflict, or exploiting their stamina to propagate anger and violence, they are deemed estranged from Ogun and consequently distanced from the path of spiritual progress.

The personality traits, physical characteristics, and inclinations of an individual are believed to be strongly influenced by their head-Orisha. In particular, someone whose head-Orisha is Yemanja may exhibit pronounced traits such as affection, a fondness for familial connections, a fuller physique, and, usually, long hair. On the other hand, an individual whose head-Orisha is Yansa (Oya) might display characteristics such as a loud speaking voice, an affinity for colorful accessories like necklaces and rings, a propensity for laughter, a quick temper, deep affection, and sensuality. Nevertheless, the primary attributes underlying all of these traits revolve around the life path within the context of the family, as exemplified by Yemanja, and the pursuit of independence, as exemplified by Yansa.

Another significant influence on an individual's spiritual journey is the ancestral-Orisha. Unlike the head-Orisha and counter-Orisha, the ancestral-Orisha does not shape the individual's personality traits but is closely associated with one's spiritual essence. In certain Umbanda branches, the ancestral-Orisha is viewed as the divine aspect from which the monad originated – a concept[18] akin to

---

18 In Theosophy, it is asserted that the creation of the monad, which delves into other planes of reality to gain enlightenment, is generated by one of seven Rays, where seven masters lead each Ray. Therefore, if an individual has been generated by the 6th Ray, it means that for eternity, that individual will retain their essence and will one day return to that domain to be a part of that Ray or divine domain.

theosophic schools where the monad is seen as a fragment of God or the solar Logos responsible for generating the core portion of an individual's spirit.

The ancestral-Orisha remains constant throughout all the individual's lifetimes on Earth. For instance, if an individual's ancestral Orisha is Oshala, then Oshala certainly was their ancestral Orisha in their previous lives and will continue to be their ancestral Orisha in their future lives. Notably, the ancestral-Orisha serves as a constant presence that connects the individual to their spiritual origin and provides a profound sense of continuity across lifetimes.

Overall, individuals of both genders have the potential to embody either male or female head-Orishas as well as counter-Orishas. or ancestral-Orishas. Consequently, it is conceivable for women to naturally embody head-Orishas such as Ogun or Shango, while men may naturally exhibit head-Orishas such as Oshun or Yansa.

Worship and Cult

Engaging in worship of an Orisha in Umbanda is not obligatory; rather, it signifies a deliberate and direct alignment with a particular divine emanation. Within this framework, each Orisha is perceived as a distinct emanation, characterized by unique attributes that manifest in various facets of worship. The rituals include the selection of cleansing herbs, the composition of offerings in terms of food and beverages, and the observance of specific colors associated with each Orisha. These material expressions, mirroring the frequencies of the Orishas, are considered manifestations of the divine essence, serving as tangible connections to the cosmic order within the physical realm.

Perceiving Orishas as manifestations of the divine is analogous to recognizing the diverse languages and varying tones through which

God communicates. Revering a specific Orisha can be compared to engaging in conversation using a particular language and adopting a distinct accent. It is imperative to duly acknowledge that the manifestation of power within the Orishas is accompanied by their phalanx or spiritual workers. These entities operate under the vibratory influence of the Orishas, contributing to the intricate fabric of the broader spiritual realm.

The spiritual entities operating under the influence of the Orishas function as intermediaries, often utilizing incarnate mediums to establish a connection between the two planes. Direct communication with the Orishas is non-existent, as they are regarded as divine emanations. Consequently, the initial spiritual entities that manifested in Umbanda brought forth additional insights into the Orishas and their relationship with the divine and humanity. However, it is essential to note that the Orishas transcend the concept of mere archetypes; they are esteemed and, therefore, worshiped as deities.

The Orishas' omnipresence extends across all realms of Earth, as their inherent connection is exclusively to this planet. Their vibratory influence is notably felt in specific natural landscapes, including rivers, woodlands, fields, and mountains. These natural spots are believed to provide ideal settings for reverential practices, offerings, and spiritual communion.

The cult of Orishas in Umbanda encompasses the veneration of divine energy that establishes a connection between God and an individual's crown chakra, particularly when worshiping one's personal head-Orisha. In the context of other Orishas, such as during ceremonies held at a temple dedicated to a specific Orisha, the objective may primarily be to fortify the bond with that deity and assimilate its attributes into one's own life. In essence, there are two main motivations for veneration or devotion to an Orisha: the desire to strengthen one's relationship with the divine through reverence for one's head-Orisha or the act of requesting blessings or expressing gratitude for accomplishments.

Within each Umbanda center, it is customary to honor all Orishas revered in that specific temple, placing particular emphasis on that house's patron Orisha. However, in personal settings, individuals have the freedom to create their own home altars, enabling them to pay homage to their head-Orisha or any other Orishas they choose to revere.

In the initial years of Umbanda, significant emphasis was placed on seven primary Orishas: Oshala, Yemanja, Shango, Oshossi, Ogun, Oshun, and Yansa. While other Orishas were not entirely overlooked, this was not due to a lack of knowledge or intent. Instead, Umbanda aimed to maintain simplicity to cater to its humble practitioners. Additionally, it was believed that these seven Orishas wielded such expansive influence that most other Orishas not explicitly mentioned fell under their overarching sphere.

As Umbanda evolved and expanded, an increasing number of Orishas garnered recognition, thereby enriching the religious tradition with complexity. Simultaneously, the introduction of supplementary classes of spirits aligning themselves with both traditional and newly embraced Orishas within Umbanda gave rise to the concept of "thrones" or "domains" of Orishas, which essentially categorizes the Orishas based on their dovine traits and their respective fields of influence. These conceptual frameworks aided devotees in comprehending the diverse, multifaceted expressions of the divine on Earth. Nevertheless, it is crucial to note that the classification of Orishas and their recognition may diverge depending on the specific branch of Umbanda one follows.

Orishas: Attributes and Stories

Umbanda, as a cohesive religious tradition, maintains a unified framework but diverges into distinct branches that revere, acknowledge, or contemplate varying numbers of Orishas—ranging from 7 to 11, or 14 to 16, and sometimes even more. Therefore, this study aims to compile a comprehensive list of Orishas, presented without a specific hierarchy. Nevertheless, it starts with Oshala, often regarded as the patriarch of all Orishas, and concludes with Eshu, representing the absolute counterpoint to Oshala in terms of vibratory signature within the divine realm reflected on Earth.

Oshala

Oshala, pronounced o-shah-LAH, derived from the proto-Yoruboid term Òrişànlá, which translates to "the great Orisha," is the epitome of faith and peace and is considered the most important and father of all Orishas. This revered Orisha is alternatively recognized as Obàtálá, pronounced o-bah-tah-LAH, a name which is believed to have originated from the combination of the terms "Oba," meaning king, "ta," which is a contraction of *Ìdèta* representing an esteemed organization and town, and *la*, meaning big or great.

Oshala holds paramount significance among the Orishas, being attributed with the pivotal role of receiving divine light from God and subsequently disseminating it to all other Orishas. In this capacity, Oshala is perceived as a unifying force, embodying the collective essence of all other Orishas. Traditionally regarded as the supreme Orisha, statues of Oshala or representations symbolizing him, such as those of Jesus Christ, are positioned atop every Umbandist altar. Nevertheless, it is worth noting that Oshala may garner comparatively lesser popularity in Brazil when compared to other revered Orishas such as Yemanja.

Oshala is the central figure within the category known as the "white Orishas." Within this category, Oshala himself embodies two distinct aspects: Oshalufan, representing his elder manifestation, is often depicted as delicate and fragile, displaying exceptional adherence to moral principles and a profound sense of fraternity. Similarly, individuals whose head-Orisha is Oshalufan often exhibit these qualities as well; and Oshaguian: representing the younger depiction of Oshala, characterized by eloquence, optimism, and a relaxed demeanor. Interestingly, those whose head-Orisha is the youthful version of Oshala are often perceived as taller than the average individual.

Oshala serves as a catalyst for fostering faith, peace, and a grounded perception unobstructed by illusions. Through the amplification of faith, Oshala empowers individuals irrespective of their religious inclinations, guiding them towards a trajectory aligned with higher universal principles. Amidst tumultuous circumstances, Oshala instills serenity; in moments of anxiety, patience emerges; and amidst despair, tranquility prevails. Those who hold reverence for Oshala embody these virtues, reflecting the limitless essence of peace encapsulated within his divine energy.

Individuals whose head-Orisha is Oshala are widely recognized for their remarkable patience and composed temperament. Occasionally exhibiting shyness, they are characterized by their studious nature, commitment to justice, kindness, and a profound sense of spirituality. Conflict and competition are consistently avoided by these individuals, who possess a notable ability to manifest their desired realities—a defining trait that perhaps stems from their unwavering belief in the power of their convictions. Conversely, it is also acknowledged that those whose head-Orisha is Oshala, but who have deviated from the path aligned with divine laws, may experience a life of illusions. In this state, they not only exhibit a tendency to believe in anything indiscriminately but, more regrettably, become excessively immersed in mundane pursuits, thereby losing sight of life's inherent purpose. Also, they may become rather arrogant and snobby, believing that others are not as "spiritually advanced" as they are.

The Orishas, being vibrations that represent the divine, can be manifested or evoked through various elements such as colors, plants, stones, symbols, and mantras. Each Orisha possesses distinct associations with specific elements that reveal similar vibrations, albeit in their own material kingdoms. In this context, Oshala is particularly connected with the color white, which symbolizes not only peace but also the harmonious fusion of all other colors. In this sense, Oshala represents the synthesis of all other Orishas. White flowers, particularly white roses without thorns and lilies, are often considered to be linked to Oshala. Botanical elements such as boldo leaves, rosemanry, green grapes, pears, white rice, white sugar, and various white vegetables also embody his energetic essence. Clear and white crystals and stones are believed to have a special association to Oshala, particvularly clear quartz.

Oshala's domain is primarily found in open fields and meadows. As an expansive Orisha, his cult thrives in spacious and airy environments. These serene and open spaces are the ideal settings for invoking Oshala, as his energy is most easily accessed there, even without formal rituals or invocations.

His symbol, the ringing-staff, reminiscent of a walking cane, represents profound reverence for his experiences and wisdom. It consists of three disks, each representing a fundamental realm. The first disk symbolizes the realm of the Orishas, the second embodies the realm of the Spirits, and the third encompasses the realm of human beings. Atop the staff, a dove rests, symbolizing the divine grace that harmoniously unifies these interconnected realms. The ornate decorations adorning the disks hold deep significance, portraying Oshala's transformative journey and emphasizing his inherent wisdom. Each life experience is likened to a cherished souvenir collected along the path, symbolizing the places visited and the invaluable lessons learned.

The white dove depicted on his staff serves as his animal symbol.

In Umbanda, practitioners commonly vocalize the invocation and perform the clapping ritual before presenting an offering or commencing a service in honor of a specific Orisha. It is worth noting that salutations for the Orishas can vary, and this book presents the customary salutation, which is not a rigid requirement for the worship of an Orisha, meaning that one may simply say "save" followed by the name of the Orisha. The salutation, or incantation, used to invoke Oshala before a ritual is "Epa, baba," pronounced AY-pah baBAH. This phrase derives from the proto-

Yoruboid language, specifically "gba baba," meaning "Save, father." The salutation is often accompanied by three claps or a series of seven claps, as is customary for all other Orishas.

The worship of Oshala is characterized by its simplicity, as reflected in the offerings made to him. His favorite dish consists of rice pudding, or white rice cooked with sugar or honey poured on top. Accompanying the dish, a glass of water or, occasionally, white wine may be offered. The presence of one or seven white candles is also common. For more elaborate offerings, flowers, fruits, and white shells may be included.

Oshala holds the esteemed position of being the father of all Orishas, granting him the ability to assist with various matters. However, his specialty lies in instilling faith and bringing calm to any situation. When faced with abstract challenges such as a lack of mental clarity, inner peace, or feelings of stress, anxiety, or depression, Oshala can swiftly restore equilibrium. In cases involving physical or material issues, he imparts resilience and inner strength, enabling individuals to overcome obstacles and manifest improved results effortlessly. Oshala is also sought after for resolving conflicts and animosities both at home and in the workplace, transforming the perspectives and attitudes of those involved. When forgiveness is needed, Oshala can influence the minds of both parties, fostering a greater willingness to ask for and grant forgiveness. Among all the Orishas, Oshala is renowned for his mercy and compassion.

While fields and meadows are ideal locations for summoning Oshala, a simple white candle and a glass of water can suffice at home, provided there is faith. Organic offerings, such as fruits and juices, can be discarded in nature, while bowls, glasses, and other objects used in rituals can be washed and reused in the future. If natural spaces for discarding organic matter are unavailable, they can be disposed of in the appropriate waste can. When it comes to home altars dedicated to Orishas, they can consist of various elements that resonate with the specific Orisha. These elements include compatible crystals, symbols, imagery, colors, and flowers.

In essence, the more reverence one shows towards Oshala, the greater their resilience, patience, and overall sense of happiness become.

Old Blacks are the group of spirit workers who operate under the direct influences of Oshala. In a syncretic manner, Oshala is associated with Jesus Christ.

Yoruba Myth ○ The Waters of Oshala

One of the most renowned narratives, recounted by Beniste (2006), is the myth of the "Waters of Oshala," where Oshala decides to visit King Shango.

In the customary tradition of the Orishas' land, Oshala sought the guidance of an oracle to inquire about the journey. Despite the advice to reconsider, Oshala had already resolved to travel to Òyó. The oracle cautioned him, saying, "Carry three sets of white clothing, as Eshu may hinder your path." Additionally, he was advised to bring three white cloths, chalk, and soap and to accept all requests made along the way without complaint, regardless of the circumstances. This was seen as a means to protect his life.

With these precautions in mind, the Orisha embarked on his journey towards Òyó. While traversing the forest, he encountered Eshu, who struggled to lift a barrel of palm oil onto his back. Eshu beseeched Oshala for help, and without hesitation, Oshala offered his assistance. However, Eshu deliberately spilled the palm oil on Oshala and swiftly departed. Oshala cleansed himself in the river, changed his attire, and resumed his journey.

Further along the path, Oshala encountered Eshu once more, this time struggling with a sack of charcoal. Again, Oshala extended his aid, only to have Eshu spill the charcoal on him. Undeterred, Oshala cleansed himself in the river, changed his clothes, and continued his journey to Oyó.

On yet another occasion, he encountered Eshu attempting to lift a barrel of molasses, and the same pattern repeated itself.

As Oshala approached the city, he came across a white horse that had escaped from Shango's stables. He took it upon himself to return the horse to its rightful owner. However, before reaching the city, guards, misunderstanding the situation, mistakenly accused Oshala of theft and subjected him to violent assault, resulting in broken limbs. He was then imprisoned within the palace, where he languished for seven years, forgotten by all.

During this time, Shango's kingdom was plagued by pestilence and misfortune. The land experienced severe drought, leading to a compromised harvest, and thus widespread hunger. Epidemics, diseases, and frequent deaths befell the people, causing them to revolt against Shango. Desperate for a solution, Shango sought the counsel of a local oracle, who revealed, "An innocent man wearing white clothes is unjustly imprisoned. The current revolt is a natural response to the injustice committed. Life remains imprisoned in your dungeons, akin to an elderly man suffering unjustly as a prisoner, paying for a crime he did not commit."

Upon receiving the revelation, Shango hastened to the prison, where he discovered Oshala in a state of neglect and distress. Without delay, he brought Oshala to the palace and summoned all the Orishas for help.

Each Orisha carried a vessel filled with water from a sacred spring, pouring it over Oshala, symbolically cleansing him. The king of Òyó commanded his subjects to attire themselves in white and observe silence as a respectful gesture of seeking forgiveness from Oshala. Shango himself donned white garments and carried the elderly king on his back, leading a procession in celebration of his liberation. The entire population joyfully greeted Oshala and Shango.

Once the misunderstanding was resolved, rainfall graced the land, crops flourished, and diseases waned.

This myth alludes to the unwavering resilience embodied by Oshala and those who hold Oshala as their head-Orisha. It also emphasizes the significance of the Oshala cult, which rejects the use of palm oil, charcoal, and molasses. Furthermore, the myth suggests a correlation between Shango, the Orisha of Thunder, and the concept of justice.

Logunan (Oya-Tempo)

Logunan, alongside Oshala, is recognized as the Orisha of faith. However, while Oshala's influence fosters and expands religiosity in one's life, Logunan's polarity absorbs and restricts it. Pronounced logoon-NUN and formerly referred to as Oya-Tempo, associating her nature with Orisha Oya, the deity of movement, and "tempo," meaning "time," Logunan's existence is subject to ongoing discussion and interpretation. Logunan holds a lower position within the framework of Umbanda's tradition, primarily due to the more recent introduction of the polarity concept through the teachings of Sacred Umbanda. Her cult appears to be part of Sacred Umbanda but is nearly absent in other branches. Nevertheless, given the widespread acceptance of the concept of Divine Thrones among Umbandists, it was relatively easy to identify Logunan as the counterpart of Oshala. However, her cult is generally limited or even absent in most Umbanda practices. In Sacred Umbanda temples, on the other hand, Logunan may be honored alongside Oshala, playing a role in maintaining a harmonious balance within the cult of the Throne of Faith. According to Saraceni (1993), the medium and Umbanda leader who introduced the concept of Logunan (as well as that of Egunita), Logunan brings order to religious chaos and counteracts excessive blind faith, guiding fanatics back to a point of equilibrium. Logunan exposes and drains moral hypocrisy, particularly that exhibited by false religious leaders and moral puritans.

It is Logunan's energy that holds accountable those who exploit faith for personal gain and those who work towards corrupting faith.

Logunan represents the concept of physical time, which can be understood as the dimension of movement. This is the temporal realm in which individuals and masses evolve during their earthly existence. Moreover, Logunan is believed to assist individuals in effectively managing their time and establishing clear priorities based on their personal circumstances.

Individuals whose head-Orisha is Logunan may exhibit traits such as mild introversion, optimism, emotional intelligence, and, when on the regrettable side, jealousy, disorganization, and anxiety. Those who are understood to be misguided in faith and have false moral values are believed to be out of balance with Logunan's vibration. However, it is particularly rare to encounter Logunan as one's head-Orisha, as Yansa typically assumes that role when the unveiling is assessed.

The colors associated with Logunan are white, silver, and a touch of black. The crystal symbolizing Logunan is smoky quartz. The chosen symbols for Logunan are the hourglass and the spiral. Her domain are the open fields.

Logunan is connected to specific herbs such as rosemary and eucalyptus. As for fruits, offerings can include pineapple, coconut, and any other white fruit with a lower water content than usual.

To invoke Logunan, the salutation used is "See the time, mother!"

The worship of Logunan shares similarities with that of Oshala, and it is possible to revere both Orishas simultaneously. However, in certain circumstances, Logunan may be specifically honored with offerings of cooked rice topped with slices of coconut. This offering can be accompanied by a white, silver, or dark blue candle and a glass of anise liqueur.

Cowboys are the group of spirit workers who operate under the influences of Logunan, and she is syncretically associated with figures such as Joan of Arc and Saint Clair.

Yoruba Myth ○ The Creation of Time

According to the teachings of Rubens Saraceni, the myth of Logunan says that Olorun, the creator of the world, observed that things were not happening, remaining stagnant and unchanging, as if life did not exist. Everything appeared as a grand painting, rich in intricate details but lacking the magic of existence. There was no division between past, present, and future, and nothing was evolving, or altering. It was then that Olorun decided to create Logunan, bestowing upon her the power to infuse movement into all things.

Through Logunan, time finally emerged, and existence manifested itself. And finally, the interplay of the past, the nourishment of the present, and the projection of the future that all that is synchronously revolves in the wheel of life.

Oshun

Pronounced *o-SHOON*, the name Oṣun carries various meanings derived from its Yoruba roots, all of which complement each other. It can signify "from the sea," "calming streams," or "that who sleeps." In Nigeria, Oshun lends her name to a river and is regarded as the Orisha of love, encompassing not only romantic love but also maternal love and unconditional love for all beings and things. Oshun emanates qualities of mercy and nurturing kindness. As the Orisha of freshwater, rivers, waterfalls, and streams, she breathes life into plans, partnerships, pregnancies, and all manifestations. While Yemanja is believed to generate the seeds of life, Oshun nurtures and develops them, whether they are physical lives or the seeds of thoughts, projects, or ideas.

Oshun's domain is closely tied to the essence of gold and occasionally copper, symbolizing prosperity and material comfort. She represents abundance and self-worth. Many individuals who struggle with self-love or feelings of unworthiness find solace in the influence of charming Oshun, as she instills a sense of being loved, valued, and beautiful. Beauty is one of Oshun's primary attributes. As the queen of beauty, she inspires people not only to care for themselves but also to create beauty and harmony in their surroundings, wherever they may be. Oshun's concept of beauty extends beyond mere appearances; it encompasses the transformation of spirits who once rejected their own worth and appearance into beings who are now invited to embrace themselves with extra care and attention, besides promoting the divine via the beauty of things. Above all, Oshun is revered as the embodiment of divine love.

Oshun is an adored mother, and tracing a parallel with Neopagan traditions, Oshun would represent the maiden, whereas Yemanja would be the mother, and Nana would be the crone. Oshun is youthful, emotional, and delicate, yet she also possesses exceptional diplomatic skills, rivaling Oshala; and strategic acumen, second only to Oshossi. This is rooted in Oshun's aversion to conflict. She abhors arguments, confrontations, and combat, preferring instead to seek resolution through dialogue, persuasion, or occasionally by discreetly working behind the scenes, where she invariably achieves success.

Overall, Oshun is renowned as the most peace-loving among all the Orishas.

Oshun is deeply associated to divination and serves as a guardian and patron of mediums and psychics. She holds a particular affinity for oracles such as tarot readings, palmistry, and similar practices.

Often affectionately referred to as "Mommy Oshun," she has a group of spirits working under her influence who exude a gentle and nurturing demeanor, specializing in matters of love and prosperity.

While Oshun is known as a nurturing mother figure, those with Oshun as their head-Orisha may exhibit a self-centered focus rather than attending to the needs of others. Their speech is characterized by sweetness and they usually display a refined sense for fashion. They may have soft and rounded features in their bodies and faces, as well as fairer skin and hair compared to their family members. Males with Oshun as their head-Orisha may display feminine traits and have an interest in fashion and exquisite collectibles. Regardless of gender, individuals with Oshun as their head-Orisha often possess a strong sense of intuition, are drawn to esoteric subjects, and may seek comfort in crystals, incense, candles, but also in profoundly occult schools of thought. Individuals with Oshun as their head-Orisha tend to steer clear of conflicts, opting for dialogue in positive situations. Yet, in their negative polarity, they may resort to manipulation, place extreme significance on appearance and occasionally show signs of vanity and superficiality.

Oshun is commonly associated with the color yellow, symbolizing her esteemed status as the custodian of all that is gold. However, she is also frequently depicted in dark blue, particularly in temples where her links to Yemanja, another water deity, is emphasized. The depiction of colors in Oshun's imagery or the choice of candle colors offered to her do not alter the essence of her cult. However, in centers where yellow is favored—which is the vast majority—the associations with gold, prosperity, and beauty are stressed. On the other hand, in centers where her cult leans towards blue, the focus is on her association to water, symbolizing the life-giving properties of water and her qualities as a nurturing mother. In Umbanda centers, the mediums who channel Oshun's phalanx spirits frequently use weeping as a way to externalize her emotions.

Renowned for her fondness of lilies, Oshun is closely associated with various yellow flowers as well, including the likes of yellow roses and sunflowers. Chamomile, anise, and lemon balm are the herbs that resonate with her vibrant energy. Among her favorite fruits are yellow melons, peaches, apples, pears, and grapes. As for more elaborate offerings, mashed, cooked black-eyed peas with honey are commonly the best choice. Champagne, fruit juices, especially those from her favorite fruits, and mineral water are the best choices of drinks.

When it comes to crystals, rose quartz and pyrite are deemed the most harmonious with Oshun's essence.

Her predominant symbol, the golden hand mirror, embodies the concepts of self-love and abundance, and is widely recognized. Her animal symbols are the hens and peahens.

Oshun's sphere of influence, wherein her energy emanates most powerfully, primarily encompasses waterfalls, cascades, and serene rivers and streams. Nevertheless, any freshwater body serves as a suitable conduit for tapping into her harmonious vibration.

The customary salutation employed to invoke Oshun before a ritual is "Ora Ye-Ye O, Mommy Oshun," pronounced as "aura yay-yay O," signifying "graces of mommy" in the proto-Yoruboid language. Similar to other Orishas, this salutation frequently includes three claps or a series of seven claps.

Oshun is primarily invoked to address matters pertaining to love and romantic relationships. Her energy is known for its ability to strengthen and nurture the bonds of love. Consequently, conducting worship and rituals dedicated to Oshun is best suited in serene environments near waterfalls or flowing rivers. As part of the offering, fruits, flowers, and champagne may be arranged alongside 1, 3, or 5 yellow candles. Alternatively, beverages can be directly poured into the water without the need for glasses. After approximately 15 minutes, the candles can be extinguished, taken home, and relit at a later time.

At home, honoring Oshun can be as simple as lighting a yellow candle and having a glass of juice as an offering.

Prior to venerating the deity, it is advantageous for the devotee to bathe with the specific herbs or flowers associated with Oshun, as is customary for any Orisha. In the case of Oshun, one can prepare a concoction using chamomile or yellow roses (boiled if dry or mashed and strained if fresh), dilute the liquid in water, and bathe while contemplating thoughts of Oshun.

Either at home, in nature, or in an Umbanda temple, it is crucial to offer Eshu first, by lighting a red and black candle, at least.

The spiritis of Children, and pombagiras are the groups of spirit workers who operate under the influences of Oshun. In a syncretic context, Oshun is often associated with the mother of Jesus, the Virgin Mary, due to shared attributes such as youthfulness, deep compassion, and being prominent symbols of love. It is important to note that Oshun is commonly associated to the younger depiction of Mary, of the times of baby Jesus, while Yemanja, another Orisha associated with the mother of Christ, may be associated with Mary of the times of crucifixion. Additionally, goddess Aphrodite (Venus) can also be associated with Oshun.

Yoruba Myth ○ Oshun Gains Power Over Ifá

One day, Oshun approached Eshu and expressed her curiosity about the secrets of the oracle known as Ifá, which only him and Orunmila were privy to. Oshun pleaded with Eshu to share the knowledge, but he adamantly refused.

Undeterred, Oshun pondered and thought of seeking the assistance of the forest witches, believing they could help her enchant Eshu. When the witches came across Oshun in the forest, they were curious about her presence and questioned why a stunning woman like her would be there. Oshun explained that she sought knowledge of magic, but Eshu was unwilling to share it. Having harbored ill feelings towards Eshu, the witches saw an opportunity to teach him a lesson through Oshun. They offered their help but stipulated that

Oshun must make offerings to the forest whenever she uses their magic. Oshun readily agreed to their conditions.

Empowered by the witches' assistance, Oshun approached Eshu once again and requested the secrets of Ifá and its signs. Once more, Eshu declined to divulge the information. This time, Oshun revealed a magical powder in her hand and enticed Eshu's curiosity by exclaiming, "Eshu, look at what I have here!" When Eshu turned to look, she blew the powder into his face, temporarily blinding him. Startled, Eshu dropped all the cowrie shells he held. As the shells fell, Oshun seized the opportunity to trick Eshu. She asked him how she could assist, and Eshu requested that she retrieve all the shells. Oshun inquired about how many shells were there, to which Eshu replied, "16! Now, gather them all." Oshun obediently collected the shells, questioning why there were precisely 16. Eshu explained that each shell provided an answer. Oshun further inquired if there were only 16 possible answers, to which Eshu responded, "Together they can yield 256 answers." With curiosity still lingering, she asked about the presence of a larger shell, prompting Eshu to disclose even more details and meanings. By the time Oshun had gathered all the shells, Eshu had revealed the full extent of their meaning.

Having obtained what she wanted, Oshun approached Oshala, proclaiming, "Father, I now know about Ifá." Orunmila, who was present, inquired about the source of her newfound knowledge. Oshun recounted how she had outwitted Eshu. Impressed by her resourcefulness, Orunmila declared that henceforth, Oshun would share ownership of the divination system with Eshu.

This myth emphasizes the natural inclination and proficiency of individuals with Oshun as their head-Orisha in interpreting oracles, along with their occasional adeptness in manipulation.

Oshumare

Oshumare, pronounced *o-shoo-mah-RAY*, derives from the Yoruba term *òṣùmàrè*, which translates to "rainbow." This Orisha symbolizes transformation and represents the movement of life. The snake is widely recognized as Oshumare's primary symbol due to its ability to shed its skin, signifying change and new cycles. Occasionally, certain branches of Umbanda associate Oshumare's symbol of a serpent with Kundalini, a Hindu concept of spiritual energy believed to reside at the base of the spine. The rise of this energy through the spine to the head is said to lead to, among other things, consciousness expansion. In a similar vein, the colors of the rainbow can further represent each chakra. Oshumare's characteristics are closely tied to vitality and transformation, reminiscent of aspects related to Kundalini. While this concept aligns with Oshumare's ability to bring about profound life transformations, most Umbanda temples emphasize the shedding of skin and the subsequent visible change as being more directly associated with Oshumare's symbolic animal.

According to Yoruba mythology, Oshumare spends half the year as a rainbow and the other half as a snake, symbolizing water and masculinity as a rainbow, and earth and femininity as a snake. While some belief systems perceive Oshumare as bi-gender, androgynous, or alternating between male and female, it is more commonly observed that Oshumare is regarded as a male with an androgynous temperament. Consequently, Oshumare, along with Logunede and Eshu, may occasionally be associated with homosexuality and bisexuality.

Sharing the Domain of Love with Oshun, Oshumare consumes and transforms anything that deviates from the essence of love, including its disharmonies. Those who are excessively attached, despite believing they are expressing love, are said to be distanced from the energies of Oshumare. Oshumare, therefore, constricts and absorbs that which deviates from genuine love and diminishes the illusory aspects of it. As he absorbs one's disharmonies, he also emanates vibrations of renewal.

Movement, change, and overcoming are fundamental aspects directly related to Oshumare. Although not widely revered in many

Umbanda temples, Oshumare's energy is interconnected with Oshun, Nana, and Obaluaye.

The energy of Oshumare inspires profound transformations among his devotees. These changes extend beyond mere jobs or addresses, encompassing lifestyle, faith, and principles. Oshumare's influence also acts as a catalyst to remove barriers that hinder the manifestation of prosperity. As a result, Oshumare is regarded as an Orisha that fosters wealth and abundance. Oshumare also upholds continuity, ensuring that what is good remains preserved despite any circumstances or challenges that may arise.

Individuals who have Oshumare as their head-Orisha are frequently characterized by their childlike qualities, extroverted nature, optimistic outlook, and gentle demeanor. Oshumare's protegees are recognized for their eloquence, inquisitiveness, enjoyment of life, and dynamic nature. They often embody a remarkable absence of prejudice or bias, exemplifying an open-minded and inclusive stance towards others. Physically, they are often slender, possessing exotic beauty, and an allure that is unique, complemented by their piercing gaze.

Despite encountering early-life adversities, their path unfolds as a profound transformative journey, reminiscent of the symbolic transformation from water to wine. During this process, various aspects of their lives, such as their spiritual beliefs, financial circumstances, lifestyle, and other fundamental elements, undergo remarkable and substantial changes.

When individuals are in opposition to Oshumare's vibration, they may exhibit traits such as insincerity, persistent dishonesty, arrogance, sadness, and unkindness. Additionally, they may display a tendency to flaunt their possessions or status and portray a snotty, insolent behavior.

Oshumare is associated with all colors as he is the rainbow Orisha, although candles in his cult and bead necklaces worn by his followers tend to be yellow and green more often than multicolored.

Any colorful crystal is associated with Oshumare, including obsidians and opals. Pyrite and green jade can also be incorporated into his altar to reflect his nature.

Oshumare enjoys a wide variety of vibrant flowers, and his herbs include hibiscus, chamomile, bay leaves, and oregano. Offerings to Oshumare often include melons, bananas, papayas, and passion fruit.

Oshumare's domain is primarily found at powerful waterfalls where water meets earth, symbolizing the convergence of his two elements. Open spaces with rain are also favorable for his energy. Additionally, the margins of turbulent rivers are believed to be associated with his energetic movement. The serpent or snake is the natural animal symbol of Oshumare, and his tool is the snake and rainbow, often depicted as two snakes ascending a rainbow.

The salutation used to praise or invoke Oshumare is "Arroboboi, Oshumare" pronounced as "*ah-ho bo-BOY.*" The origins of this salutation are uncertain, and while some claim it means "lord of the cycles" or "save Oshumare," these interpretations are grammatically and etymologically inconsistent with Yoruba or proto-Yoruboid roots. However, it seems to have evolved from a phrase meaning something along the lines of "come crawling."

Oshumare's presence is usually summoned to address matters related to stagnation, deviations of love, and lack of prosperity. His energy is also known for renewing all that is antiquated or imbalanced in life. For those whose head-Orisha is Oshumare, exalting their Orisha aims to strengthen their bonds and maintain the continuity of Oshumare's vibrations in their lives.

As part of the offerings, bananas, chosen for their shape, are a good option. Colorful flowers and white wine may be arranged alongside either one multicolored candle, a candle half yellow and half green, or seven candles of each color.

Oshumare's most common offering consists of mashed sweet potatoes and honey, shaped into a snake biting its own tail. The snake can be adorned with black-eyed peas, or at least two eyes. This offering can be placed in a clay bowl or on leaves and left in nature.

Similar to other water deities, beverages for Oshumare can be directly poured into the water without the need for glasses. After approximately 15 minutes, the candles can be extinguished, taken home, and relit at a later time.

At home, honoring Oshumare can be as simple as lighting a yellow or green candle and offering a glass of juice.

It is a good practice to bathe with specific herbs or flowers associated with Oshumare before worship. In the case of Oshumare, one can prepare a concoction using mugwort, bay leaves, or yellow roses (boiled if dry or mashed and strained and if fresh).

In Umbanda centers, the mediums who channel Oshumare's phalanx spirits frequently crawl like snakes moments after channeling. However, Oshumare's spirits are less commonly found in Umbanda centers, where most of them identify themselves as working under the influence of Oshun, in cases where that particular center does not revere Oshumare.

Children are the group of spirit workers who may operate under the influences of Oshumare. Oshumare is not commonly syncretized with other entities, but there are occasional associations made with Saint Bartholomew. This connection arises due to saint's patronage over commerce, tailors, and shoemakers, which aligns with Oshumare's symbolism of shedding skin, akin to changing clothes, besides the energy of exchange.

Yoruba Myth ○ The Rainbow Serpent's Gift

There was a village in the ancient Yorubaland that was suffering from a terrible drought. The rivers ran dry, the crops withered, and the people suffered. So, they sought the assistance of their divine pantheon, entreating the gods and goddesses to bring forth rain and relieve their misery.

Among the deities who heard their pleas was Oshumare, the Rainbow Serpent. Oshumare possessed the ability to bring life-giving rain to the earth, and the people held great hope in their hearts when they learned that the deity would intervene.

Oshumare descended from the heavens and coiled around the tallest palm tree in the village, with his shimmering scales casting prismatic hues upon the surrounding landscape.

Oshumare spoke to the villagers in a gentle voice, promising to bring forth rain and end their suffering. However, the Orisha requested a precious offering in return. Oshumare desired the village's most treasured possession, a golden crown adorned with precious gemstones, passed down through generations.

The villagers were torn. They cherished their crown as a symbol of their heritage, but the drought had left them desperate. After much reflection upon it, they decided that the lives of their people were more valuable than any material possession. Reluctantly, they presented the crown to Oshumare, placing it at the base of the palm tree.

Impressed by their sacrifice, Oshumare began to transform. The deity's form shifted, taking on the appearance of a magnificent rainbow that arched across the sky. Moments later, a soft rain began to fall, gradually turning into a gentle downpour. The villagers rejoiced as the parched earth soaked up the revitalizing water, and new life blossomed all around them.

As the rain continued to fall, Oshumare spoke to the villagers once more. The deity explained that the golden crown had served as a vessel to channel their collective sacrifice, transforming it into life-giving rain. Oshumare expressed gratitude for their selflessness and assured them that their village would forever be blessed with abundance and prosperity.

This may allude to the changing nature of Oshumare, transitioning from a snake to a rainbow to rain. It also signifies Oshumare's connection to abundance and the dramatic life changes experienced by his protégés, ranging from poverty to prosperity and vice versa, as well as Oshumare's call for detachment from materialism.

Oshossi

Oshossi, pronounced *o-SHAW-see* (from Yoruba Ọ̀ṣọ́ọ̀sì, rooted in *Ọṣọ́tókanṣoṣo*, meaning "the famous guardian"), is the Orisha who embodies the pursuit of knowledge. In Umbanda, Oshossi is revered as the representative of the throne of Knowledge.

Oshossi, the hunter Orisha, embodies the pursuit of knowledge and material gain. He is characterized by resolute focus, personal effort, and determination. Closely associated with gains, particularly in relation to the fruits of labor, Oshossi is also the embodiment of abundant crops, profits, and overall prosperity through work.

As a seeker of knowledge and work, Oshossi's presence is particularly felt in places like libraries, schools, universities, stores, and markets. Despite being exceptionally charming and physically strong, he values knowledge and intellect above sheer physical power. Oshossi extends his assistance to those seeking employment, financial stability, and career advancement. He also supports individuals in their pursuit of educational endeavors, whether it be preparing for exams, writing books, or conducting research. In a similar vein, Oshossi is an Orisha who inspires art, including painting and music, making him one of, if not the most prominent, supporters of the arts among the Orishas.

Individuals with Oshossi as their head-Orisha are often diligent, dedicated, and efficient in their endeavors. They tend to maintain long-lasting employment or follow the same career paths throughout their lives, showcasing their strong work ethic. These individuals have an appreciation for the arts and possess sociable traits while still maintaining a sense of discretion. Due to their strong inclination towards intellectual pursuits, they seldom open up or express their emotions, resulting in occasional feelings of loneliness. Their diligent nature allows them to acquire wealth easily, as they are unafraid of hard work and tirelessly pursue their goals.

These individuals possess a natural charm and are commonly perceived as physically attractive. They often exhibit a tall, slender physique and possess a youthful appearance and behavior. Above all, their strong capacity for focus is considered their most prominent characteristic. However, when they are not aligned with the divine influence of Oshossi, they may squander their resources, opportunities, and time. They may also develop antisocial tendencies, social phobias, and become overly materialistic or workaholics. Cynicism and sarcasm are also strong traits developed by those unaligned with Oshossi's energy.

Oshossi is commonly associated with the color green, which represents the lushness and abundance of the woodlands. On rare occasions, he may also be associated with the color dark blue or even turquoise. He finds affinity with various flowers, as none of them seem to contradict his nature. Some of his preferred herbs and botanicals include laceleaf, fern, and rosemary. When it comes to fruits, coconut, pineapple, limes, oranges, avocados, and other green fruits are considered most compatible with Oshossi's vibrations.

Green quartz, amazonite, green aventurine, lapis lazuli, sodalite, and green agate are among the gems associated with Oshossi. As for his animal symbol, birds such as parrots, cockatiels, and toucans represent his intelligence.

Oshossi is the protector of forests, woodlands, and pristine woods. It is believed that Oshossi's energy flows through the trees and the wildlife inhabiting these areas.

His symbol is the bow and a solitary arrow, representing his resolute focus.

When invoking Oshossi before a ritual, the salutation used is "Oke aro, Oshossi!" pronounced "okay ah-ROE." It translates to "look out; be vigilant" and likely derives from the Yoruba phrase "wo ke o," which carries the same meaning.

A suitable offering for Oshossi would be a bowl of assorted fruits accompanied by a glass of lager beer and a green candle. For a more elaborate offering, consider boiling corn cobs and adorning them with coconut pieces. On top of the corn cobs, molasses or any syrup can be drizzled (it is advisable to avoid honey, as it may not align with Oshossi's frequency). Besides beer, white wine or coconut water are also good choices.

During rituals conducted in natural settings, it is appropriate to place the foods and fruits on leaves such as lettuce or kale and pour the drink onto the ground, unless a cup made of coconut shell can be used. In the domains of the Orishas, candles are not essential, as their energy is already abundant. However, if candles are used, it is recommended to extinguish them and take the remaining candle home for later use.

To enhance the connection with Oshossi, certain herbs can be burned as offerings, including tobacco (such as lighting a cigar), or any herb that produces fragrant smoke, especially bay leaves, can be utilized in this manner.

Mestizos are the group of spirit workers who operate under the influences of Oshossi.

The Class of spirits known as the Mestizos work under the direct influence of Oshossi. They serve as representatives of his energies and act in alignment with his nature, which inspires determination and focus.

In a syncretic manner, Oshossi is symbolically associated with Saint Sebastian. This connection stems from Saint Sebastian's usual depiction in paintings and sculptures as a young man bound to a tree with arrows piercing his body.

Yoruba Myth ○ A Solitary Arrow

King Odudua hosted a grand celebration within the confines of his palace, extending invitations to all except three enigmatic witches, the Eleye, dwellers of the nearby woods.

As revenge, these witches, possessing an unholy power, unleashed a sinister enchantment upon the kingdom. Their malevolence materialized in the form of a menacing bird, haunting the palace grounds.

Despite the king's valiant efforts, his forces were unable to vanquish this monstrous avian creature. The kingdom found itself besieged, with neither resources nor individuals able to enter or depart. In a bid to quell this crisis, the kingdom proclaimed a reward: the individual capable of defeating the bird would be granted half the kingdom and the king's daughter as a spouse.

Many valiant souls attempted to conquer the beast, yet none succeeded in their endeavors.

However, Oshossi, filled with unwavering determination, vowed to be the one to prevail. Recognizing that an incantation surrounded the bird, Oshossi's mother resolved to venture into the woods in search of the witches. She approached the witches, inquiring if any magical influence enveloped the bird. The witches confirmed the existence of such magic and stipulated that an offering must be made to them within the woodland before Oshossi embarked on his mission.

Undeterred by fear, Oshossi ventured into the kingdom, armed with nothing but a solitary arrow. In an astonishing display of prowess, he successfully struck down the monstrous bird with a single shot.

This myth exemplifies the determination and fearlessness inherent in Oshossi, attributes vital for triumph. It also highlights Oshossi's remarkable focus, symbolized by the single arrow he employed. The arrow serves as a representation of his capability for concentration, undeterred by distractions. It may also highlight the importance to acknowledge the forest's dwellers.

Oba

Oba," pronounced as "oh-BAH," originates from the Yoruba word *ọba*, meaning "king," and is also linked with the river Ọba. Oba is acknowledged as the female Orisha governing rushing and turbulent rivers, as well as the wheel of life.

As a warrior deity, Oba represents the masculine aspect among the female Orishas, embodying strength, resilience, and the essence of justice. Although her presence is not as commonly observed in Umbanda centers, her vibrations are often equated with Oshossi or, less frequently, with Yansa.

Within the realm of knowledge, Oba complements Oshossi by absorbing distractions and removing obstacles that hinder individuals' progress. Oba's energies offer assistance to those seeking balance in their lives, especially in combating the excesses of intellecualism and the excess of false knowledge, including misinterpretations of sciences and religious teachings. As Oshossi enhances focus, Oba curtails external influences that lead to alienation. Additionally, Oba is widely recognized as a symbol of vigor, assertiveness, and physical strength. Individuals facing challenges requiring stamina and energy often seek her aid.

Individuals with Oba as their head-Orisha may exhibit traits of being indomitable, strong, courageous, and passionate. Hose under the influence of Oba are focused towards work, but they also experience intense emotions, which are openly displayed. Children of Oba may not communicate very effectively, as they can come across as blunt or inflexible. They tend to have a simple demeanor, both in their attire and in their professional aspirations, although their profession and work hold great importance to them. They are loyal, possessive, and intense in all aspects of life. On the downside, they may be prone to dramatic tantrums, exaggerated complaints, and accusations, magnifying even minor setbacks and potentially hindering their success and well-being.

The appearance of those with Oba and their head-Orisha can sometimes be mistaken for children of Ogun, Yansa, or even Shango, but they typically have strong and sturdy bodies, round faces, a natural tan, and are generally not distinguished by pronounced beauty.

The colors associated with Oba are magenta and terracotta. Her primary symbols are those of war: the sword, shield, symbolizing courage; and sometimes the bow and arrow, symbolizing focus. Her gemstones are rose agate, pink alexandrite, and any magenta or shocking-pink stone.

Her flowers include the orange tree flower and red roses. Acceptable fruits for offerings to Oba are watermelons, oranges, red apples, plantains, and mangoes. Other botanicals associated with her include tamarind and cilantro (coriander).

Oba's domains are turbulent and tempestuous rivers, making her worship more potent along the banks of fast-flowing waters.

The greeting and salutation used to invoke Oba is "Oba Shere!," pronounced *she-RAY*, which derives from proto-Yoruboid and means "running Oba," signifying a sense of rushing.

It is believed that the more one worships Oba, the fewer distractions and deceptive obstacles they will encounter in life. Offerings to Oba may include fruits, flowers, a magenta candle, and red juices. For more elaborate arrangements, mushroom soup with salt can also be a suitable choice. The mushrooms symbolize Oba's resilient nature and may be connected to the myth where she cuts off her own ear.

Another highly intricate offering, reserved for powerful petitions, is a black-eyed pea dough made with onions, palm oil, and chilies, wrapped in leaves, and boiled. This can be adorned with thornless red roses, mango pieces, and other decorative elements. Prior to presenting the offering, water taken from the tumultuous shores can be poured onto the ground.

While reverence for Oba is not widespread in Umbanda centers, her cult is steadily gaining popularity among followers of Sacred Umbanda. Mestizos, a group of spirit workers, also operate under the influence of Oba. Additionally, she may be syncretized with Saint Rita of Cascia, known for her practicing mortification of the flesh while praying.

Yoruba Myth ○ The Ear Soup

Shango was married to Oshun, Oya, and Oba. Among his wives, Oshun held a special place in his heart, which led to Oba's constant attempts to steal the secret recipes that Oshun prepared for her husband.

Growing increasingly irritated with Oba's behavior, Oshun devised a plan to expose her rival's actions. She invited Oba to witness the preparation of a dish that she claimed delighted Shango immensely.

Upon Oba's arrival in the kitchen, she discovered Oshun wearing a headscarf to conceal her ears. Oshun was in the process of preparing a soup for Shango, with two mushrooms floating on the surface of the broth. Oshun, however, convinced Oba that those mushrooms were actually her own ears.

When Shango tasted the soup, he savored it, licking his lips.

Inspired to replicate the recipe, Oba proceeded to cut off her own ear and include it in the soup. However, when Shango saw the ear, he found it repugnant. Oshun then removed her headscarf, revealing her intact ears.

Enraged by the deception, Oba engaged in a heated confrontation with Oshun.

Shango, consumed by anger, thundered his fury at both of them.

Filled with terror, Oba and Oshun fled, transforming themselves into rivers.

This legend highlights Oba's vulnerability as she succumbs to believing false information. It also underscores her thorough dedication to love, despite the differences she had with Oshun. To this day, the waters of the rivers Oshun and Oba remain turbulent and agitated at their confluence.

Shango

Shango, pronounced 'shun-GO,' derives from the Yoruba name *Sàngó*, which was borrowed from the Nupe language's Sòkó referring to a lightning deity that the Yoruba people assimilated into their religious practices as Ṣàngó. Shango is revered as the Orisha of thunder, fire, mountains, opulence, and, most significantly, justice.

According to legend, Shango was a Yoruba king, the son of Oranian, the ruler who established the Empire of Oyo around the year 1400. After his death, Shango, who was deeply beloved by the people, was elevated to a divine state.

Shango holds a prominent position among the Orishas due to his pivotal role in the pantheon, representing divine and impartial justice. Undoubtedly, Shango is recognized as one of the most powerful Orishas in terms of influence. He embodies determination, and as the deity of volcanoes, he is symbolized by the forces of nature that imply strength. He is celebrated as the king of grand festivities, not limited to ordinary gatherings but rather significant celebrations. Furthermore, Shango is believed to provide assistance in legal matters concerning financial gains, documentation, and bureaucratic procedures. As the primary deity associated with balance, he ensures equilibrium. Additionally, Shango is attributed the responsibility of assessing an individual's karmic burden and granting mercy by alleviating it. Although metaphorical in nature, his essence as the embodiment of divine justice establishes a profound connection to that fundamental law.

Apart from being sought after for wishes of self-esteem and prosperity, it is common to find devotees who believe that Shango's justice will grant them victories, regardless of whether they are on the right or wrong side. However, Shango is believed to represent a divine aspect, and hence he only operates in alignment with the highest standards of righteousness. Therefore, Shango can help individuals rectify their past wrongdoings by instilling a deep understanding of moral rightness and justice, thus inspiring them to cultivate an elevated sense of justice, embrace truce and reconciliation, demonstrate generosity, and actively seek to correct their past mistakes.

Individuals who have Shango as their head-Orisha are characterized by their determination, generosity, and a strong sense of self-righteousness. Their commanding presence is difficult to overlook, as they possess an air of importance even in ordinary circumstances. People influenced by Shango, particularly those with Shango as their head-Orisha, often excel in entrepreneurship, self-employment, or hold high-ranking positions within their organizations. Shango's energy embodies that of a leader, someone who assumes great responsibility and prefers giving orders rather than taking them. Their desire for power stems from a commitment to maintaining what they perceive as just, often aligning with their actual intentions. Financial stability is frequently associated with these individuals, often through inheritance, property ownership, or their own businesses.

They tend to indulge in lavish possessions such as luxury, large items, such as spacious houses, and big cars, as they have a preference for grandeur. Their self-esteem commands respect wherever they go, yet they may harbor a fear of being forgotten or not admired. The children of Shango are highly sociable and enjoyable companions, frequently hosting celebrations, parties, and dinners with a preference for large gatherings. This same inclination extends to their families, where they assume the role of the family's pillar, providing support and taking responsibility for its overall structure, both financially and otherwise. These individuals are passionate by nature and often exhibit strong displays of emotion, which includes being overly flirtatious. However, in their negative aspects, when disconnected from Shango's positive influence, they can become excessively egoistic, selfish, domineering, and ostentatious. Additionally, they may also develop deadbeat behavior, by not meeting their financial obligations.

Typically, those influenced by Shango are recognized by their solid and bulky physiques and a penchant for wearing fashionable, expensive, and high-quality attire.

Shango is commonly associated with the color red, symbolizing his fiery nature, but brown, white, and hints of gold are occasionally attributed to him due to his association with mountains and wealth. Shango's preferred flowers include red palms, red carnations, red daisies, and red birds of paradise. His selection of herbs includes bay leaves, basil, mulberry leaves, plum leaves, and coffee leaves. Fruits that are his favorites include quince, persimmon, mango, red chilies, and okra. Dark beer is Shango's main beverage of choice. Red jasper and garnet are among the stones connected to Shango's vibration. Volcanic rocks are especially significant as they resonate with Shango's energy of strength, vitality, and potency. However, any stones related to mountains, or rocky places may also pertain to Shango. His animal symbol is the lion, which is also associated with Saint Jerome in a syncretic sense. Saint Jerome is often depicted with a lion by his side, representing an act of kindness and mercy when he removed a thorn from the lion's paw. The lion became devoted to him and served as his companion and protector. Apart from the lion, eagles and turtles are also symbols of Shango.

Shango's sphere of influence is primarily encountered in mountains, volcanoes, rocky regions, and mines. His energy can also be found in justice courts, tribunals, restaurants, theaters, and police stations, which he shares with Ogun.

Shango's emblem is the two-faced ax, often depicted engulfed in flames, symbolizing his impelling sense of justice. Additionally, he is associated with other symbols such as the crown, the throne, and the mountains (except the ones with snowy peaks).

The customary salutation used to invoke Shango before a ritual is "Kao Kabecile" pronounced as 'kah-O kah-bay-SEE-lay,' likely derived from the Yoruba phrase "káwò kábíèsí le," meaning "come, strong majesty." Occasionally, due to historical mistranslations, it has been erroneously rendered as 'come salute majesty' or 'let me see you, majesty.' This salutation often involves three or seven claps and can be accompanied by placing both hands around one's head, symbolizing the king's crown. Besides Christian syncretism, it can be proposed that Shango has various similarities with other thunder gods from different mythologies, not only for sharing thunder as the epitome of their power but for their position as kings, central figures in the pantheon, or their deliberate sense of justice. Religious and mythological associations could be made with Zeus, Thor, and Raijin, from Greek, Norse, and Japanese mythologies, respectively.

Revering Shango not only benefits those with him as their head-Orisha, stimulating the development of positive traits within them, but it also serves as a means to seek assistance in matters related to justice, legal affairs, court proceedings, and document processes. Additionally, it is common to seek Shango's intervention for prosperity and to establish solid foundations in one's life. Devotion to Shango instills individuals with a profound sense of inner strength and a 'can-do' attitude. Shango's personality is renowned for its remarkable courage, making his vibrations particularly effective for those in need of courage. Justice permeates Shango's essence, and by revering him, one may cultivate a heightened sense of justice, benefiting from both mundane justice and becoming more just in their interactions with others. Shango's influence can also extend to supporting business endeavors and fostering through business.

While the worship of Shango is often associated with grandiosity, it is important to note that such pompous characteristics are not obligatory or demanded by the Orisha.

One of Shango's most intricate offerings consists of okra cooked with onions, palm oil, and honey, presented in a wooden bowl. Surrounding the dish, seven brown or red candles are lit, accompanied by seven glasses of dark beer. For more elaborate offerings, flowers and burned bay leaves can be included. The optimal locations for worshiping Shango, aside from a dedicated temple, are mountains, particularly rocky ones. Mines or solitary rocks also serve as suitable choices. If the matter at hand involves legal affairs, offering the Orisha near a court may be ideal, but it is important to exercise discretion to maintain urban hygiene and uphold local integrity. At home, creating a portal for Shango's blessings can be as simple as having a glass of dark beer and a brown or dark red candle lit once a week.

Gypsies are the group of spirit workers who operate under the influences of Shango.

Yoruba Myth ○ The Discord Between Omolu And Shango

Shango was on top of the world, celebrating yet another glorious victory in the city of Oyo. He was so joyful that he decided to throw a massive feast in his kingdom, inviting all the revered Orishas. As the preparations unfolded and the guests started arriving, the kingdom buzzed with excitement, except for one missing guest: Oshun.

Oshun, with Omolu in tow, as she had asked him to join the feast, made their way to the kingdom, eager to join the party. When they entered the grand hall, Shango wasted no time expressing his disapproval to Oshun, saying, 'What took you so long? And why did you bring this poorly dressed man to my fancy feast?' Shango gave Omolu a thorough once-over with his eyes. Feeling uneasy, Oshun replied in frustration, 'This is Omolu. Can you not see his true essence?' Shango shot back, 'Sure, I see him! But his clothes do not fit the royal class of my kingdom, let alone deserve a seat at my fancy table.'

Yansa, witnessing Shango's disdain and feeling her anger rise, got up and summoned a powerful gust of wind that blew away the straw covering Omolu, revealing his handsome face and perfectly fitting attire for the occasion. Caught off guard and unsure how to react, Shango quickly grabbed one of his fancy golden chairs and urged Omolu to sit. But Omolu, hurt and humiliated, could not hold back a tear and told Shango, 'You may be the king with a grand empire, but remember, I am the guardian of the very land that everyone, including you, walks upon. So, I am leaving your kingdom now. Enjoy the festivities, everyone!'

The party went on, but Shango, burdened by guilt, retired to his chambers for the night, haunted by his actions. The next morning, when he opened a window, he was greeted by a devastating sight. The once-thriving crops had withered, and the land itself seemed to decay beneath them. Desperate to understand what was happening, Shango sought guidance from Orunmila. The oracle's words pierced his heart: 'You disrespected the God of the earth, and now your kingdom is cursed.' Consumed by remorse and unsure of how to make things right, Shango set off on a journey to seek forgiveness from Omolu.

Omolu, being a humble man, embraced him and reassured him, saying, 'Find peace; your lands will be restored to their former glory.' Relieved by the forgiveness Shango received, he left. In return, Omolu decided to host his own celebration, inviting all the Orishas, including Shango. Everyone enjoyed the festive atmosphere at Omolu's gathering, and to everyone's surprise, Shango made an appearance. Omolu warmly welcomed him, saying, 'Come in, Shango; this house is yours. Let's feast and celebrate together.' However, all eyes were fixed on Shango, questioning why he was there after what he had done to Omolu. Unable to bear the scrutiny and feeling unwelcome, Shango left, realizing he was not fully welcome.

And so, every year, the grand banquet is held with all the Orishas in attendance, except for Shango.

This story highlights the contrasting vibrations and energies of Shango and Omolu among the Orishas. One moves swiftly while the other is slow; one brags while the other remains humble; one is loud while the other is quiet. Therefore, it is advisable to worship these two Orishas on different days. If their worship happens on the same day and at the same place, it is best to keep their offerings far apart, as their vibrations can clash. While the Orishas are not enemies, these tales remind us that their fields of operation can be vastly different, requiring caution to avoid weakening their respective powers.

Egunita

Egunita, pronounced Ay-goo-nee-TAH, is a name borrowed from the Yoruba language, combining *éégún*, which refers to bones and signifies ancestors and the dead, and *ita*, which may jointly connote "lady of the dead," alluding to one of Yansa's characteristics as lady of the dead. Alternatively, Egunita is referred to as Oroina, pronounced O-roy-NAH, also borrowed from Yoruba: *ara* means character or nature, and *ina* means fire, whereas altogether they signify "that of fiery nature," or even "fury of fire". This Orisha is a more recent addition to the pantheon, particularly embraced by followers of Sacred Umbanda..

As the Orisha of purifying fire, Egunita[19] does not have a historical presence in the Yoruba or African pantheon. Rather, she is observed as a newly recognized counterpart to Shango, specifically associated with justice and fire. Often regarded as a variant or aspect of the Orisha Yansa, Egunita represents a cosmic fire that purifies addictions, particularly those stemming from a sense of injustice, exaggerated emotions, or an excessive attachment to mundane sentiments. According to Saraceni's (1993) explanation, an unbalanced individual possesses an inherent negative magnetism that draws, concentrates, and stores this cosmic fire. Once this cosmic fire reaches a state of intense consumption, it depletes and ultimately neutralizes the imbalances.

Despite a relatively recent cult, which not only lacks tradition but also details, it may be challenging to indicate what best fits this Orisha. Notwithstanding, the cult of Yansa tends to look like the base for that of Egunita.

Nevertheless, Egunita is frequently sought to pair with Shango in petitions or to emanate their energies together in favors related to justice, strength, and the purifying of stagnant and deleterious

---

[19] Although Egunita is a relatively recent addition to the pantheon of Orishas, it is important to recognize the profound significance of her existence within the framework of Umbanda. Some individuals may mistakenly assume that Egunita was solely created by men or dismiss her as an unnecessary variation of Yansa. However, it is crucial to realize that the Orishas are observed as vibratory manifestations of a single God, and that local mediums and sensitives have observed and understood their manifestations throughout history. Egunita's inclusion enriches the tapestry of Orisha worship, allowing practitioners to access a broader range of spiritual energies and attributes.

energies via the divine throne of fire. When working with Ogun, Egunita intensifies his winds, whereas when working with Shango, she enhances his fire.

Egunita is related to the core of the Earth, for its magma, and the core of the Sun, for the same reason, indicating her association with potential fire and heat (but not necessarily the sunshine, like Shango and Oshala are).

Unsurprisingly, individuals with Egunita as the head-Orisha are rare and may often be designated with Yansa as their head-Orisha, for the latter is the closest Orisha to Egunita's nature, including the fact that both of them are cosmic Orishas. That is, they tend to consume that which is out of balance to allow spiritual progress to unfold. Yansa, however, is aligned more with the element of air, whereas Egunita is linked to fire.

Those who manage to obtain the precise designation of their head-Orisha as Egunita tend to be loyal, self-righteous, and are usually loud. They have a temper to defend the weaker, and they are the type of people who can solve any troubles that cross their way or the way of their loved ones.

As Egunita is associated with the Sun, those born with her as head-Orisha tend to shine, including in terms of physical magnetism. They also tend to work outside home, being fatigued easily if confined. In their negative side, these individuals may loose their temper easily and lack patient.

Egunita's main color is orange but also with red or shocking pink, symbolizing the essence of lava and magma. The presence of pink may be attributed to the traditional interpretation of one of Yansa's manifestations, which likely influenced the emergence of Egunita as an individual entity.

Her favored flowers include sunflowers, daisies, stone-breaker, and tansy, while her primary herbs and botanicals include peppermint and rue. Fruits that align well with Egunita's nature are pineapples, plums, blackberries, citrons, raspberries, and currants. Among the recommended beverages for offerings are mint brandy, rose bubbly, or orange juice.

Hematite, red jasper, and tiger's eye are stones associated with Egunita, although any volcanic stone falls within her domain. Her main tools typically consist of a lightning bolt, a six-pointed star, or a sword, often accompanied by a fire torch.

The lioness, tigress, and golden meerkat serve as animal symbols representing Egunita. Her domain includes the vicinity of volcanoes as well as hot deserts and rocky mountainous areas.

The customary salutation used to invoke Egunita before a ritual is "Kali Ye," pronounced *kah-lee YAy,* referencing the Hindu goddess Kali (and also the Romani patroness Sara Kali), and "ye," derived from the Yoruba term for "graces."

As Egunita was not actively worshiped during the time of slavery and the subsequent prohibition of African cults, no Christian saint was syncretized with her. However, in contemporary syncretism, Saint Sara Kali is often regarded as the closest representative. Kali, the Hindu goddess who purifies illusions through her sacred fire, may also be compared to Egunita. Additionally, it is a common practice to call upon her divine fire to purify locations that might be rife with negative energy or haunted by traumatic memories. Egunita's fire is also potent against curses and dark magic, whether directed at individuals or at specific places. Furthermore, individuals who require a more logical and analytical approach to their circumstances can also benefit from her guidance, as her fire consumes irrational thoughts and behaviors.

Offerings presented to Egunita typically include tangerines, oranges, lemons, mint brandy, sunflowers, and seven orange candles. When performing rituals in natural surroundings, the fruits can be placed directly on the ground. However, when conducting ceremonies at home, it is advisable to use a copper or golden bowl as a receptacle for Egunita's offerings. While her offerings are relatively simple, their presentation can be enhanced by selecting a red glass cup for her brandy and arranging sliced fruits to resemble flames. Similarly, the seven candles can consist of one yellow, four orange, and two red candles. Additionally, Egunita may be revered through bonfires or burning cauldrons dedicated to her, where written wishes and petitions are cast into the flames to be consumed by her transformative energy.

Assembling an altar to Egunita at home provides one with a point of force that continuously absorbs destructive energies, which are rapidly consumed by her flames.

Gypsies are a group of spirit workers who operate under the influence of Egunita.

Umbanda Myth ○ She is Magma

According to legend, Earth was once a massive, incandescent mass of fire. Olorun, being aware that there would be no possibility of life, sent Yemanja, the wife of Oshala, to extinguish this immense fire with her waters. Yemanja labored diligently, and with each emanation of her power, a layer of land formed. When the Earth's crust was ready, the fire had been entirely extinguished, and most of the land became completely covered by saltwater.

With this, Egunita became imprisoned at the center of the Earth. Unhappy with this fate, the Orisha of Fire sought out Olorun, who admonished the deity for its previous desire to have the Earth solely for herself. However, with His kindness and wisdom, the Supreme God said, 'You are paying for your own guilt. You will have complete dominion only over the center of the Earth. However, at periodic intervals, you may demonstrate your fury to the Earth's inhabitants through the power of your voice and your offspring.'

The voice portrayed in this myth is the roar of volcanoes during eruptions, and the offspring refers to the incandescent lava.

This myth alludes to Egunita's inner fire, which is more closely related to internal imbalances of temper and impatience than to the energy to manifest events, as is the case with Eshu and Shango.

Ogun

Ogun, derived from the Yoruba term *ògún*, meaning war, and pronounced as "o-GOON," is revered as the Orisha of war, battles, conquest, technology, protection, iron, and pathways. Ogun stands as a primordial Orisha, having always existed alongside other prominent deities such as Oshala, Yemanja, Oshun, and Oshossi. Resolute and disciplined, Ogun exemplifies the true essence of a warrior, confronting obstacles with robust determination. The ruler of the divine throne of Law, Ogun shares the responsibility of executing divine justice with Yansa, as dictated by Shango.

While Ogun holds immense popularity among the Orishas, it is worth noting that his images and statues are not commonly found in Umbanda centers, where veneration of the Catholic saint Saint George is more prevalent. Ogun and Saint George share many similarities, leading to a powerful syncretism that has also influenced the adaptation of colors in the cult, special days, and other aspects of Ogun's worship to align with Saint George's traditions.

Conflict has always been an inherent part of human existence, and through Ogun and his vibratory nature, individuals gain the courage to face daily battles and overcome obstacles.

Known as the Orisha who initiates action with fearlessness and swiftness, Ogun is associated with the element air, although his mastery of blacksmithing and occasional displays of fiery temperament may also relate him to earth and fire.

Ogun is an Orisha who is often considered a sibling of Eshu and Oshossi, as the three share many traits. Revered as a symbol of martial prowess and unwavering loyalty, Ogun embodies strength, determination, and courage. Known for his seriousness, steadfastness, and tenacity, Ogun is regarded as the epitome of a heroic figure.

Individuals born with Ogun as their head-Orisha possess a remarkable sense of determination and a conquering spirit. When aligned with Ogun's positive influence, these individuals confront challenges without complaint, inspiring others with their perseverance. Invariably impulsive and impetuous, they may thrive in leadership positions and those where physical stamina is needed.

They typically exhibit extraordinary physical energy and a vibrant sense of humor. However, if they fail to tap into their inherent Ogun essence for personal growth, they may experience extreme anger over trivial matters and display confrontational and violent behavior and suspicion, leading to financial struggles and turbulent relationships.

Sons and daughters of Ogun typically have a slender physique, expressive eyes, quick movements, and a commanding voice. They often have a penchant for fashion and may dress in a youthful manner, though this does not reflect immaturity in their personality unless they are out of sync with Ogun's vibrations.

Engaging with individuals who are under the influence of Ogun can be challenging, as they may appear to be stubborn and have a constant drive to compete. However, once they commit to a path of righteousness, they become relentless in their efforts to assist others, taking responsibilities, providing aid to the less fortunate, and offering protection to those in need.

Ogun is associated with the colors red and dark blue, depending on the manner in which his cult is practiced. The cult of Ogun is closely intertwined with that of Saint George when the color red is prominent, while a more traditional approach favors the color dark blue. These color variations have minimal devotional implications, as they primarily indicate a change in aesthetics. Some Umbanda temples may even interchange Ogun's imagery and name with that of Saint George, while still utilizing the color blue for candles and special adornments on his altar. It is believed that centers emphasizing the color red focus on Ogun's aspects related to battles, courage, and audacity, while those dressing him in dark blue prioritize his qualities as a protector and guardian. Nevertheless, both colors are within the domain of Ogun, just as yellow and sometimes dark blue are associated with Oshun.

Offerings to Ogun often consist of fruits such as mangoes, as well as yams, black beans, and palm oil, preferably obtained from sustainable sources, as the Orishas represent the energy of nature itself. Ogun's associated plants include the snake plant (specifically the variety without the yellow line surrounding the leaf, as that is associated with Yansa), lemongrass, sweet basil, eucalyptus, and mango tree leaves. Flowers such as red anthurium and red carnations can be offered as well.

Crystals and stones that resonate with Ogun's nature include carnelian, red jasper, blue topaz, magnetite, and other stones containing significant amounts of metals, such as hematite, which contains notable quantities of iron.

Ogun's domains are primarily straight roads and rails, with train tracks being particularly significant due to their connection to technology and metals. It is worth mentioning that stones obtained from locations near rail tracks possess a strong emanation of Ogun's energy.

Symbols and emblems commonly attributed to Ogun include the sword, as well as metal chains, nails, screws, and other objects related to metallurgy.

The salutation used to praise or invoke Ogun is 'Ogun Ye,' pronounced as 'o-GOON YAY,' which translates to 'save Ogun' or 'graces to Ogun.' Additionally, it is common for devotees of Ogun to say 'patakori Ogun,' pronounced as 'pah-tah-koe-ree,' derived from the Yoruba words pataki (important) and ori (head), signifying that Ogun is the main lord of their heads.

In addition to his strong syncretism with Saint George, Ogun may also be associated with several gods of war from different cultures, embodying and exemplifying their main traits related to warfare, impulsiveness, and other general characteristics. Examples include Ares and Mars from the Greek and Roman pantheons, Guan Yu from Chinese mythology, and Tyr from Norse mythology.

Ogun bestows courage, strength, and, most importantly, the determination to conquer and endure hardships. One of Ogun's most revered qualities is protection against lower magic, possessive spirits, and negative energy. Consequently, the veneration of Ogun is often motivated by either the desire for strength or the need for protection.

A simple ritual for invoking Ogun's strength within oneself may involve a single red candle and a glass of lager beer. However, a more elaborate ceremony would typically include seven red candles, a bowl of black beans cooked with onions and palm oil, and a glass of lager beer. It is worth noting that complex rituals, whether performed at home or in an Umbanda center, do not need to be repeated frequently. After an initial elaborate offering, subsequent days or weeks may suffice with just a candle and a glass of beer.

For petitions seeking protection for oneself, one's home, for a business, or for family members, a ritual can be conducted using seven dark blue candles arranged around semi-grilled or lightly baked yum, pierced with 21 toothpicks, and accompanied by palm oil poured over it on a metal plate. A glass of lager beer should be placed beside it. Similarly, to maintain the energy flow in the following weeks, a single blue candle and a glass of beer suffices.

If one chooses to honor Ogun solely in his blue tradition, or opt for his red qualities, it is advisable to adhere to one color consistently, irrespective of whether the ritual is for determination or protection. It is also important to emphasize that before any complex rituals involving the Orishas, one must first offer homage to Orisha Eshu, or to his workers, namely Eshus and Pombagiras, at least with a red or red and black candle. If possible, a glass of rum or champagne, and a lit cigar or straw cigarette can also be added.

Bohemians, cowboys, and various Eshus are the groups of spirit workers who operate under the influences of Ogun.

Yoruba Myth ○ Ogun Sees Red

Ogun, a courageous warrior and the son of a prominent king, embarked on a distant journey to engage in battle.

After years away, he returned to his kingdom, only to find that his presence went unnoticed. People passed by him without recognizing or acknowledging him.

Feeling ignored and disregarded, Ogun approached the people, inquiring if they knew him, but each person denied any knowledge of him. Overwhelmed by anger, Ogun, wielding his sword, confronted everyone, demanding recognition. But as they continued to deny knowing him, Ogun's fury escalated, leading him to unleash violence and wreak havoc. Consumed by rage, he lost control and killed many of his own people.

However, Ogun's son, who had remained in the kingdom during his father's absence, approached him with a platter filled with Ogun's favorite dishes, including beans, yams, palm oil, and beer. The son calmly spoke, 'Father, do you not understand why they remain silent? Do you not remember that you asked everyone, once a year, to observe silence and fasting?' With this reminder, Ogun was overtaken with regret and embarrassment.

In an act of repentance, he plunged his sword into the ground, causing the earth to crack open, and he descended into the chasm.

Oshala, witnessing this series of events, decided to transform Ogun into an Orisha, granting him the domain over war, battles, conquest, and pathways.

This myth may allude to Ogun's nature as a warrior, but more importantly, to his impatient temper and thus his tendency to act impulsively and regrettably when unaware of the situation.

Yansa

Yansa, pronounced *ee-un-SUN*; derived from the proto-Yoruboid Ìyá Èyánsàn (as modern Yoruba *iya-ẹẹsan*) meaning "mother of nine," is the esteemed Orisha associated with lightning, winds, tornadoes, hurricanes, cyclones, and storms. Yansa is also commonly referred to as Oya, pronounced *oy-AH*, originating from the Yoruba word *Ọ* (honor; respect) and *iya* (mother). As the Orisha of movement, audacity, and agility, Yansa holds a revered status as the most resolute and strong-willed Orisha, embodying feminine empowerment and transmitting fearless daring, courage, and self-sufficiency.

Yansa's influence promotes profound changes and upheavals, leading to new beginnings. While the changes brought about by Yansa differ from the transformative destruction of the Hindu god Shiva[20], Yansa acts as a cosmic force that impels movement and repositioning of things, ideas, people, and all other elements so that they can be readjusted and renewed. She has the ability to shift thoughts and situations from their established positions, allowing for realignment and progress.

Yansa is often sought after to expedite the pace of progress and to promote agility in all cases that seem stagnant. In addition to her role in movement and change, Yansa shares the patronage of the throne of Law with Ogun. This divine domain governs karma and divine justice based on merit, where the law must be implemented. While Ogun establishes order along straight lines, Yansa absorbs and dissipates any deviations from that order through circular motion. When individuals find themselves overwhelmed by destructive emotions linked to addictions or excessively driven by instinctual urges, Yansa channels and dissipates these emotions. This process allows individuals who have veered off the path of divine law to regain rationality and be redirected back onto the correct course.

Yansa is also associated with cemeteries and the spirits of those who struggle to detach from earthly addictions, or from the negative

---

20 The philosophy behind Shiva's destruction is not rooted in arbitrary or chaotic motives but rather in the transformative and regenerative dissolution necessary for new cycles to emerge.

emotions lingering from their past actions. Consequently, Yansa's vibrations is responsible for guiding and relocating these spirits.

Occasionally, Yansa's emanations align with those of Shango, working in tandem to promote active justice. While Shango establishes justice in a fixed and settled manner, Yansa facilitates movements and actions that contribute to the pursuit of it.

There are several manifestations and variations of Yansa and Oya, each encompassing unique aspects and characteristics. One example is Oya Bale, which represents the aspect of Yansa associated with her dominion over the realm of the deceased. This particular manifestation is invoked in spiritual work involving entities such as spiritual vampires. Another example is Oya Afefe, who is connected to the winds and embodies agility and swiftness. Additionally, there is Oya Maganbelle, representing the qualities of being unable to bear children (which is not common, but neither a rare condition in women whose head-Orisha is Yansa).

While Egunita is sometimes considered a variation of Yansa, it is important to note that this Orisha of Fire possesses distinctive attributes that set her apart and prevent her from being categorized solely as a variation of Yansa.

Another noteworthy variation is Oshun Opara, which represents a unique facet of Oshun herself. Oshun Opara combines the radiant energy of Oshun with the fierce essence of Oya. This fusion gives rise to a dynamic and intense manifestation of Oshun, where the emphasis shifts from delicate beauty to fearless feminine deity.

It is worth mentioning that all Orishas encompass variations within themselves, showcasing different qualities depending on specific rituals or religious practices. However, in the context of Umbanda, practitioners typically focus on a single manifestation of an Orisha, referred to by one name. It is important to recognize that these variations and multiple names are more closely associated with Candomblé than with Umbanda's theological framework.

Individuals born under the influence of Yansa exhibit many warrior-like characteristics, displaying impulsiveness, courage, and extroversion, and often exaggerating their manner of speaking, dressing, and adorning their bodies. Women who have Yansa as their head-Orisha often dress provocatively and exude sensuality. However, unlike Oshun, Yansa's expression can be more provocative and, in its negative aspect, even vulgar, while Oshun invariably maintains a sense of elegance.

Children of Yansa also tend to have a slim appearance, an energetic demeanor, and a cheerful disposition. These individuals are known for their exuberant joy and loudness, appearing to fear very little. They also demonstrate a remarkable ability to endure hardships for extended periods when others might succumb more quickly. Having Yansa as their head-Orisha grants them agility and a natural inclination towards action and change. They often feel a strong desire to protect and defend those close to them, which gave rise to the myth of the "mother of nine."

In this myth, Yansa, initially unable to conceive, managed to give birth to nine children after making an offering. Paradoxically, those with Yansa as their head-Orisha tend to prefer independent lives and have fewer children.

In their negative aspects, the children of Yansa may exhibit traits of loud troublemakers, often reacting excessively to situations in an uncultured manner.

Yansa is commonly associated with the color red, but orange, yellow, and occasionally brown are also found in her cult. As a result, bead necklaces, candles, stones, fruits, and flowers often follow this color preference.

Yansa has an affinity for a variety of red and orange flowers, including red roses, poppies, and chrysanthemums. Bamboo is her primary plant, symbolizing her ability to bend without breaking. As such, bamboo groves and open spaces with gusts of wind are considered her domains. The snake plant, with its yellow-bordered leaves, is also an important symbol of her energy. Herbs used in her cult include bay leaves, bamboo leaves, lettuce, cinnamon, and the petals of the aforementioned flowers. Yansa's preferred fruits are mangoes, red apples, pomegranates, and oranges.

The symbolic crystals of Yansa are citrine, jasper, and carnelian.

Yansa, the Orisha of strong winds, is primarily represented by a sword but can also be depicted with a torch or a pom-pom made of horsetail hair, which she uses to generate gusts of wind to repel spirits.

The salutation used to praise or invoke Yansa is "Epahey Yansa!" (or "Epahey Oya"), pronounced as *ay-pah-HAY*. This expression originates from Yoruba and carries the meaning of "oh, hello" with a respectful tone of utter surprise, possibly reflecting her association with loudness and lightnings.

Yansa is recognized for her ability to invigorate stagnant or slow-paced causes by instilling movement and agility. Her dynamic energy generates excitement and motivation, particularly in work-related matters, spiritual obsession, and romantic relationships. A recommended ritual offering for Yansa involves the use of either one or nine red candles, a glass of rosé champagne, and natural incense made from herbs and botanicals associated with her (most incense sticks are typically made of bamboo, which aligns favorably with Yansa's nature).

During the ritual, the candles and incense are lit, the champagne is poured, and a respectful clap is followed by loudly verbalizing "epahey Oya!"

For a more elaborate ritual, it may be suitable to incorporate nine candles, fruits, flowers, incense, and champagne. In addition, a recommended dish that harnesses Yansa's powers of agility and intensity consists of a bread-like pastry dough made from mashed black-eyed peas, onions, and red chilies, fried in palm oil.

When performing the ritual at an Umbanda center, in a natural setting, or at home, it is customary to offer Eshu at least a glass of rum beforehand. To maintain Yansa's emanations on the altar, it is advisable to light a red candle and pour some rosé champagne at least once a week.

Cowboys and elves are the groups of spirit workers who operate under the influences of Yansa.

Yansa is syncretized with Saint Barbara due to their shared connection with lightning. In the story, Saint Barbara was condemned to death by her own father, who was later struck by lightning on his way home.

Yoruba Myth ○ Oshun's Mirror

As told by Prandi (2000), Oshun lived in a palace and would spend her days in her room, gazing at her mirrors. Her mirrors were made of polished seashells and gold, in which she admired her beautiful reflection. One day, Oshun left the room and left the door open. Her sister, Oya, entered the room and was mesmerized by the world of mirrors she found. Looking at her own reflection, the seashells revealed an astonishing truth to Oya: that she was beautiful! The most beautiful! The most stunning of all women! Oya discovered her beauty in Oshun's mirrors.

Oya was enchanted but also frightened: was she more beautiful than Oshun, the Beautiful? Overwhelmed with happiness, she shared her discovery with everyone. But Oshun Opara, consumed by bitter envy, was no longer the most beautiful of women. As a result, she sought revenge.

One day, Oshun went to the house of a disembodied spirit and stole their mirror—the mirror that only shows death, the horrifying image of all that is ugly. She then placed the specter's mirror in Oya's room and waited.

When Oya entered her room, she looked into the mirror and despaired. She tried to escape, but it was impossible. Her terrible reflection had trapped her. She ran through the room in hopelessly, throwing herself on the floor and banging her head against the walls. She could not escape from the room or the horrifying vision of ugliness. Oya went mad, and eventually she left this world. Oshala, who witnessed everything, reproached Oshun Opara, and subsequently transformed Oya into an Orisha. He also made the decision that Oshun would never forget Oya's image by forcing her to dress in Oya's colors and adorn herself with the same metal that her sister used in her jewelry and warrior weapons.

This myth alludes to the fact that Oya, or Yansa, although beautiful and sensual, is not to fit into the terms of conquering the world for her beauty, so much so that when she sees herself beautiful and is thus excited by it, something bad happens to her. The myth also focuses heavily on Oshun's negative sides of jealousy and revenge, besides mentioning why that particular aspect of her—Oshun Opara—is so similar to Yansa.

Obaluaye

Obaluaye, pronounced "o-bah-loo-ah-YAY" and derived from the Yoruba *ọba lúw áiyé,* meaning "king in the earth," is a prominent Orisha associated with the cure of diseases, the earth, respectability, and decency.

Obaluaye is renowned for his influence over various diseases, including skin-related conditions, infections, airborne illnesses, epilepsy, and convulsions. Obaluaye embodies healing properties rather than being solely the source of afflictions. In the Yoruba tradition, when his presence was associated with disease, he would be called Ṣọpọna, meaning "be cautious." While this distinction is not commonly observed in Umbanda, the brazilianized name "Xapanã" is occasionally used in specific Umbanda centers to refer to both Obaluaye and Omolu.

Obaluaye's healing abilities emanate from his earthly energy, effectively dispelling these ailments.

This Orisha also staunchly opposes falsehoods and lower forms of magic.

While closely connected to the earth, Obaluaye should not be fully equated with underworld deities found in other cultures, such as Anubis in Egyptian mythology or Ades in Greek mythology. Nevertheless, Obaluaye represents the transitional aspect, facilitating the transformation from one state to another or from one plane of existence to the next. Obaluaye's energy is dedicated to exhaustive healing efforts before concluding one phase and initiating the next. In this capacity, he is then correlated to the realm of the underworld, as he navigates among those on the brink of death, offering them a cure.

Obaluaye and Omolu are often mistaken for each other and erroneously believed to be the same Orisha. However, these were originally distinct entities and were later merged due to their numerous similarities, particularly in relation to disease healing and the underworld. Obaluaye came to be regarded as a younger manifestation of Omolu. In Umbanda, both Orishas are worshiped interchangeably, forming a unified cult. Despite this fusion, their energies remain consistent, with Obaluaye primarily associated with the daylight and Omolu with the night, although this fact is seldom observed.

As a universal Orisha, Obaluaye irradiates transformative principles, sharing with Nana the responsibility for the divine throne of Evolution. Together, they aid the spiritual evolution of individuals in all aspects.

Obaluaye symbolizes wisdom, similar to Oshala, albeit with a greater emphasis on earthly journeys, whereas Oshala is more closely associated with the air and represents wisdom through faith.

Obaluaye governs the realms of medicine, treatments, and general change with great authority. He also serves as a guiding force for spirits as they embark on a new beginning after death.

In the realm of Orishas, which are aspects of God akin to how each color in a rainbow is part of the same white light, certain Orishas represent opposing aspects, similar to the relationship between yellow and violet in the color wheel. In this vein, Obaluaye and Omolu are considered the counterbalances to Shango. While Shango embodies extroversion, exuberance, movement, laughter, and prosperity, Obaluaye represents timidity, silence, delicacy, and restraint. Similarly, Ogun stands in direct opposition to Nana, and Oshala opposes Eshu. It is important to note that the Orishas are not adversaries, nor does one aspect of God antagonize another aspect of God itself. Instead, they operate in distinct realms, focusing on different matters. For instance, when venerating Shango, it is advisable to avoid immediately revering Obaluaye, and vice versa. This principle extends to the positioning of their altars and offerings, ensuring that one vibratory activity does not interfere with the other. For instance, the energies that Nana embodies—old age, peace, and tradition—are in contrast to those that Ogun represents, which include youth, war, and technology. Due to their inherent differences, these energies are considered incompatible and have the potential to compromise one another when brought together. Therefore, it is preferable to have separate altars for each, or honor them on different days. Additionally, one should never use fruits, colors, or elements associated with one Orisha as offerings to another on opposite spectrum.

Individuals whose-head Orisha is Obaluaye often display traits of timidity, reserve, and notably, self-righteousness. It is not uncommon to find Obaluaye's sons and daughters having experienced severe illnesses early in life or enduring prolonged periods of illness for 20 to 30 years. However, and usually surprisingly, at some point, complete healing occurs, resulting in a robust physique and a strong immune system. In fact, individuals with Obaluaye as their head-Orisha are regarded as exceptionally healthy, possessing the capacity to readily channel their healing energies to others, thus becoming great healers in spiritual healing. The benevolent and curative properties emitted by their chakras, particularly the heart, spleen and solar plexus chakras, are abundant, making engagement in spiritual healing highly recommended for these individuals. This restorative process often allows those born under the influence of Obaluaye to live long lives, reaching above the average age.

They possess the ability to not only heal others physically but also emotionally, knowing the appropriate methods and words to employ. Emotionally, those governed by Obaluaye are deeply sensitive, although they do not exhibit dramatic tendencies. Their voices tend to be low and calm, and they may often prefer traditional fashion, house decor, and values while remaining open-minded and tolerant.

These individuals may also possess a higher propensity, compared to the average person, for mediumship or paranormal abilities, allowing them to provide additional assistance to others in need. It is advisable that those born under Obaluaye's influence remain connected to a spiritual path and faith to prevent them from developing diseases, especially mental ones, that belong to others and to the places they go, as they tend to absorb the environments.

On the negative side, in cases where someone has Obaluaye as their head Orisha but is not aligned with the deity's true nature, they may become excessively grumpy, prone to complaining, and experience depressive tendencies. They are often observed to be in a bad mood and may also become rather ironic and rude.

One distinctive characteristic of individuals with Obaluaye as their head-Orisha is their inclination towards secrecy. It is common for them to keep many aspects of their lives confidential or to be advised to do so. It is important to note that this inclination towards secrecy does not imply dishonesty but rather a preference for not divulging extensive information.

Individuals who have Obaluaye or Omolu as their head-Orishas may find themselves living with a sense of perpetual limitation. It is important to note that the energy of the Orishas themselves does not cause this unfavorable situation. Instead, it is the individual's own spirit that already possesses inherent limitations prior to reincarnation, and thus the Orishas step forward and play a crucial role in assisting these individuals on their journey of incarnation.

Physically, individuals governed by Obaluaye may bear visible signs of the challenges faced throughout life, such as blemishes or skin roughness. They may also appear and act older than their actual age in the earlier stages of childhood and adolescence and slightly younger as they progress through old age.

White is a common symbol for Obaluaye, representing his authority over souls, while black and white signify his connection to the earth. Although his frequency aligns more with violet, this color is not typically observed in his cult.

White chrysanthemums, iris, and daisies are among the flowers associated with Obaluaye, the plants of the Orisha (namely cacti) often exhibit a tough and spiky exterior, yet they possess abundant water within them. This duality reflects his nature, symbolizing outside strictness and discipline while harboring an enormous heart within, filled with deep emotions. Lavender and coriander are some of the herbs associated with him.

Obaluaye has a preference for fruits such as soursop, jackfruit, plantains, and coconut—all of which depict hard shells but softness within. Mineral water, black coffee, and dry wine are considered suitable drinks for him. Smoky quartz, howlite, and onyx are among the crystals associated with his vibration.

Obaluaye's tool is a club or cane, but the Christian cross is also linked to his cult, alluding to cemeteries, which are within his sphere of influence.

When presenting offerings or candles to Obaluaye, it is customary to respectfully utter the phrase "atoto, Obaluaye!" (pronounced ah-toe-TOE), a term derived from the Jeje culture, meaning "silence." This signifies reverence for his presence as a respected authority.

Obaluaye is primarily invoked to address matters related to health, and his energy is renowned for its healing capabilities and its capacity to facilitate spiritual progress for individuals, groups, and situations. This energetic influence often manifests as physical change, experienced through purging processes. While it is unlikely that anyone would ask Obaluaye to inflict illness for the sake of personal progress, it is common to request his assistance in alleviating burdens and promoting favorable health outcomes. In such cases, individuals may also seek the aid of Omolu to reduce illnesses and karmic burdens.

For those seeking to enhance their connection with Obaluaye or aiming for general well-being, a simple offering can consist of a large white candle (preferably a 7-day candle) and a cup of black coffee. For more complex offerings that harness Obaluaye's potent earthly energy, such as protection against low magic or the cure of severe or terminal illnesses, a large bowl of popcorn (preferably popped solely by heat and without salt) is placed in a straw basket, with coconut pieces atop used as a garnish. Additionally, a glass of dry red wine can be included.

In cases where a specific illness requires healing, one can pass 14 small white bread buns over their own body in a wiping motion before placing them in a basket alongside candles, which can either be white or violet in color. A glass of water is also included in this offering. After 7 days, all the organic components of the offerings should be disposed of in nature.

Obaluaye also governs the transition from physical life to astral life, assisting in the transmutation of physical remnants before full discarnation occurs. In these instances, a simple white or violet candle can be offered while requesting a smooth passage for a loved one. As Obaluaye also governs cemeteries and graveyards, lighting candles there or at their local shrines is indeed the recommended choice.

Old Blacks are the group of spirit workers who also operate directly under the influences of Obaluaye.

In a syncretic manner, Obaluaye is associated with Saint Lazarus, as the Christian saint is renowned for his wounds. Additionally, in one of Obaluaye's ancient myths, his physical ailments transform into the emotional pain of exile, which draws parallels to Chiron from Greek mythology. Chiron was a wise and compassionate centaur who possessed extensive knowledge of medicine but could not heal himself. However, this association is not observed in Umbanda.

Yoruba Myth ○ The Journey of Wisdom

According to the legend, young Obaluaye, a mere boy of twelve summers, found himself cloaked in despair. Ignored and overlooked by those around him, he felt the weight of loneliness settle upon his shoulders like an unyielding shroud.

Yet, within the depths of his soul, a flicker of determination burned brightly. With resolve as unyielding as the roots of the sacred iroko tree, Obaluaye embarked on a quest to carve his destiny anew. Through verdant forests and tangled undergrowth, he ventured forth, guided only by the beacon of his own unwavering spirit.

But fate, fickle as the wind, had other designs. As he journeyed deeper into the wilderness, he found himself beset by a swarm of relentless mosquitoes, their buzzing chorus echoing through the canopy like a cacophony of tiny drums. Each bite left behind a mark, a testament to the trials he endured.

Yet, despite the agony, Obaluaye pressed on, his spirit unbroken. With each passing day, the welts upon his skin began to fade, a testament to his resilience in the face of adversity. And when weariness finally overcame him, he surrendered to the embrace of sleep, nestled amidst the roots of an ancient baobab tree.

It was in this slumber, beneath the watchful gaze of the moon, that Obaluaye heard the whisper of the spirits, their voices a symphony of ancient wisdom. They spoke of trials endured and lessons learned, of the strength that lies dormant within every soul waiting to be awakened.

Awakening to the dawn's gentle caress, Obaluaye felt the weight of newfound knowledge settle upon his shoulders like a mantle. With each step homeward, he carried not only the scars of his journey but also the wisdom of ages past.

As he returned to his village, he beheld a scene of desolation, a shadow cast upon the once-thriving community. It was then that he understood the true depth of his purpose—to heal not only himself but also those around him.

With compassion as boundless as the ocean, Obaluaye extended his hand to those in need, offering solace to the wounded souls who had once overlooked him. And in the warmth of his embrace, the village found hope anew, their hearts alight with gratitude for the boy who had become their guiding light.

This story may allude to the ailments that individuals born with Obaluaye as their head-Orisha may experience, but more importantly, it highlights his profound willingness to assist others through the wisdom gained from his own past hardships and trials.

Nana

Nana, pronounced "nun-NUN," derives from the Yoruba term for 'grandma,' signifying her venerable status as one of the most ancient Orishas in both symbolic age and the history of her cult. Revered as the embodiment of purification, wisdom, and motherhood, Nana Buruku, as she is occasionally referred to, holds dominion over the sacred throne of Evolution.

Nana's primary role entails purifying and separating dense and obscure matter from clear and subtle ones. With her exceptionally high-frequency vibration, she facilitates the dissolution of addictions, residual negative influences, toxic thoughts, and uncontrolled activities that lead to violence and accidents.

Nana is strongly associated with elements such as mud, sludge, mangroves, and the depths of rivers and lakes, which symbolize physical existence and the process of purifying and decanting residues.

As an embodiment of wisdom, experience, and maturity, Nana serves as the repository of ancestral memory and governs the domain of remembrance, including the memory of past lives. As a guardian of tradition, she finds tranquility in serene environments, the night, and the ethereal realm of still bodies of water and gentle rainfall. Nana's sphere of influence is characterized by a slow and deliberate pace, symbolized by a gentle drizzle.

Known for her kindness and deep affection for children and animals, Nana assumes the archetype of a loving grandmother figure. It is believed that those who actively rescue and care for animals align themselves with Nana's nurturing vibrations.

Nana bears significant responsibility for human life and is regarded as one of the primary deities overseeing its existence. The overflowing of rivers, which brings fertile mud, played a crucial role in the flourishing of ancient civilizations such as those of Mesopotamia, Egypt, the Indus Valley, and the Yellow River in China.

Just as Yemanja is linked to the generation of life and Oshun with its sustenance, Nana represents the cycles of life, including both its inception and conclusion. However, she is also associated with the symbolism of death. In addition to Omolu/Obaluaye, and Yansa, Nana assumes responsibility for the realm of discarnate spirits. She is believed to separate ordinary spirits from those with malevolent intentions or perverse manifestations, guiding them accordingly.

Traditionally, Nana exhibits a strong aversion to metals; therefore, offerings dedicated to her must not include any objects composed of or containing metal. This principle arises from the stark contrast between Nana's fast oscillation and short wavelength and that of Ogun, who embodies the opposite and is characterized by swiftness and agility, particularly linked with the elements of iron. Thus, within the cult of Nana, the avoidance of metals is crucial to preventing conflicting energies from arising. This principle is rooted in their distinct domains and characteristics and is further exemplified in myths recounting conflicts between Nana and Ogun.

Nana's essence manifests in various forms of purification, encompassing chemical, energetic, and spiritual processes. Activities such as cleaning, resting, or engaging in fasting are also linked to this venerable Orisha. Nana's deliberate and unhurried nature facilitates the gradual separation of elements, allowing for the progression of evolution.

Individuals born under the influence of Nana are characterized by their cautious demeanor, calm disposition, and strong attachment to their homes. They have a deep connection with their physical dwellings, maintaining an orderly and pristine living space. To them, domicile transcends its role as a mere residence—it becomes a sacred temple. Consequently, the children of Nana are destined to own their own homes, often opting for modest simplicity in appearance. They embody a conventional personality, appreciating traditional objects, art, and customs.

Individuals guided by Nana as their head-Orisha are known for their inherent kindness, genuine friendship, and compassion towards animals. It is not uncommon for them to care for multiple animals, often adopting those in need.

However, if individuals with Nana as their head-Orisha succumb to negative influences, they may exhibit tendencies towards constant grumbling, habitual complaints, excessive judgment, and a prematurely aging appearance. It should be noted that Nana's association with the mysteries of magic often intrigues those influenced by her, leading to an interest in the occult. Depending on their level of spiritual progress, some may even delve into obscure spell-casting and witchcraft practices. As Nana is intimately connected to the realm of conjuring, it is widely recognized that those under her guidance bear a significant responsibility in oral enchantment. Consequently, the curses or desires verbally expressed by these individuals possess significant power to impact others. Nevertheless, by cultivating a mindset of altruism and kindness, their desires find greater fulfillment, and they may experience an extended life with robust health.

Nana is commonly related to the color lilac, but also violet, symbolizing her transmutative and mystical nature.

Bellflowers, violets, lavender are among Nana's preferred flowers, while compatible plants and herbs include red cabbage, fir needles, rosemary, and sage. Fruits that hold significance for Nana include purple grapes, blueberries, apples, plums, and eggplants.

Rainwater, coconut water, rosé wine, and light berry liquors are the preferred beverages attributed to Nana.

Amethysts hold a close connection to Nana, with other violet or lilac stones also being relevant to her energy. The frog is the animal symbol associated with this Orisha, signifying her domain of power in swamps as well as the bottom or margins of serene rivers and lakes. Owls are also commonly associated with her, for being a nocturnal animal that symbolizes wisdom. Additionally to swamps, Nana exerts influence over cemeteries, maternity wards, and the home.

Nana's emblem or tool is a curved and adorned branch of a tree, which she cradles and cares for as one would a baby. Symbols such as pentagrams or the waning moon are also tied to her cult.

The customary salutation used to invoke Nana before a ritual is "Saluba, Nana!" pronounced as 'sah-loo-BAH,' originating from the proto-Yoruboid term *sa luwa*, meaning 'we escape to you.'

The worship of Nana, whether by those who bear her as their head-Orisha or by others, bestows protective qualities against witchcraft spells and curses, particularly those related to death. Additionally, it facilitates the cultivation of wisdom, serenity, and, most importantly, the purification of one's thoughts, emotions, and spiritual energies, resulting in a renewed and revitalized life.

A simple act of reverence to Nana at an altar can involve lighting a violet candle and placing a glass of water. For a more elaborate offering, typically performed once a year, seven violet candles surrounding a wooden or straw bowl filled with fruits and a glass of water can be arranged near the margins of a lake, river, or, preferably, a serene swamp or still puddle. The fruits can be elegantly placed on red cabbage or lettuce leaves, while sage can be burned, and violet flowers arranged around it. The chosen beverages, which may include red wine, can be poured onto the soil or into the river. If the altar is situated at home, water from a river, lake, or fine rain can be offered in a glass.

Old Blacks and Witches are the classes of spirit workers who directly operate under the influences of Nana.

While there may be occasional syncretism between Nana and Saint Anne, Jesus' grandmother, as well as with the crone goddess of pagan religions, Nana is predominantly observed independently and distinct from such syncretic connections.

Yoruba Myth ○ Nana Confronts Ogun

The myth recounted by Verger (2019) revolves around Nana, an ancient water deity whose origins trace back to a distant era in the past. Ogun, a formidable warrior chief, always took the lead in any endeavor. However, their paths converged one day at a gathering—the assembly of two hundred Orishas on the right and four hundred on the left. There, they discussed their powers extensively, paying homage to Oshala, the creator of all humans, and honoring Orumila, the master of human destinies. Eshu, the vital messenger, was also a topic of discussion.

In the midst of their discourse, the significance of Ogun's tools for survival and agricultural activities was emphasized, prompting the Orishas to hail him as the most crucial among them. Yet, Nana contested this notion, questioning the reliance on Ogun's works. Despite the consensus of the others, Nana chose not to pay homage to Ogun, suggesting the possibility of another Orisha being more paramount. In response, Ogun, noting the homage paid to him by all other Orishas, expected Nana to do the same. However, Nana adamantly refused to acknowledge Ogun's superiority, sparking a heated debate between them.

Challenged by Ogun, Nana confidently affirmed her intent to render him dispensable. In retaliation, Ogun asserted, "Very well! You will know that I am indispensable for all things."

He then questioned how Nana planned to accomplish tasks without utilizing his expertise as the master of all metals—tin, lead, and iron. Unfazed, Nana declared that henceforth, she would eschew anything crafted by Ogun yet still achieve all her objectives.

This tale illustrates the contrast between the modern, aggressive, and fast natured of Ogun and the ancestral, gentle, and slow nature of Nana. And it also reminds why offerings to Nana should not contain metals.

Yemanja

Yemanja, pronounced *yay-mun-ZHAh* (with the "zh" sound as in "measure"), derives from the Yoruba phrase *iye ọmọ ẹja*, meaning 'mother of the fish children.' She is revered as the Orisha of waters, seas, motherhood, family, and the mind.

Yemanja holds a significant position among the Orishas, being perhaps the most revered and popular Orisha in Umbanda, with her influence extending beyond the confines of religious temples. Often regarded as the mother of all Orishas, though this position is disputed but not fiercely contested with Nana, Yemanja represents and safeguards the essence of the family. As the foremost maternal Orisha, Yemanja exemplifies nurturing qualities, displaying exceptional kindness and a strong familial orientation.

Apart from her role in family matters, Yemanja also governs the realm of the mind, encompassing thoughts and all aspects related to the head, including the physical brain and skull.

Yemanja presides over the divine throne of Generation alongside Omolu. Consequently, she holds authority over the conception and emergence of all forms of life, whether the birth of new life itself or the birth of endeavors and projects. While the concept of "generation" is commonly sewed with the conception and fertilization of human cells, the dominion of Yemanja and Omulu extends beyond human reproduction. It encompasses the fertilization and emergence of all physical life forms, as well as the generation of thoughts, ideas, and emotions. Yemanja's sphere of influence extends beyond fertility and pregnancy; she also generates ideas, opportunities, and occasions. All seeds of creation and fecundation originate from Yemanja's divine emanation.

In Umbanda, Yemanja is honored as the queen of the seas, even though her African roots primarily associate her with rivers, including the Ogun River in Nigeria, for which she serves as the patron. Upon her arrival in Brazil, Oshun became more closely associated with rivers and waterfalls, while Yemanja claimed dominion over the vast seas[21].

---

21 Due to Brazil's urbanization being more coastal-oriented compared to Western African nations, the sea holds a more significant role in Brazilian society. This coastal influence

Yemanja, like Oshun, possesses a caring nature. However, while Oshun focuses on self-care, as evident in the hand mirror that she gazes into, Yemanja's hand mirror is turned outward, reflecting others and encouraging them to see their own reflections. This demonstrates that Yemanja's focus lies in assisting others in their personal growth.

Transparency is a key principle she upholds. Typically calm and gentle, Yemanja rarely exhibits irritability or egotistical behavior.

While wealth is not typically associated with Yemanja (as it is more aligned with Oshun, Shango, and Logunede), she possesses the power to manifest abundance wherever it is lacking. Additionally, Yemanja is believed to strongly protect against malevolent spirits, owing to her vast number of followers and the collective belief in her guardianship. This spiritual influence is further amplified through the concept of Umbanda's egregore, or collective belief.

Yemanja is also referred to as "the mermaid queen" and "the great mother of the seas," and, alongside Oshala, she is perhaps the Orisha most closely associated with peace, tranquility, and serenity.

Yemanja holds the esteemed position as the ruler of the divine throne of Generation, signifying that the very essence of life originates from her profound emanations.

Yemanja continuously emits the vital energy known as *ashe*, which serves as the driving force behind the generation of thoughts. As the Orisha closely linked to the realm of the head and the mind, Yemanja's influence extends to matters of mental clarity, inner peace, and the perception of reality.

Through harmonious alignment with Yemanja's energy, individuals can find enhanced creative inspiration and the ability to manifest their thoughts and ideas into reality. Conversely, mental difficulties, disturbances, confusion, and various mental challenges, as well as physical injuries that may affect cognition, memory, and balance, are believed to arise from a misalignment with Yemanja's frequencies. Thus, seeking solace and resolution within Yemanja's realm of influence can bring healing and restoration. The power of Yemanja resonates deeply with the intricate workings of the human mind, encompassing both its conscious and subconscious aspects.

---

naturally extends to religious cults, shaping the associations and significance of deities such as Yemanja. As a result, Yemanja's dominion over the vast seas became more pronounced, reflecting the cultural and geographical context of the country.

In essence, the physical head, the conscious mind, and the subconscious mind all fall within the sphere of Yemanja's influential reach.

Individuals born with Yemanja as their head-Orisha display a profound dedication to their family. They possess a highly emotional nature and regard their home as a nurturing sanctuary. They extend their caregiving tendencies beyond their homes, and they usually treat friends and even their own parents as if they were their children.

These individuals are characterized by their exceptional kindness, amiable disposition, and friendly demeanor. While they may sometimes appear vulnerable, they possess an underlying strength of will, determination, and a fiercely protective nature towards those they hold dear. They thrive in the company of others and are not particularly fond of solitude.

The children of Yemanja often demonstrate open-mindedness and have modern perspectives that are seldom antiquated or overly traditional. They excel in professions related to food and cuisine, childcare, home decor, literature, education, and psychology.

Yemanja's sons and daughters harbor a deep love for the sea, appreciating open spaces, luminosity, and indulging in culinary delights.

It has been observed that those aligned with Yemanja typically have a slightly robust physique with invariably long hair. They hold a sophisticated sense of style, though never to the extent of Yansa's flamboyance or Oshun's over-preoccupation with beauty.

While the children of Yemanja are known for their emotional and gentle nature, they may occasionally display superficial behavior or engage in excessive gossip. They have a tendency to hold onto anger for extended periods and struggle with forgiveness and letting go. In their less positive manifestations, they may become overly controlling, excessively attached to the material world and people, promote gossiping, and seek solace in overindulgence or emotional coping mechanisms such as drinking or overeating. Their selflessness sometimes leads them to neglect their own needs.

Yemanja is commonly linked to the colors pale blue, deep blue, and white, symbolizing the vastness of the seas and her serene temperament. The Orisha of the Seas favors white flowers such as roses, lilies, and orchids, which embody purity and grace. Her preferred herbs include jasmine and lavender, which align with her delicate energy. Basil, despite its association with fire and movement, also holds significance in Yemanja's domain. Among her favorite fruits are green grapes, yellow melons, peaches, green apples, pears, lychees, and other water-rich and white fruits. Her beverage choices range from mineral water to champagne and clear cider. Coconut water and sparkling water are also suitable options.

In terms of crystals, clear quartz and aquamarine harmonize well with Yemanja's essence. Lapis lazuli and sodalite are also associated with her energy.

Yemanja's primary symbol is the silver hand mirror, representing the ability to help others see themselves and cultivate self-care. Other symbols associated with her include the five-pointed star, sea stars, seashells, and pearls. The fish, particularly when in a group, serves as her animal symbol.

Yemanja's sphere of influence radiates most powerfully within the seas and oceans. However, beaches and shorelines also provide a suitable conduit for connecting with her vibration.

The customary salutation used to invoke Yemanja before a ritual is "Odo ya!" pronounced as 'o doe yAH,' meaning "mother of the river" in the Yoruba language. According to custom, there are frequently three claps or a series of seven claps following this salutation.

Yemanja is revered for promoting inner peace, improving family dynamics, and addressing various aspects related to home and the mind. The cult of Yemanja, therefore, fosters family harmony and mental clarity.

To invoke her transformative vibrations, a simple ritual can be performed using a white candle, a glass of champagne, and a white flower.

For a more intricate ritual, conducted by the beach to establish a closer proximity with Yemanja, one should bring white flowers, champagne, and grapes and offer dedications while leaving the flowers after passing seven waves and pouring the drink into the ocean. Prior permission should be sought from the spiritual guardians of the beach, who operate under Yemanja's umbrella.

To address familial issues, seek fertility, or seek healing for mental ailments or brain injuries, a ritual can be performed using a miniature head made of wax, glass, paper, wood, or plaster. This head should be placed in a basket surrounded by fruits and flowers, with

Yemanja's preferred beverage, white roses or white orchids, seven pale blue candles around it, lavender or rose water poured on the basket, or even sprayed with perfume. Small mirrors and seashells can also be included as garnish. At the beach, offer a blue candle and champagne to the local guardian, and then proceed with the Yemanja's offering, invoking her powers and mercy.

If the ritual is conducted at the beach, only organic items should be left behind, while bottles, candles, mirrors, etc. must be brought back home. In the case of a home ritual or at a temple, the organic matter should remain for at least 16 hours and then be brought to the sea, or at least taken to a woodland, while the other objects can be retrieved after three days for future use.

Sailors, and Ondines are the groups of spirit workers who operate under the influences of Yemanja.

In a syncretic context, Yemanja is sometimes associated with the mother of Jesus during Christ's adulthood, due to shared attributes such as deep compassion and being prominent symbols of love.

Yoruba Myth ○ Yemanja's Resentment

Yemanja is the daughter of Olokun, the god of the seas. A caring father, Olokun gave Yemanja a pot with a potion to be used in times of great danger. Faced with such a situation, Yemanja was to break the pot, and a solution to the problem would magically appear.

Time passed, and Yemanja grew up and married Odudua, considered the creator of the universe. Together, they had ten children, each becoming an Orisha representing an element or natural phenomenon such as fire, forest, storms, and so forth. However, Yemanja and Odudua did not live happily ever after.

Tired of her marriage, Yemanja left her hometown and aimlessly journeyed westward. Upon reaching another city, Yemanja met Okere, who fell in love with her and proposed marriage. Yemanja agreed but set one condition: Okere must never make any comments about her breasts, which had grown larger after breastfeeding her ten children. Okere accepted the condition, but one day, after drinking too much wine, he made a joke about his wife's large breasts. Offended and deeply saddened, Yemanja decided to leave.

Yemanja ran as quickly as she could to elude Okere's pursuit. However, in her haste, Yemanja stumbled and dropped the pot containing the protective potion given to her by her father. In a magical instant, a river sprang forth, carrying Yemanja towards the ocean. Wanting to obstruct her path, Okere transformed into a mountain. Unable to progress, Yemanja called upon her son, Shango, who hurled a lightning bolt, splitting the mountain in half. Yemanja reached the sea, where she remained as its queen, ruling with grace and majesty.

This myth may suggest that Yemanja, despite her nurturing nature, is not immune to feelings of resentment, which result in her own uncontrolled emotions.

Omolu

Omolu, pronounced 'o-moo-LOOH,' derives from the Yoruba language, specifically from the words *ọmọ* (son), *olúwa* (lord), and *bí* (born as), and is thus abbreviated to *ọmọ lú*. Omolu is recognized as the Orisha of both death and healing. Regarded as the elder manifestation of Obaluaye, this cosmic Orisha holds authority over the divine throne of Generation, alongside Yemanja.

Omolu's influence prevents anything that disrupts the process of generation or rebirth. This Orisha's frequencies render ineffective those intending to extinguish or harm lives, as his purpose is to preserve them. Genocidal schemes, misuse of pesticides, and the distribution of harmful drugs may also be thwarted by Omolu, potentially resulting in the demise of those involved in such activities. Under Omolu's vibration, such plans or actions cease to exist.

Being a cosmic Orisha, Omolu's role involves the constriction and elimination of obstacles that hinder the work of the universal Orisha (Yemanja). His purpose is to safeguard and ensure the integrity of the energies propagated by Yemanja and prevent their dissipation or corruption. If Yemanja generates and emanates life, whether in the form of embryos or as projects and ideas, Omolu's task is to protect and preserve that vital energy.

Omolu demands the utmost respect due to his rulership over strictness, which is necessary for bringing about transformative change. Symbolically, Omolu's actions relate to one's karmic burdens and serve as a metaphorical judgment of whether one will descend to lower realms after passing away, evaluating their karma and merits for future rebirth.

Omolu's energy is strongly tied to the root chakra located at the base of the spine, and it resonates with the Earth's energy.

Depictions of Omolu, similar to those of Obaluaye, often portray him wearing a long straw hat that covers his entire body. This imagery symbolizes the wounds on one's soul, representing karmic afflictions.

As the lord of death itself, Omolu should not be feared. Paradoxically, this essential Orisha within Umbanda promotes life and health, despite his relatedness to diseases and mortality. Despite being renowned as the lord of physical death and known for his seriousness, Omolu is also recognized for his immense kindness. In his cult, he may show compassion by delivering individuals from severe illness or even death, dramatically alleviating their burdens.

Individuals who are born under the influence of Omolu as their head-Orisha exhibit traits of strictness, determination, reticence, adherence to tradition, and a willingness to support others. These individuals tend to have a pessimistic outlook, even in favorable circumstances. They are known to be stubborn, resistant to changing their opinions, and occasionally express a darker perspective.

Financial struggles are not typically severe for those influenced by Omolu, but they are unlikely to experience great wealth or opulence in life.

The self-esteem of these individuals may fluctuate, leading to episodes of depression or social insecurities. However, due to their resolute nature and strong work ethic, they do not rely solely on external factors for their success.

They often have an air of mystery, maintain a serious demeanor, and have only a few close friends. Similar to the children of Obaluaye, individuals associated with Omolu tend to appear older during childhood and adolescence. This pertains not only to their physical appearance but also to the level of responsibility and maturity they exhibit. Additionally, they may exhibit rough skin, poor posture, shorter stature, and a low voice.

Those influenced by Omolu have a preference for quiet and traditional activities. They may excel in professions such as librarianship, research, psychology, medicine, and spiritual leadership.

On the negative side, when individuals do not align with Omolu's vibration, they may lean towards witchcraft, extremist beliefs, or even experience homelessness or life-long illnesses.

Omolu is commonly associated with the colors white, black, and occasionally purple, influencing the choice of bead necklaces, candles, stones, fruits, and flowers attributed to his cult.

A wide array of plants and flowers align with Omolu's energy, including purple chrysanthemums, violets, and clematis. Additionally, plants like aloe vera and cacti, known for their thorns and spikes, are also within his vibration.

Preferred fruits for Omolu include black cherries, black grapes, black currants, soursop, and figs. In terms of stones, Omolu's vibrations resonate strongly with onyx and black tourmaline, while occasionally deep purple amethyst may also be included.

Cemeteries serve as Omolu's sacred domains, where his energy is particularly potent, and his devoted workers stand guard over these sacred grounds. Cemeteries hold profound significance as sites of energy transmutation, symbolizing the transition from culmination to new beginnings. They serve as locales where spirits who still maintain connections to their physical bodies draw upon residual energies before undergoing a complete transition to the astral plane. Energetically, graveyards stand unparalleled on Earth as the places where transmutation is most present.

Omolu shares tools and symbols with Obaluaye, employing a short cane made of straw and cowry shells, as well as a cross.

The salutation used to praise or invoke Omolu is "Atoto, Omolu," pronounced 'ah-toe-TOE.' Similar to Obaluaye's salutation, it invokes a profound silence as a mark of respect. The nature of the salutation reflects Omolu's frequency, which is one of the shortest and fastest oscillations among the Orishas, in contrast to the longer and slower frequencies of Eshu, and Ogun.

In Umbanda, Omolu and Obaluaye are often regarded as aspects of each other or as closely related Orishas, leading to similarities in their worship and rituals. The plants, flowers, herbs, and fruits used in their rituals may overlap, although Omolu's offerings typically include drier, harder, and spikier elements compared to Obaluaye's, as well as darker hues of purple. The candles used for both Orishas are typically white and black, with the addition of darker purple tones specifically for Omolu.

One cleansing ritual associated with Omolu involves preparing a bowl of popcorn and lighting seven candles. The purpose of this ritual is to direct negative energy towards the popcorn, which acts as an energy absorber. After the ritual, typically within a period of 24 hours, it is recommended to dispose of the popcorn in a cemetery.

It is highly recommended to seek permission from Omolu and his attendant Eshus before entering a graveyard. This involves requesting permission upon entering the cemetery's gates and showing reverence by lighting a candle for the local guardians before proceeding with any rituals or candle lighting dedicated to Omolu or to the discarnate spirits.

Old Blacks, Eshus, and occasionally Sailors, are the groups of spirit workers who operate under the influences of Omolu.

While Omolu is syncretized with Saint Lazarus, he can also be perceived as an interpretation of Anubis due to their shared associations with cemeteries, the assessment of karma, and guiding individuals in the afterlife. However, it is important to note that this interpretation is not observed within the Umbanda tradition.

Umbanda Myth ∘ The Wounds of Omolu

Omulu, born as the son of Nana, who bewitched Oshala, came into this world marked by deep wounds. His disfigured appearance haunted him, and Nana, his own mother, cast him away to the vast sea. It was there, amidst the rolling waves, that Yemanja, the majestic queen of the salty waters, found the abandoned child and took him under her wing. Yemanja raised Omolu as her own, sharing with him the sacred knowledge of healing that eases human suffering.

As time passed, Omolu grew with his scars, burdened by shame.

During a grand celebration among the revered Orishas, he felt overwhelmed by the fear of judgment and sought solace in the shadows, standing alone in a distant corner. However, Ogun, the warrior Orisha, recognized Omolu's pain and crafted a remarkable straw hood that covered him completely. This ingenious creation allowed Omolu to dance freely, shielded from prying eyes that brought him torment.

Yansa, the tempestuous goddess of winds, was captivated by the enigmatic figure concealed in straw. With a desire to reveal Omolu's true essence, she unleashed her powerful gusts upon him. In that transformative moment, a spell took hold. Omolu's wounds underwent a remarkable metamorphosis, turning into a cascade of popcorn that shimmered and gleamed like sunbeams, radiating a newfound brilliance and Omolu's beauty.

Ibeji

Ibeji, derived from the Yoruba term *ibeji* meaning twins, is pronounced as 'ee-bay-ZHEE' ("zh" sounding like the "s" in the word vision). Within Umbanda, Ibeji is revered as the Orisha embodying the essence of infancy, playfulness, and innocence.

Perceived as two Orishas, Ibeji manifests as twins, although symbolizing a uniform emanation. As the Orisha in the form of children, Ibeji epitomizes the purity necessary for spirits to liberate themselves from malice, embarking on a new life or phase unburdened by their past or the arduous disciplinary trials in their spiritual journey.

Ibeji signifies a new beginning, wherein innocence is granted another opportunity, and it is imperative for individuals to periodically renew their perspectives through the eyes of a child.

Despite being portrayed as children, Ibeji's power and prominence among the Orishas are profoundly respected and esteemed. The spirits working under the Umbrella of Ibeji are renowned for their extraordinary skills, gaining access to any knowledge or location with remarkable ease.

Radiating happiness and kindness, the mere presence of Ibeji dissolves stubbornness, excessive seriousness, and resentment. However, it is essential to distinguish Ibeji's happiness from that of Yansa, associated with empowerment, and that of Eshu, tied to humor. Ibeji's happiness emanates from a sense of perfect balance—a profound feeling that no hurt or pain has ever existed and that the present is an immensely thrilling moment.

Ibeji serves as a catalyst, inspiring individuals to wholeheartedly embrace the profound yet simple joys of genuine smiles and hearty laughter. With the vibrant vigor reminiscent of a sunrise and the delicate unfolding of a flower, Ibeji emanates an aura of spirited playfulness and childlike exuberance, a demeanor that transcends mere folly.

Moreover, Ibeji's presence engenders an atmosphere conducive to forgiveness and the initiation of novel life ventures. Yemanja generates the seed, Oshun germinates it, and ibeji brings forth its blooming. Within the Umbanda tradition, it is firmly held that the absence of Ibeji's invigorating essence in life, in the household, or in enterprises could potentially lead to stagnation, curtailed growth, or untimely conclusion.

Revered across numerous Umbanda temples during celebrations of children's days and in harmony with the Christian syncretism, Ibeji's influence extends beyond cultural boundaries.

Individuals who have Ibeji as their head-Orisha exhibit distinctive traits that reflect youthful and lighthearted behavior. Characterized by their joyful and often playful mannerisms, these creative individuals embrace life with an effervescent childlike spirit, which is evident in their attire choices, communication style, and preferences for recreational activities.

Their predisposition towards happiness is remarkably pronounced, and instances of resentment or vengeful intentions are exceedingly rare among them. Similarly, tendencies toward depressive states are notably uncommon. When their childlike attributes are prominently expressed, it is worth noting that they may encounter scenarios where they become inclined towards stubbornness or obstinacy.

In situations where their disposition does not align harmoniously with the essence of Ibeji, there can be instances of temperamental outbursts, an inconsequential carefree attitude, and a tendency to not take life's more serious aspects as seriously as warranted. Occasionally, they may also become rather dependent on others.

Occasionally displaying an inherent innocence, these individuals may find themselves susceptible to external influences. Paradoxically, they also possess the ability to evoke feelings of empathy and compassion in others, thus effectively safeguarding themselves from potential malicious intentions. Physically, individuals influenced by Ibeji often possess a distinct appearance, characterized by their relatively shorter stature, round countenance reminiscent of a youthful child, and notably animated laughter, often sparked by trivial matters. Their perspective on the world is notably akin to that of a child, fostering a unique and captivating outlook.

Ibeji is commonly associated with the colors pale blue and pale pink, symbolizing purity and love, as well as representing the two polarities in their more innocent form.

Their favorite flowers include forget-me-nots, daisies, and other small, colorful blooms. Among the herbs associated with Ibeji are lavender, chamomile, and vanilla. Fruits that harmonize well with Ibeji's nature include grapes, strawberries, peaches, watermelon, bananas, and pears. Recommended beverages for offerings include sweet fruit juices with added sugar, sugary soda, and water sweetened with sugar.

Rose quartz is their primary stone, although aquamarine and blue aventurine can also complement their cult. Their principal tools typically consist of a pair of gourds, symbolizing the twins. Additionally, toys are often employed as part of their ritual.

Rabbits are animals that signify a connection to Ibeji, while puppies and kittens may also reflect their essence.

Their domain encompasses gardens, parks, playgrounds, and kindergartens.

The customary salutation used to invoke Ibeji before a ritual is 'Oni Ibeji' or 'Oni Beijada,' pronounced as "on-nee bay-ZHAH-da," derived from the Yoruba phrase *wọ́n ni ibejì*, meaning "they are twins."

The worship of Ibeji resembles a joyful child's birthday celebration, complete with toys, an abundance of sweets, fizzy soda, and colorful balloons. Emphasizing a lively and cheerful atmosphere is essential to their worship, making decorative elements and sugary delights central to their rituals.

Ibeji's protective sphere encompasses new beginnings and youthful aspects, including children, budding plants, and nascent projects. Thus, their veneration is particularly beneficial for these areas, fostering not only their growth but also their overall happiness in life.

To create a home altar for Ibeji, two candles are essential: one a pale pink and the other a gentle blue shade. Additionally, a glass of a sugary beverage should be present. As Ibeji as energetically close to Oshun, their altar may be placed near that of the Orisha of love, and in case an altar of Ibeji is nonexistent, Oshun's can serve as their temporary place of worship.

For an annual offering, special festival, or significant petition, an assortment of candies, toys, and soda should be included. In natural settings, fruits and juices can be placed near flowers. During an Umbanda session involving the working spirits of Children, who operate under the influence of Ibeji, they often magnetize the candies and pieces of cake, imbuing them with healing properties and spiritual particles of happiness. Devotees are encouraged to consume these candies, as they hold important spiritual significance. If one cannot consume them, preserving the candies and later placing them in a garden for the local "spiritual children" is a respectful alternative.

Syncretism with Ibeji is evident in the veneration of Christian saints, Saint Cosmas and Saint Damian. These saints were twin brothers, who dedicated their lives to tending to the ill with selfless charity and boundless compassion.

Yoruba Myth ○ Ibeji Challenges Death

Lady Death arrived in the village, intent on taking the lives of the community members before their appointed time.

As Death claimed countless lives, an increasing tide of sorrow and despair swept through the village.

Feeling helpless, the villagers turned to Ifa, the oracle, for guidance. Ifa's response was clear: "Only the Ibejis can challenge death." The villagers were puzzled: "What? These children? These mischievous little ones?" they questioned incredulously.

However, knowing Ifa's wisdom to be unerring, they decided to beseech the Ibeji for assistance. The Ibeji agreed to help, but under a condition: "Once we have triumphed over death, we shall be rewarded with copious amounts of sweets."

And so the Ibeji commenced playing music. The melodic strains beckoned Death, who approached and began to sway to the rhythm of the Ibeji's melodies. The music persisted throughout the entirety of both the day and night. As time passed, Death grew weary. Filled with exhaustion, Death implored the Ibeji to halt their music.

Yielding to Death's plea, the Ibeji finally stopped, extracting a promise from Death to depart the village.

With Death's departure, a newfound sense of jubilation returned to the village. From that point on, the villagers held the Ibeji in the highest esteem. In celebration of their triumph, a lavish feast of candies was prepared in their honor.

This myth may allude to Ibeji's nature of facing the adversities of life with happiness, besides being a hint for adults to believe in children and in their capability of solving problems in a simple, innocent manner. It also connotes to Ibeji's nature being the opposite of that of death.

Logunede

Logunede, also spelled Logun Edé, is pronounced *loh-goon-ay-DEH*. The name is occasionally believed to derive from Yoruba terminology, drawing from two distinct sources: *olóògun* refers to the concept of knowledge in the arts of medicine, while *èdè* refers to the city of Ede, an important location in Yorubaland believed to be the birthplace of certain Orishas. However, the Orisha's name is more likely the result of an amalgamation of *ologun*, which means 'military,' connoting his qualities as a warrior, and *ode*, which means 'hunting.' Hence, the name Logunede all but certain means 'hunter warrior.' Despite his name's association with hunting and warrior qualities, Logunede is most commonly linked to wealth, beauty, and intelligence.

Considered the offspring of Oshun and Oshossi, Logunede exhibits qualities that reflect aspects of both his parents. With the grace and beauty reminiscent of his mother, Logunede also possesses the intelligence and a thirst for knowledge akin to his father's traits. He encompasses a harmonious blend of the personalities of Oshun and Oshossi, where the throne of Love intertwines with the throne of Knowledge. This young Orisha symbolizes material wealth as the owner of all gold, like his mother, and the provider of abundance, akin to his father.

The essence of Logunede lies in his inherent polarity, which strikingly balances feminine and masculine attributes. This characteristic occasionally grants Logunede the recognition of an androgynous Orisha, although he is predominantly observed as a masculine entity. In certain Candomble sects, Logunede is perceived as a masculine aspect of Oshun, paralleled in polarity, similar to the relationship between Yemanja and Olokun or Oshala and Odudua.

Logunede, the esteemed prince among the Orishas, holds a significant position as the adolescent entity within the pantheon, revealing both youthful traits in appearance and personality.

Exhibiting exceptional charm, Logunede embodies delicacy and strength, remaining calm and gentle while occasionally displaying the prowess of a hunter.

Numerous accounts describe Logunede as a fearless warrior, often portrayed in tales where he receives instruction from Ogun and Yansa in the arts of war, and, naturally, from his father, Oshossi. However, Logunede represents, according to most devotees, a distinct type of warrior: that who employs diplomacy and strategy to achieve victory, as opposed to physical combat. Additionally, Logunede is believed to possess an innate aptitude for magic, bestowing proficiency upon those under his patronage.

In mythology, it is recounted that Logunede is the sole male Orisha to forge connections or affinity with the frightful forest witches. Furthermore, Logunede may occasionally be observed assuming the role of protector of fauna, sharing with Nana the position of a lover of animals.

Logunede also assumes the role of the Orisha associated with seemingly impossible causes, intervening when situations appear unsolvable or require prompt resolution.

As a prominent advocate of wealth and beauty, Logunede aids his devotees in cultivating a sense of self-worth, prompting them to prioritize self-care and the absorption of knowledge. Furthermore, the vibratory influence of Logunede proves highly advantageous for individuals engaged in the study of multiple complex subjects simultaneously.

In Umbanda, the veneration of Logunede is uncommon. In many instances, mediums, priests, and other practitioners are told that Oshun or Oshossi is their head-Orisha, when in reality, they may actually have Logunede as their head-Orisha.

Those born under the influence of Logunede remain forever youthful, possessing both the allure typically related to Oshun and the intellect of Oshossi. Although somewhat vain, they utilize this trait without much arrogance. They are drawn to luxury, high-quality items, and display elegance when desired.

Given their exceptional intelligence, the children of Logunede seem to possess knowledge on a wide range of subjects. Regrettably, they may become accustomed to believing that they hold the absolute truth, which can lead them to dismiss others' perspectives.

Despite their modern outlook and appearance, the offspring of Logunede can occasionally portray a hunter-like focus on acquiring resources and wealth. These individuals tend to have ample material resources, often appearing wealthier than they truly are. However, they may become overly reliant on external sources to achieve their desires—depending on parents, spouses, or others. On the negative side, they may exhibit fickleness, laziness, vanity, and egocentric behavior. Additionally, they might succumb to the allure of material pleasures, leveraging their charm and persuasion skills to achieve their wishes. Nevertheless, the sons and daughters of Logunede are known for their remarkable adaptability, as Logunede is able to show the qualities of Oshun, Oshossi, Ogun, and Yansa as needed. As a result, Logunede's attributes are among the most diverse within the pantheon, which reflects on those with him as head-Orisha.

Logunede is regarded as the most beautiful Orisha, imparting his children with distinct and delicate features reminiscent of those seen in Oshun and Oshossi. They may possess exotic facial traits, consistently exuding a harmonious and angelic appearance.

Individuals born with Logunede as their head-Orisha often exhibit distinctive physical characteristics, such as lighter eyes and hair, irrespective of their ethnicity or ancestral background. Typically slender in build, these children of Logunede maintain an appearance reminiscent of adolescence throughout their lives, a quality that also finds expression in their sense of fashion and opinions.

The colors associated with Logunede are golden yellow and turquoise blue. His crystals include pyrite, blue sapphire, and green aventurine, while gold is also a significant element for him. Most stones are related to Logun, except dark-colored or red stones and those of volcanic origin.

Logunede's animal symbol is the seahorse, but peacocks and colorful little birds are also directly associated with him, symbolizing beauty, youth, and purity.

Grapes, apples, and other sweet fruits are linked to Logunede, while his preferred beverages are coconut water, champagne, lager beer, white wine, and yellow juices.

His sphere of influence is primarily strong in waterfalls, cascades, rivers, woodlands, forests, and places where young adults gather, such as schools, universities, and parks.

Logunede's emblem is the golden mirror and the arch and bow, representing his mother and father's tools, and denoting his relation to vanity and a thirst for knowledge.

The customary salutation used to invoke Logunede before a ritual is "Loci Loci, Logun," pronounced as 'LO-see LO-see, loGOON,' a Yoruba term meaning something like "come on, Logun, go!"

Logunede is an exuberant Orisha known for emanating continuous vibrations of knowledge and beauty. Despite being traditionally perceived as both a warrior and a delicate deity, Logunede's intelligence and charms are undeniably profound, inspiring others to seek knowledge and elevate their self-esteem through various means.

Devotees often seek to connect with Logunede in their quest to embody his admirable qualities. Others may turn to him to petition for assistance with so-called "impossible causes," to attain youthful attributes, and to foster a more positive outlook on life. Notably, Logunede is frequently sought as an intermediary between Oshun and Oshossi, particularly for matters concerning prosperity.

A simple altar dedicated to Logunede may include a yellow or green candle, a glass of white beer or white wine, and a piece of pyrite. For more elaborate rituals, a bowl of cooked corn adorned with coconut pieces and poured with cane or maple syrup may be utilized. Additionally, offering fruits, yellow flowers, and sweet incense can further enhance reverence. In natural settings, offerings to Logunede are best received near a river, where the shore meets the woods, symbolizing the harmony between water and earth. For those seeking to absorb Logunede's energies more effectively, it is advisable to avoid wearing red clothes, or consuming meat.

In an Umbanda center, where Logunede is not customarily worshiped independently, his rituals and offerings can be appropriately placed alongside those of Oshossi or Oshun.

Logunede does not appear to govern any particular class of spirits; nonetheless, spirits may belong to groups overseen by other Orishas and collaboratively operate within the framework established by Logunede. Hence, spirit workers such as Mestizos, Children, Pombagiras, and Eshus can occasionally operate under Logun's vibration.

Logunede may, though rarely, syncretize with Saint Expeditus, the patron of urgent causes, and may also be associated with Archangel Michael, the Greek god Eros (and the Roman Cupid).

Yoruba Myth ○ The Birth of Logunede

Oshossi was wandering through the forests in search of game. During his travels, he encountered Oshun, the epitome of femininity—charming, delicate, and sensual. Despite his awareness of the danger Oshun represented, he couldn't resist her allure. Oshun, using her wily charm, tempted Oshossi by adorning herself with leaves and herbs, making him mistake her for Ossain, the male Orisha of herbs and leaves, to whom Oshossi had a great affinity. Captivated by the illusion, Oshossi fell in love with her.

However, upon discovering the deception, Oshossi became infuriated and denied the paternity of the child Oshun later gave birth to—Logunede. Oshossi withdrew to the forest, refusing to accept the truth.

But Nana, the venerable and experienced Orisha, intervened and took an active role in Logunede's life. She convinced Ogun, who was in love with Oshun, to accept and raise Logunede as his own son. Oshun, however, left the child and embarked on a marriage with Shango.

Over time, Ogun's love for Logunede grew immensely, and he treated the boy as if he were his true son. Yansa was a loyal companion of Ogun, and as a result, Logunede started to display a unique blend of characteristics typical of Ogun and Yansa. But as he grew older, his nature as the child of Oshun and Oshossi revealed itself.

Since he was a young child, Ossain has assisted Logunede in learning the secrets of medicinal herbs as well as the craft of making potions and the power of healing hands.

As Logunede matured, he became a beloved figure among almost all Orishas, admired not only for his beauty and kindness but also for his youthful bravery. He showed a deep appreciation for both the forests, inherited from his father, and the waterfalls, inherited from his mother. This unique blend of attributes made him a bridge between different aspects of nature, besides possessing the traits he had acquired from Ogun, Yansa, and Ossain.

Amidst this journey of self-discovery, Logunede sought to reconcile his father's denial of paternity. Despite Oshossi's initial reluctance, Logunede's determination and kind-hearted nature eventually touched his heart. Moved, Oshossi admitted his true parentage and embraced Logunede as his son, inviting Logunede to stay with him in the forest for half the year, as he would spend the other half in the waterfalls with his mother. Oshun, seeing the possibility of being with Oshossi, accepted to continue raising Logunede with Oshossi that way.

Logunede, Oshossi, and Oshun formed a close bond as a family. Logunede's presence brought harmony and unity among the his parents as they recognized his special role in bridging the realms of forests and waters, uniting knowledge and love.

This myth alludes to the dual polarity of Logunede, who not only depicts the blended qualities of his biological parents—knowledge, beauty, and wealth—but also the traits of Ogun, Ossain, and Yansa.

Ossain

Ossain, pronounced "o-SAin" and originating from the Yoruba *òsányin* (*òsà* alluding to 'deity,' and the suffix *nyìn* relating to medicine), is the Orisha associated with all plants and herbs, particularly those recognized for their healing or magical properties. He is also considered a great wizard.

Within Umbanda cults, Ossain is rarely worshipped; consequently, it is uncommon to find anyone whose head-Orisha is that Orisha, and thus spirits working under the tutelage of Ossain seldom manifest. They may instead appear as workers of Oshossi or, perhaps, Omulu. However, his name is known for its association with leaves, which hold a significant place in the rites.

As a reclusive Orisha, Ossain's vibration resides within virgin woodlands and forests, where it aids in harnessing and enhancing the power of natural remedies. It is believed that, for an herb or any part of a plant to be energetically activated, one must seek Ossain's blessings. Although this belief is rooted in mythology and is nearly unknown among Umbandists, some adherents do revere Ossain, especially if they are particularly inclined or fond of herbs, botany, or the secret powers of plants.

While not commonly acknowledged within Umbanda, Ossain's recognition may, in fact, surpass that of Logunan and Egunita.

The myth, and to some extent, the nature of Ossain, bears resemblance to that of the Greek centaur Chiron. Chiron was known for his kindness and wisdom (Lawrence, 1994), especially in the fields of medicine. Both Ossain and Chiron possess profound knowledge to heal others; however, they seem to encounter difficulty when it comes to treating themselves.

Within the Umbandist pantheon, Ossain is perceived to be situated between Oshossi and Omulu. As an Orisha related to cure and healing, alongside Omolu and Obaluaye, Ossain differs in the sense that he heals through the use of herbs, and thus, earthly medicine.

Individuals born under the influence of Ossain are characterized by their reserved nature, much like the Orisha itself. Exuding a sense of shyness, these individuals are exceptionally quiet, yet possess great intelligence, enabling them to excel in intricate manual tasks that require precision, dexterity, and attention to detail. Despite their quiet demeanor, when they do speak, they often exhibit a humorous and easily laughable side.

The children of Ossain exhibit strong character, showcasing qualities of strength and loyalty. They are often recognized for maintaining neutrality in various circumstances and may occasionally display a degree of coldness, which should not be misconstrued as apathy but rather as a firm commitment to justice and impartiality. Additionally, they are characterized by patience and resilience.

Similar to Ossain's family members in the myths (Nana and Obaluaye), individuals influenced by Ossain appreciate norms, and adhere well to laws and rules, reflecting well-mannered traits.

Naturally, these individuals may have an affinity for plants and prefer consuming teas and natural medicines over modern pharmaceutical preparations. Nevertheless, they are intelligent enough to heed the advice of modern doctors when necessary. Overall, all sons and daughters of Ossain tend to be tolerant, materially detached, studious, and charitable.

On the negative side, if someone with Ossain as their head-Orisha leans towards spiritual negativity, they may incline towards revenge, witchcraft, and drug use.

Ossain is commonly associated with the colors green and white. White carnation is his favorite flower, while eucalyptus, collard greens, and rue are his favored herbs. It is important to emphasize that all herbs fall under Ossain's domain; therefore, any of them is compatible with his nature. Avocados and figs are his preferred fruits, and his beverages include rum and other clear or green drinks mixed with mint. The animals associated with Ossain are goats and roosters.

Instruments related to his cult include chains, coins, and crutches (for his bad leg). However, his primary work tool is a central rod with a bird at the tip, and from the middle of this rod, seven points extend.

The customary salutation used to invoke Ossain before a ritual is "ewe o!" pronounced as "'eh-oo-ay-O,' a term derived from the proto-Yuroboid *ewé wọ̀*, meaning "save the leaves!"

The veneration of Ossain is advisable for individuals undergoing medical treatments and those engaging in the use of plants for ritual baths, potions, and remedies.

In a sylvan setting, consider placing collard greens cooked with palm oil on a large leaf; or offering boiled yams. Avocados, figs, and other green fruits are highly appreciated too. While a solitary green candle may suffice, it is recommended to extinguish the candle after a minimum of 14 minutes to mitigate the risk of fire accidents.

In the Umbanda temple, candles and herbs may be place by an altar near any other Orisha, like Oshossi or Omulu. For worship within one's home, a straightforward arrangement comprises a green candle, a glass of mint liquor, and dark leaves such as spinach.

Syncretism with Ossain is rare, as the Orisha is seldom venerated in most Umbanda centers. However, Saint Benedict and occasionally Saint Joseph appear to be considered his syncretic saints.

Yoruba Myth ο Ossain Present His Leaves

As told by Prandi (2000), Ossain, the son of Nana and brother of Oshumare, Ewa, and Obaluaye, held dominion over leaves, herbs, and science. He possessed the knowledge of healing and the mysteries of life. Ossain, known for his kindness, provided magical preparations such as baths, teas, infusions, ointments, and potions. His healing abilities extended to curing various conditions, including pains, wounds, bleedings, dysenteries, swellings, fractures, plagues, fevers, corrupted organs, purulent skin, and bruised blood, effectively purging the body of all evils. All the Orishas relied on Ossain to cure any ailment or bodily affliction, making him an indispensable figure in the battle against diseases.

One day, Shango, the god of justice, decreed that all the Orishas should share Ossain's power and knowledge of herbs and healing. So, Shango ordered Ossain to share his leaves with the other Orishas. However, Ossain refused, prompting Shango to instruct Yansa to release her powerful winds and gather all the leaves from Ossain's forests for distribution among the Orishas.

Then, Yansa created a hurricane, collecting the leaves and carrying them towards Shango's palace.

In response, Ossain commanded the leaves to return to his forests, and they obediently followed his orders. Almost all the leaves returned to Ossain, causing those already in Shango's possession to lose their *ashe*, the power of healing.

Recognizing Ossain's exclusivity of his leaf power, Shango, a just Orisha, acknowledged Ossain's victory. Despite this, Ossain generously gave one leaf to each Orisha; each with its energies and activation chants essential for their function.

While the Orishas could perform wonders with these leaves, Ossain retained his deepest secrets. The Orishas expressed gratitude to Ossain, reverencing him whenever they utilized the leaves.

This myth allude to the importance of revering Ossain before using any herb for magic or healing works.

Eshu

Eshu, pronounced 'ay-SHOO' and derived from the Proto-Yoruboid term èṣù, holds multiple interpretations for his name, including the most accurate one, "harmonizer." However, there is also a belief, though less likely, that it may have emerged from the meaning "to confuse." In different cultures, the deity known as Eshu is also referred to as Eleggua and Elegbara, originating from the Yoruba term Alagbara, meaning "strong" or "powerful."

The Orisha of vitality, paths, portals, and fire, Eshu is the intermediary between heaven and Earth, playing a crucial role in conveying petitions from individuals to the Orishas and facilitating the transmission of their responses back to Earth. As the Orisha of movement and magic, Eshu possesses formidable power. Notably, alongside Oshala, Eshu is among the select few Orishas capable of directly accessing Olorun, the omnipotent God.

Eshu embodies vigor and drive, being also an astute guardian and, more importantly, the Orisha who accomplishes what was sentenced by other Orishas, meaning that "without Eshu, nothing can be done." Overall, Eshu has the ability to open and close any path, any road, and any door.

As the foremost Orisha to be venerated and propitiated before other Orishas, Eshu's presence as an object of adoration does not extend to every Umbanda center, owing to the unfortunate influence of misleading Christian dogma. Erroneously, Eshu has been associated with Satan due to his mischievous character, his distinct preferred colors (red and black), and his primary symbol, which incorporates a phallic representation—an ancient symbol denoting virility and fertility. Consequently, the cult of Eshu, much like that of other less prominent Orishas such as Ibeji or Oshumare, remains relatively uncommon. Nonetheless, the profound understanding and significance attributed to Eshu have motivated numerous newly established Umbanda temples to incorporate the veneration of this Orisha within their practices.

Even within Umbanda centers where the worship of Orisha Eshu is not directly practiced, his existence is still recognized and acknowledged. However, the cult associated with this Orisha is entrusted to his phalanx of spirit workers, namely the Eshus (who bear the same name as their master) and Pombagiras. These Eshus and Pombagiras serve as direct manifestations of Orisha Eshu, representing him in their spiritual endeavors. As a customary practice in Umbanda centers, it is habitual to offer reverence and homage to the temple's guardians, Eshu and Pombagira, prior to commencing any service or act of worship. This serves not only as a symbol of recognition for the forthcoming spiritual undertaking but also as the invocation of the energies and movements that only Eshus can yield.

Orisha Eshu assumes the role of protector and guardian of portals. He represents the cycles of life and holds immense power, capable of profoundly reshaping one's life through a simple request.

Eshu is also known as the agent of karma, bringing forth both challenging experiences, which align with his mischievous nature, as well as favorable outcomes based on the individual's deserving and merits. These favorable outcomes encompass various aspects such as acts of heroism that may save one's life, unexpected lottery wins, the redirection of potential harm, and, more importantly, the enhancement of one's willpower, youthfulness, and overall motivation. The inherent nature of orchestrating both positive and negative circumstances bestows upon Eshu the designation of being the Orisha of duality. Nevertheless, it is important to emphasize that Eshu is not an Orisha to be feared, and he would never inflict harm without just cause. His character embodies that of a jovial individual who refuses to tolerate mistreatment and maintains friendly relations with everyone.

Eshu has the ability to unlock pathways, imbue individuals and endeavors with vitality and momentum, and ensure the safeguarding and triumphant outcome of rituals. In essence, Eshu embodies the deity of action, facilitating progress and efficacy in various undertakings.

While Eshu shares the status of being an Orisha like the others, he is revered for having a unique polarity that sets him apart. Symbolically represented by the concept of the vacuum, Eshu comprises a broader essence in comparison to the other Orishas, as he holds the remarkable distinction of being the Orisha with the closest proximity to humanity in terms of vibratory nature.

Orisha Eshu is closely associated with the colors red and black, which symbolize dynamic and expansive movement (red) as well as the void or nothingness (black).

Red carnations are his corresponding flowers, while botanical elements such as chilies, limes, ginger, garlic, belladonna, high john the conqueror, and castor bean leaves also embody the fiery and agile nature of Eshu.

Black crystals and stones are all believed to be connected to Eshu, but rubies hold a particular resonance due to their embodiment of his vital force and intrinsic power.

The Domain of Eshu are primarily crossroads, as he serves as the guardian of passages and portals. The convergence of energies at the crossroads encapsulates the inherent duality within his nature. Thus, crossroads hold profound spiritual significance and are optimal locations for conducting rituals dedicated to Eshu, ensuring their utmost efficacy.

Despite traditionally having a phallic baton as his symbol, in Umbanda the trident is Eshu's most commonly attributed tool, and his symbol animals are roosters and black dogs.

The incantation used to invoke Eshu before a ritual is "laroye eshu," (pronounced lah-ro-YAY), often followed by "Eshu emojuba," (pronounced *ey-mo-joo-bAH*). These phrases originate from the Yoruba and proto-Yoruboid languages, respectively, and translate to "Save Messenger Eshu; I bow to you, Eshu." It is important to note that while "emojuba" conveys the meaning of "I bow to you," practitioners of Umbanda are advised against physically bowing down to Eshu as they would to other Orishas. This distinction arises from the belief that other Orishas represent energies from higher realms, while Eshu's energy is more closely tied to the earthly plane. Therefore, a specific hand gesture is adapted to symbolize bowing to Eshu: interlacing the fingers with palms facing downward and making a circular motion, representing the sphere [planet Earth] that Eshu embodies.

Before making offerings to any other Orisha, it is customary to observe the practice of offering to Eshu first, as he assumes the role of commander, overseeing the flow of energy sent to and received from other Orishas. However, when solely honoring and seeking assistance from Eshu within his specific cult or while celebrating his name, the act of making offerings follows a similar pattern as when he opens the service for other Orishas. Notably, Eshu's offerings are considered relatively straightforward and uncomplicated.

In Umbanda centers, the worship of Eshu typically involves the use of black and red candles, rum, cigars, and a cassava or corn flour-dish. This flour-dish is prepared by combining raw cassava flakes (gari) or dry corn grits with palm oil. This mixture, sometimes adorned with one, three, or seven red chilies or a lime divided into three parts, serves to provide fuel for the ritual or petition. The beverage is believed to enhance swiftness and cleanse whatever is required, while the energetic leaves of the cigar are thought to cleanse and carry *ashe*, or divine energy.

After arranging the dish, glass of rum, and candle on the floor, one can proceed by clapping three times and uttering the phrase "laroye eshu." It is at this moment that requests, petitions, and favors can be sought, along with asking for permission to initiate the worship of other Orishas. Eshu is the quickest among all Orishas to respond to petitions and invocations.

It is crucial to offer Eshu on the floor, as his energy is deeply connected to the earth. When offering Eshu prior to worshiping another Orisha, it is essential to show reverence to Eshu outside the temple premises or, in the case of home worship, outside the house or by the balcony of the apartment. This precautionary measure is taken because Eshu's vibration is exceptionally potent and more pronounced compared to the energies of other Orishas. Bringing his direct energy into one's home is believed to result in temporary insomnia, electronic equipment malfunctions, or overall instability for a few hours.

The potency of the offerings and ritual is augmented when conducted at a crossroads. However, due to considerations of respect for public spaces and concerns regarding littering, it is advisable to perform these rituals primarily in rural areas. In such settings, the individual making the offering has the opportunity to collect and dispose of the offerings the following day or within a span of three or seven days. This approach ensures proper reverence while also maintaining cleanliness and adhering to environmental responsibilities. The plate and glass can be washed and reused.

In an Umbanda temple, however, there is a specific place for the offerings to Eshu, as well as offerings for the spirits of Eshus and Pombagiras, called "doorway." A doorway is a very small room, like an external altar, usually outside the main salon. It is typically built close to the temple's gate. There, the energy of Eshu is thus enhanced, and those who enter the temple may be promptly spiritually scanned by the forces of Eshu before walking in.

Those whose head-Orisha is Eshu are persistent yet ambiguous in their speech and desires. They work hard due to their abundant physical energy; however, they can afford to be capricious and, as a result, end up back at square one. While they are extremely kind and benevolent, they can also be troublesome and mischievous. Nevertheless, most of the time, they act in accordance with the law.

Those who have Eshu as their primary Orisha may not have the most beautiful appearance, but they are highly sensual and magnetic, attracting both the opposite sex and the same sex. They have luck in gambling and invariably find a way to get out of situations with their sense of humor.

Individuals who have Eshu as head-Orisha, but who stray from an altruistic mindset may manifest negative traits typically associated with Eshu, such as engaging in mundane addictions, committing minor crimes, participating in irresponsible activities, lacking drive, and experiencing financial hardship. It is crucial to emphasize that Eshu himself does not possess these qualities. Therefore, the absence of his presence may be linked to the manifestation of these unfortunate circumstances.

While it is common for many followers of Umbanda to have Eshu as their head Orisha, depending on the Umbanda center, they may be mistakenly perceived as children of Ogun during clairvoyance or occasional divination with cowrie shells, as Ogun shares a close frequency with Eshu.

Yoruba Myth ∘ That Who Must Receive Offerings First

One of the numerous myths surrounding Eshu, as retold by Prandi (2001), recounts the tale of the mischievous younger sibling of Ogun, Ode (Oshossi). Eshu's playful nature often stirred up chaos and turmoil wherever he roamed.

One day, unable to endure Eshu's malevolent tricks any longer, the king of the gods decided it was time to take action. But to evade punishment, Eshu's brothers advised him to flee the kingdom. During his exile, while his siblings continued to bask in festivities and adoration, Eshu faded into obscurity, with his whereabouts unknown. Eshu cunningly disguised himself in various forms, stealthily visiting his homeland and often lurking near the entrances of ancient sanctuaries on joyous occasions. Unfortunately, none could discern his true identity, resulting in no offerings being extended to him.

Fueled by a desire for retribution, Eshu sowed seeds of unrest, misfortune, and confusion across the entire kingdom.

In desperation, the king decreed a ban on all religious activities until the source of the troubles was revealed. Seeking guidance, the priests consulted the oracle at the city gates, unwittingly communing with Eshu himself through the divination.

Through the oracle, Eshu demanded recognition and sacrifices, warning of further misfortune if his demands were not met. Ignoring the warning, the priests continued in their revelry, dismissing Eshu's words as mere folly. But Eshu was not to be ignored. Using his powers, he ensnared the priests in their seats, forcing them to heed his demands. Only through the wisdom of the oracle were they released, realizing the folly of their ways.

Following the oracle's counsel, the priests made offerings to Eshu, appeasing his restless spirit and restoring harmony to the kingdom.

This myth alludes to the importance of acknowledging and offering to Eshu so that balance can be established.

Other Orishas

Different branches of Umbanda uphold specific pantheons that they deem paramount, however, this does not imply that any given Umbanda temple disregards the existence of other Orishas. In cases where an Umbanda center venerates seven primary Orishas, it is understood that all other absent Orishas are variations or manifestations of those central entities, albeit not directly worshiped. For instance, if a center does not include Oshumare in its ritual practices, it signifies that the influence of this Orisha is encompassed within the cult of Oshun, as both Orishas share closely related divine origins and attributes associated with love and prosperity. Similarly, if the cult of Ossain is absent, it implies that his energy frequency and accompanying classes of spirits are subordinate to the governance of Oshossi. This is due to their similar roots and shared connection to woodlands and botanical elements.

Various forms of Umbanda acknowledge seven Orishas, whereas others see fourteen, indicating that each Orisha has a complementary counterpart to maintain energetic equilibrium and harmonize the divine energy. Other Orishas that may be occasionally mentioned, although they likely do not receive much exposure in any Umbanda segment, include, but are not limited to:

Iroko – time and ancestry

Iroko embodies the concepts of ancestry and wisdom. Often depicted in the form of an ancient African tree, *Ficus insipida*, this Orisha bridges the realm of the Orishas with that of the Earth, according to its myth. More significantly, Iroko is the Orisha of time, and therefore influences how one observes and experiences it. Also, it is believed that the more spiritually ancient an individual is, the more aligned they are with Iroko, and consequently, their perception of time on Earth appears to pass more quickly.

Ewa – intuition and creativity

Ewa, the Orisha of intuition, governs clairvoyance and purity. Symbolized by mist, she guides individuals to dispel the veils of illusion. Additionally, Ewa is closely associated with beauty and creativity, inspiring artistic expression and aesthetic appreciation. It is said that rarely will Ewa be the head-Orisha of an individual born as a male.

Orunmila – knowledge and prophecy

Orunmila, the Orisha of destiny, is the patron of the oracle Ifa and is responsible for foreseeing the destinies of individuals. He is also considered one of the chiefs of wisdom in mythological cosmogony. In this perspective, situated only below Olorun, Orunmila also influences devotees to be less revengeful.

Olokun – mysteries ans secrets

Olokun is regarded as an Orisha shrouded in mystery, symbolizing secrets and hidden truths. Known as the sovereign ruler of the oceans, Olokun elicits both fear and reverence. This enigmatic deity is often associated with both formidable protection and the bestowal of wealth. According to myths, Olokun's anger is believed to serve as a catalyst for necessary destruction, paving the way for new beginnings. In this light, Olokun can be likened to a synthesis of Shiva and Poseidon.

Aje Shalunga – wealth and prosperity

Aje Shaluga, another Orisha with dominion over the oceans, is counted among the offspring of Olokun, alongside Yemanja. Aje is chiefly linked to the accumulation of great wealth, although her cult also carries associations with esoteric and somewhat obscure practices. Notably, she is entirely absent from the Umbanda tradition, and her name finds limited recognition therein.

Odudua – creation and leadership

According to mythological narratives, Odudua holds a prominent position in the celestial hierarchy, second only to Olorun, forming a divine pair with Oshala as the creators of Earth. Although Odudua is occasionally depicted as a female figure, this Orisha is traditionally regarded as male. Paradoxically, Odudua is not always classified as an Orisha but rather as a singular creator of Earth. Additionally, Odudua is intimately linked to the attributes of immense willpower and exceptional intellectual prowess.

Classes of Spirits

Umbanda revolves around the teachings and functions of a diverse array of spirits. Within the temples, these spirits are channeled by mediums to convey messages, provide cleansing, and perform rituals. Behind the scenes, in the astral realm, these spirits continue their ceaseless work, operating in their specific fields and collaborating with other entities to accomplish what needs to be done.

Typically, but not invariably, these spirits may manifest the specific appearance and personality they had in a previous life—a life that inspired them to engage in charitable spiritual aid to others. The life of a spirit who, for instance, in one of their previous incarnations was a black slave in the Americas, holds significant importance for them. They acknowledge that that particular life taught them resilience, forgiveness, and, to some extent, humility. Similarly, a spirit appearing as a child might have experienced severe emotional neglect or the destruction of their innocence in their earthly existence, leading them to choose a path that enables them to assist those whose innocence and happiness have been diminished. Likewise, a spirit presenting herself as a mistress of the night might have lived as a harlot in a past life, and the pain from those experiences allows her to help others dealing with issues related to low self-esteem and personal power. Therefore, their assistance enables them to rectify their own past misdeeds, as helping others diminishes their karma or feelings of failure from that particular existence.

The spirits active within Umbanda are not practitioners of Umbanda themselves; rather, they see Umbanda as a means to carry out their charitable endeavors. These spirits are also engaged in providing assistance in Christian churches, pagan gatherings,

Buddhist temples, and various other spiritual or religious contexts, often without the knowledge of religious practitioners. They adapt their appearances to the cultural context of those who maintain mediumistic and psychic contact with them on Earth. In a similar vein, the spirit that manifests as a bohemian man in Umbanda might display traits of a Native American to a shaman in Canada, or appear as a Scottish nurse in a Spiritualist séance in France. Likewise, the same spirit could take on the role of a devotee of Krishna for a clairvoyant Hindu follower of that deity. The founding spirit of Umbanda, Mestizo Seven Crossroads, had been a significant priest in one of his previous lives, fulfilling such a role on the spiritual plane. However, his life as an indigenous man in Brazil enabled him best to convey the message of simplicity, strength, and resignation, further connecting him to the land. Similarly, several other spirits central to the foundation of Spiritism, along with those who inspired the Kardecist books, use Umbanda as a platform. They often present themselves with different names and appearances depending on the context.

The spirits active in Umbanda—those guiding mediums, safeguarding temples, and performing astral tasks—are not merely disembodied entities seeking refuge in Umbanda. These spirits have truly transformed from their regrettable attitudes or lamentedness and are wholeheartedly devoted to serving the "light." They are thoroughly prepared, having transitioned from simple discarnate people to spiritual workers. They undergo training and simulations, and, most importantly, their genuine willingness to serve and repent is assessed before they are permitted to enter an Umbandist circle. This rigorous process is also applicable, in the spiritual plane, to various other spiritualist and mediumistic religions and groups around the world.

Upon physical death, an individual might face challenges based on their possibly flawed earthly life. A life steeped in materialism, or wasted in the pursuit of physical pleasure, or, regrettably, a life marked by criminal or cruel activities can lead the newly discarnate spirit to endure torments in the afterlife. For example, spirits who committed heinous acts, like murder, might find themselves still attached to their decaying physical bodies in their graves; hence, their appearance may mirror their former body's decomposition due to their mental conditioning to their physical bodies. Enduring accusations, abuse, and even enslavement imposed by other spirits, they may eventually begin to regret their wrongdoings. Once this newfound remorse surfaces, spiritual entities of a certain hierarchy may invite them to work on tasks related to the most menial and low-ranking jobs, such as guarding a specific entrance or clearing a putrid area in the astral. As the spirit demonstrates commitment and dedication through their work, they may acquire new abilities and learn new procedures. Eventually, they embark on a transformative journey, gaining the opportunity to work within an Umbanda center. Typically, these entities, whose spiritual bodies mirror their decayed material bodies, may maintain that semi-skeleton appearance as a remembrance of what happened to them and also as a signature of their class, connoting cemeteries and, more specifically, connoting the rescue of those whose bitter materialism led them to find no freedom from their physical vessels upon physical death.

The Two Polarities

All entities within Umbanda operate within distinct qualities of energy, which are characterized by the density and vibration of spiritual and semi-physical atoms. Some types of energy primarily serve as conduits for light from higher realms, while others exert influence over earthly energies.

The light emanating from 'above' can be conceptualized as spiritual ethers, *prana*, or *ashe*, emitted through the Orishas and other sublime forces. In such instances, spirits function by directing this light onto various matters in which they are involved, including healing, cleansing, imbuing, and other related activities. Conversely, the energies generated on Earth embody denser qualities of light, albeit still spiritual in nature and closer to material elements. This energy is collected, manipulated, and generated from the etheric-double of Earth's elements, as well as by entities capable of condensing subtle energy into a more compact form.

In Umbanda, two polarities are recognized—the "Left" and the "Right." This can also be conceptualized as the Right representing the 'above' and the Left representing the 'below.' The spirits operating within the Right polarity encompass virtually all classes, with the exception of Eshus and Pombagiras, including Juvenile Eshus. In contrast, the spirits operating within the Left polarity primarily include Eshus, Pombagiras, Juvenile Eshus, and some Bohemians.

The Left has a distinct service for itself, indicating that during a service for Old Blacks, Children, Mestizos, Gypsies, and others, the spirits who operate within the Left polarity typically do not manifest and thus chants for them are not sung, meaning they are not expected to manifest. Similarly, in services for Eshus and Pombagiras, spirits like Children, Old Blacks, and Mestizos are absent. However, it is essential to note that before services for any class or polarity, the temple's Eshus are revered and offered first, as they have the duty of protecting the service and the vicinity. Notwithstanding, after this initial ritual, they are not observed by the audience if the service is for entities of the Right polarity.

The incompatibility between these two polarities means that if one is offered or requested in the presence of their diverging polarity, the vibrations of both parties will not harmonize favorably. It is as if a specific polarity, naturally subtle for its own reasons, becomes denser, making its functions more challenging. Similarly, if the other polarity must be dense and agile, its frequencies may be influenced by the subtlety or slowness of the opposing polarity. In essence, the polarities can be analogized to ambulance drivers and surgeons – despite both working to save lives, their lines of work cannot converge, and therefore a surgeon will not work with a car, and a driver will not work with medical lancets.

The Left polarity operates within the emanations of Orisha Eshu, while the Right functions under the influence of all other Orishas. In this context, it is observed that Orisha Eshu is the sole deity with a broadly earthly role. Along with his phalanxes of Eshus, Pombagiras, Juvenile Eshus, and some Bohemians, Orisha Eshu is recognized for constricting, repelling, and dissolving, embodying the total vacuum and the absence of light. On the other hand, the spirits operating under the emanations of the other Orishas expand, attract, and coagulate light.

Class and Phalanx

The spirits within Umbanda, each unique in their traits, belong to specific classes based on their fields of operation and temperaments. These hierarchical classes comprise spirits with similar pasts and abilities, working cohesively within their designated roles. For example, the Class of Mestizos includes spirits identifying as indigenous people of the Americas, who focus on labor, courage, abundance, and resilience. Eshus and Pombagiras, spirits primarily involved in desire, will, self-esteem, and vitality, form another class. The Class of Children manifests as childlike beings, instilling purity, hope, and joy. The Old Blacks, representing aged former black slaves, dedicate to healing and teachings rooted in kindness, fraternity, wisdom, resignation, and patience.

It is worth mentioning that a significant portion of the Old Blacks were indeed black slaves in their past lives, while the majority of the Children likely experienced a significant infancy in their previous existence. As for Eshus and Pombagiras, most of them had roles and social conditions in past lives that were intricately tied to desires, power, and social status, varying based on the specific phalanx to which they belong.

Each class of spirits is guided by an Orisha, who serves as their primary leader in terms of energy source and who they report to; following the guidance and working under their influence. This means that particular groups of spirits, such as the Bohemians, the Eshus, or the Cowboys, align their fields of operation and duties with the vibrations and nature of the governing Orisha of their respective class.

Each class has a specific ruling Orisha: The Mestizos are typically associated with Oshossi as their governing Orisha; Ibeji, but also Oshun and Oshumare, are regarded as patrons of the Class of Children; Orisha Eshu is the commander of Eshus and Pombagiras; and so on. As each Orisha represents a domain, such as faith, knowledge, law, love, justice, evolution, and generation, the various classes of spirits emerge from these domains, whereby they represent and express that force.

In these terms, the Old Blacks operate under Oshala's patronage, while the Sailors adhere to the tenets and vibrations of Yemanja, and similar pattern continues for other classes. However, it is important to note that while Mestizos, for instance, are predominantly associated with Oshossi, individual spirits within that class may also work under the guidance of other Orishas. It is common to encounter a Mestizo spirit associated with Oshun, Shango, Omulu, or any other Orisha. Similarly, a Child spirit may work under the influence of Omulu, and a Pombagira may comply with the tenets of Oshala.

Most spirits operate under the influence of both their domain's ruler and their own Orisha ruler, such as Velvet Eshus – spirits who belongs to a phalanx ruled by Orisha Eshu, like all Eshus, and also by Oshun, as the Velvet phalanx is influenced by Oshun. Other spirits are influenced by all seven domains, such as the phalanx of spirits Seven Crossroads, which includes the founding spirit of Umbanda, Mestizo Seven Crossroads. Along these lines, it is understood that the Orishas govern the classes, whereas the individual spirits can be governed individually by both the class's patron and other Orishas.

In addition to the entity's self-explanation of their name, which is not a personal name like "Robert" or "Catherine," but rather a name indicative of their class and phalanx, such as "Mestizo Seven Crossroads," their sigil drawn on the floor may further unveil their specific area of work and the Orishas they align with. Taking the example of "Mestizo Seven Crossroads," class, domain, and workfield can be analyzed:

"Mestizo" refers to class; "Seven" refers all seven domains; "Crossroads" refers to his phalanx—in this case, the point of strength ruled by the Orisha Eshu). Overall, Mestizo Seven Crossroads can be understood as an Oshossi-like spirit who serves all the Orishas in the areas ruled by Orisha Eshu.

The entities who work in Umbanda should not be understood as an extension of the Orishas, as the Orishas are extensions of God. Instead, they should be perceived as workers who represent the Orishas.

Class (who; quality)	**Domain** (how; under whose influence)	**Phalanx** (where; workfield)
Mestizo	Seven	Crossroads
↓	↓	↓
Strength	Under all Orishas'	Where Orisha Eshu rules

The illustration below depicts a division between the heavenly Orishas and their respective phalanx workers, as well as Orisha Eshu and his phalanx workers.

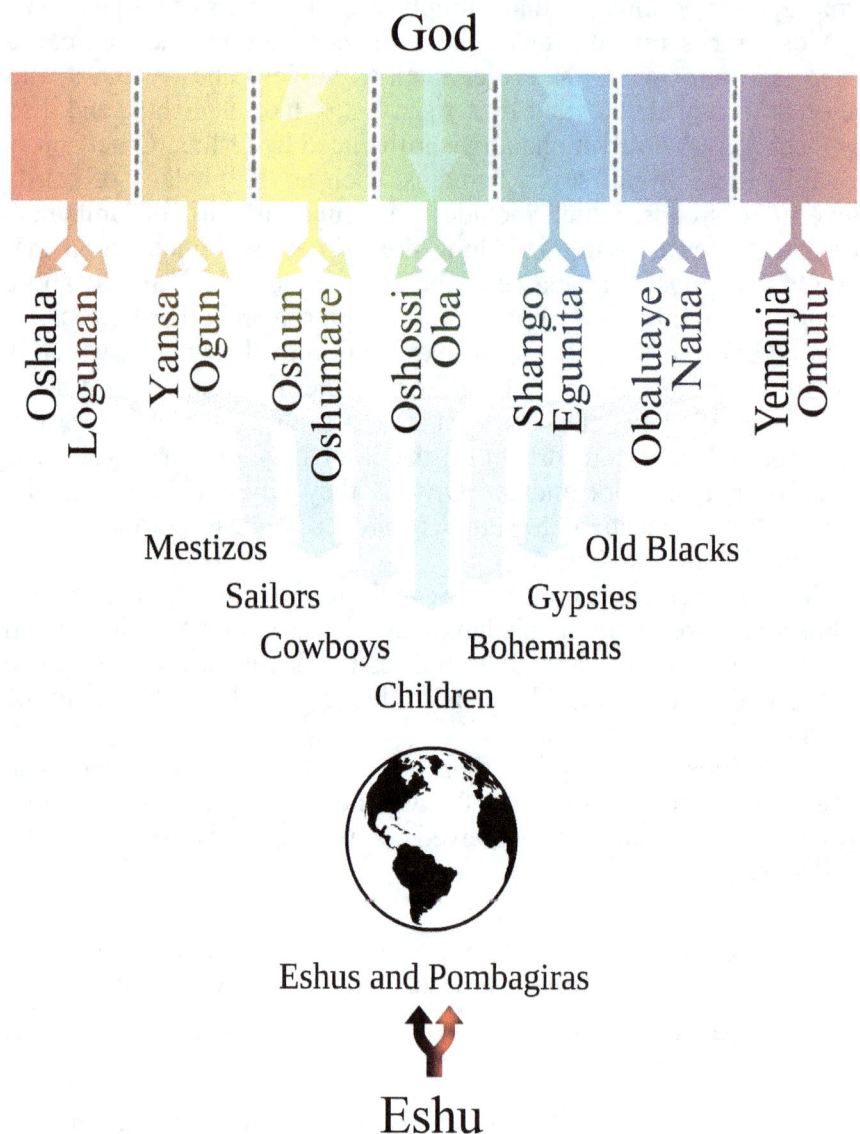

Old Blacks

As delineated in the antecedent chapters of this compendium, Father Tony emerged as the inaugural Old Black manifestation in Umbanda, facilitated through the mediumship of Zelio de Moraes. Within the framework of Umbanda, Old Blacks and Mestizos were the initial two classifications to materialize, subsequently forming the tripartite structure that includes the third component, the class of Children. While Father Tony played a seminal role in the embryonic phase of Umbanda, subsequent Old Black manifestations ensued shortly thereafter, both through Zelio and by way of other mediums.

Old Blacks are a distinguished class of spirits who manifest as former black slaves from the Americas, especially Brazil. These spirits, known for their profound benevolence, choose to appear as elderly ex-slaves to symbolize wisdom and humility.

In the early decades of Umbanda, the Old Blacks were pivotal because catering to the most underprivileged or non-white populations was of utmost importance. This group aimed particularly to impart further knowledge about Orishas and other rites of Afro-American origin. This was significant because mainstream religions like Christianity and Spiritism primarily served white communities, leading to the emergence of classes such as the Old Blacks and Mestizos.

Within Umbanda, they are revered as the highest class of spirits, capable of resolving any issue through their compassionate actions. These spirits hold significant authority not only within Umbanda centers but also extend their influence beyond religious settings. They command respect and hold sway over other spirits operating under the umbrella of the Orishas.

These benevolent spirits convey compassionate guidance, inspiring others to embrace forgiveness and patience. Manifesting as former enslaved individuals, they embody immense forgiveness and thus teach forgiveness through their own example.

When channeled by mediums in the temple, these spirits portray themselves as elderly folk healers. This manifestation often includes making the mediums appear to struggle with walking, displaying an arched back, and adopting a voice reflective of a simple, rural person. The extent to which the medium embodies the accent and traits of an elderly individual is determined by their level of animism. Animism refers to the medium's own understanding of the entity, causing them to act as if they are impersonating the spirit in their behavior and speaking traits. In this manner, mediums attire themselves in white garments reminiscent of the clothing worn by slaves in the past.

This class of spirits is renowned for their healing abilities, which encompass addressing physical, emotional, and spiritual ailments. Despite the apparent simplicity of their methods, their approach to healing is intricate. They utilize herb branches, smudge with cigars and pipes, light candles, and wear Catholic bead necklaces, all while reciting traditional Christian prayers.

The groups of spirit workers in Umbanda are widely respected, and they are even more venerated than the Orishas themselves.

Apart from the altars found in Umbanda centers, it is common for individuals to set up specific spaces in their homes where they light candles and offer various items to these entities. This practice enhances the entities' presence in their lives and turns their home altars into focal points of spiritual emanation outside the Umbanda temple.

Offerings to Old Blacks typically include coffee, mineral water, cigars, and tobacco pipes, along with white or black candles. Rue, rosemary, and boldo leaves are frequently used in their rituals, as well as white roses. The open fields are the places where offerings may be placed or where the presence of Old Blacks can be better sensed. Memorials, where people light candles to the dead are also places where candles for Old Blacks are well received; depending on the phalanx of Old Black, cemeteries are also part of their domains.

The vibratory domains of Oshala are primarily responsible for influencing the Class of Old Blacks, with occasional assistance from Obaluaye, Omolu, and Nana.

Common salutation for Old Blacks is "adore the souls!," which in Portuguese is *adore as almas*, however, that comes from the French *à doré*, meaning "make it like gold," and not to love/worship.

Chant

Child, if ever in need you find,
Just think of Grandma, her love so
kind.
She'll come to aid, without delay,
In her gentle way, she'll light your way.

Imagine a road so long, my dear,
A little white house, Grandma's here.
Sitting on a humble seat,
With a rosary, her prayers repeat.

Grandma, in your thoughts, we find,
A guiding light, so warm and kind.

Mestizos

The very first Mestizo spirit to manifest through channeling was Umbanda's own founding spirit, Mestizo Seven Crossroads. Following this, other Mestizos emerged, symbolizing a societal class that was often neglected or deemed inferior. For the first time, the mestizos assumed a significant role, utilizing the knowledge and contributions of Brazil's indigenous peoples as part of the foundation for something profound.

In Brazil, unlike in other South American nations, the indigenous peoples of the pre-Columbian era did not form grand empires or complex civilizations. Despite their smaller numbers compared to Amerindian populations in other regions, given the vastness of Brazil—comprising more than 50% of South America's land—their cultural influence has been consistently diminished and overlooked. Moreover, it has been intentionally annihilated, both physically and morally, by European-Brazilian customs and indoctrination.

Examining the core roots of religions, especially concerning their local context and the time of their founding, reveals that the iconic deities or manifested spirits are invariably responses to local issues. Old Blacks and Mestizos, in this context, represent a moment where these peoples, historically and socially, needed to assume a role and symbolically nurture their faith without feeling marginalized or less civilized.

The Mestizos, known in Portuguese as *caboclos*, represent spirits who may have had previous lives where they were of mixed European and Native American heritage. In the context of Brazil, they symbolize the indigenous people who have interacted with white settlers. These spirits are revered as the native peoples of the Americas, particularly Brazil, who are deeply connected to the land and its shamanic traditions.

Their essence is defined by immense strength, transcending their individual personalities. Physical prowess is a significant aspect of their demeanor. They exhibit remarkable resilience and a strong will to work, embodying seriousness with a touch of joviality when compared to the Old Blacks.

Mestizos play a pivotal role in every aspect of life but notably refrain from discussions related to love or passion. Due to their serious nature, they are often chosen by other high-ranking spirits as the leaders of an Umbanda center, as exemplified by figures like Mestizo Seven Crossroads.

Those who receive a magnetic pass or magnetization from the Mestizos often report feeling invigorated and revitalized, as these spirits instill a strong sense of strength and energy.

Furthermore, Mestizos are dedicated to purifying people's auras and the metaphysical aspects of various spaces. To clairvoyant mediums, they manifest themselves wearing cockades, feathers, and their faces painted in traditional indigenous symbolism. In the astral realm, they employ arch and bow, ropes, and other tools to manipulate energy, and within Umbanda centers, they utilize these holographic objects too, although these are imperceptible to non-clairvoyants.

In their rituals, Mestizos incorporate various herbs, with smudging forming a significant part of it. They also work with concoctions, candles, and other natural materials.

The points of nature where offerings may be laid, as well as where the energy of the Mestizos may be stronger, are the woodlands and forests.

Offerings made to Mestizos typically include items similar to those offered to Oshossi, such as fruits, corn, beer or white wine, coconut water, and cigars. Both green and white candles find application on home altars.

Typical salutation for Mestizos is "oke, Mestizo!" meaning 'look out.'

> **Chant**
>
> *Zambi crafted the world, every land and stream,*
> *It's Zambi's reign, in every dream.*
>
> *Zambi shaped the starry light,*
> *Oshossi roams the forest at night.*
>
> *Oke oke oke,*
> *In the forests, oke*

Children

The first manifestations of the Children transpired within the services of Mestizos, some of whom identified as child Mestizos or as infant Indigenous entities. As time progressed, this group of spirits evolved into a distinctive class of their own, distinguishing themselves as a diverse array of spirits exhibiting infantile appearances [to the mediums] and behaviors. Subsequently, they came to be recognized as *Erês*.

The entities known as the spirits of Children, commonly referred to as Erês (pronounced e-RAYS, derived from the Yoruba word irò, meaning 'to play'), form one of the three essential pillars of classes in Umbanda. This classification includes spirits devoted to the realms of innocence, purity, and joy, embodying the image and behavior of children typically aged between 3 and 7 years old.

Some of these spirits departed from the mortal realm during their childhood, while others chose to regress to their youthful state to fulfill their spiritual duties. It is also accepted that many Children may have never incarnated on Earth and thus are spirits from other spiritual planes who adapted to the archetype of earthly children, given their shared traits. Spirits who have never incarnated on Earth are known as 'enchanted' among Umbandists.

Despite their childlike appearance (observed by their mediums) and behavior, these entities possess immense responsibility and wisdom. The form they maintain is specifically for their charitable endeavors, where the archetype of childhood is crucial for them to evoke the emotions they work with and fulfill certain astral tasks while adorned in that naive guise.

When mediums channel these entities, they unfailingly assume the persona of children—laughing, crying, and speaking in a childish tone, as well as engaging in playful activities with toys. When approached by attendees seeking favors, they frequently request candy as a gesture of reciprocation and occasionally ask for gifts for living children.

The Children of Umbanda are among the most adept entities, penetrating situations where other spirits might encounter difficulty. They excel at resolving challenges deemed impossible or too late to address. Their agility is matched only by their ability to instill joy and happiness while undertaking their tasks.

These entities seem to display a level of subservience to the Old Blacks, addressing them respectfully as grandma or grandpa. Therefore, during the services, it is not uncommon to observe mediums channeling Children simultaneously with other mediums channeling Old Blacks[22]. Nevertheless, many of these children possess a spiritual depth comparable to that of the Old Blacks.

The Children represent the youthful phase of life, the Mestizo embodies middle age, and the Old Blacks symbolize old age, corresponding to purity, humility, and wisdom, respectively. This triad, forming the foundation of Umbanda, may also mirror the racial amalgamation portrayed by the spirits: whites, amerindians, and blacks coming together as a peaceful and fraternal pillar within the religion.

During festivities dedicated to Children, such as those honoring Orisha Ibeji or national Children's Day, the public is treated to banquets featuring cakes, sweets, sugary sodas, and fruits. Balloons,

---

22 Symbolically, this may allude to the coexistence of ancient wisdom and new wisdom, or the blending of old conscious knowledge and young unconscious knowledge.

vibrant decorations, and toys are also provided for the channeled Children to enjoy.

The places where the energy of Children are most felt are gardens, playgrounds, and flowery squares.

The colors associated with them are pale blue and pale pink. Therefore, their rituals typically involve lighting two candles of each color. Sugary sweets and fruit juice are essential components of their rituals. At home, a glass of juice with sugar suffices, while a candle enhances its powers.

Their elemental affinity aligns with that of Ibeji, encompassing anything associated with children, such as toys, colorful crayons, and sweets.

Sugar holds particular significance in offerings to the Children, as they utilize this element to execute their agile tasks. Moreover, sugar serves to balance their vibratory frequency, mitigating the need for mediums or devotees to compensate for any energetic disparities within their own auric fields.

Their standard salutation, like most classes, is "Save" followed by the name of the class; in this case, "Save the Children." However, "oni beijada" (on-nee bay-JAH-da) can also be used, referring to their patron Orisha Ibeji.

Orisha Ibeji is their patron, although they occasionally receive support from Oshun and Oshumare. Nevertheless, the influence of the twin saints Cosmas and Damian is pivotal in their cult, akin to St. George's role in the cult of Ogun.

Chant

Papa, send me a balloon high,
With all the children in the sky!
Papa, send me a balloon high,
With all the children in the sky!

Is there candy, dear Papa?
Is there candy in this garden, Papa?
Is there candy, dear Papa?
Is there candy in this garden, Papa?

Auxiliary Classes

Like any other class of spirit workers, the auxiliary Classes in Umbanda consist of spirits that are not exclusively tied to that religion; instead, they originate from other spiritual contexts. They offer their assistance to Umbanda, using it as a platform, but they are not the founding or primary Classes of Umbanda, meaning that they were introduced to Umbanda or given space within it later on.

Some of these Classes have gained significant popularity within Umbanda temples. As a result, their cult and presence are now widely accepted and considered integral parts of the religion.

In instances where a specific Umbanda temple does not incorporate a particular class of spirits, the spirits associated with that absent class will still naturally manifest using archetypes of other classes that are common in that temple. For example, if a certain Umbanda temple does not engage with Sailor spirits, these entities may manifest as Amerindians, Old Blacks, or even Eshus linked to Yemanja.

It is essential to note that all these spirits persistently operate within the framework of Umbanda. This religion, in terms of spiritual management, provides a platform for a wide array of spirits willing to offer assistance. Consequently, they find their rightful place within it, utilizing its space to contribute and assist those in need, irrespective of the classes they represent or are part of.

Eshus and Pombagiras

Despite not being explicitly delineated by contemporary Umbanda tenets, the classifications of Eshus and Pombagiras have been traditionally regarded as auxiliary entities within the religious framework. Historically, they were not considered the foundational figures of Umbanda and were, consequently, perceived as an additional class.

The spirits identified as Eshus and Pombagiras are known to operate across various domains, utilizing diverse spiritual and religious platforms worldwide for manifestation. However, practitioners of Umbanda did not acknowledge their presence during its nascent stages. Notably, these spirits were already prevalent within Cabula and Macumba circles. Over time, a more comprehensive understanding of this spiritual group emerged, leading to its formal inclusion in the cult.

There exists a belief that Orisha Mallet, a foundational entity in Umbanda alongside Seven Crossroads and Father Tony, was, in essence, an Eshu. This attribution is largely based on the striking parallels between his assigned tasks and those performed by Eshus in contemporary religious practices. In the earlier stages, however, he was perceived to be affiliated with the Mestizos or was even thought to have had a Malay origin in his previous incarnation.

A pivotal development occurred around the 1950s, when the spirits of Eshus were officially expounded upon and introduced to Umbanda. This elucidation, primarily found in Tancredo's seminal work *Doutrina e Ritual de Umbanda* (Doctrine and Ritual of Umbanda) published in 1951, served to distinguish Eshus from entities such as eguns or other perceived deviant spirits within the religion.

Eshus and Pombagiras are among the most well-known and revered entities in Umbanda. This class of spirits is composed of individuals who, in their past lives, were involved in matters related to power, status, or sensuality. Whereby they now work to assist incarnate humans in reclaiming their self-esteem and personal power, guiding them away from paths deemed too promiscuous or selfish.

Eshus, named after the Orisha Eshu, are male spirits primarily found to operate in urban areas. They guard streets, entrances, crossroads, and temples, revitalizing those in need and rescuing individuals trapped in nefarious astral realms.

Pombagiras are female spirits who nurture self-esteem, personal power, and enthusiasm for life. Frequently exuding sensuality and provocation, they seek to cultivate a zest for life and self-belief in individuals. During the early years of Umbanda, Pombagiras were commonly referred to as "Lady Eshu" or "Eshu Woman."

Both Eshus and Pombagiras usually present themselves as individuals of European descent, often wearing attire from past centuries. They are associated with crossroads, cabarets, bars, clubs, and cemeteries, offering protection to these places.

Additionally, there are Eshu and Pombagira Youths: child or teenage spirits, whose focus is on helping individuals manifest their intentions.

In Umbanda, the classes are categorized into two vibratory alignments known as Right and Left. The classes aligned with the Right vibration draw their powers from heavenly Orishas, while those aligned with the Left vibration derive their power from the earthly Orisha, Eshu.

When channeled by mediums, Eshus and Pombagiras customarily express loud laughter as a way to disseminate their energy. Their laughter is not necessarily a sign of happiness but serves to instill a sense of excitement for life. Within the phalanx or specific field they belong to, these entities can have individual personalities that vary from mysterious and serious to cheerful and joyous.

Eshus are frequently characterized as formidable and commanding entities, inspiring obedience and instilling fear, particularly in spirits ensnared by anger and apprehension.

In the early stages of their recognition within the cult, they exhibited a more overtly African aspect, as it was believed that they were spirits of former slaves. However, a notable transformation occurred from the 1970s onward, during which the cult of Eshus was better understood, and Eshus began to manifest with apparent European origins. During this period, there was a shift in their communication style, wherein they not only described themselves but also expounded on their previous lives and their designated roles within the religious context.

This transformative phase revealed a departure from an exclusively African persona, with Eshus adopting European characteristics, which were more aligned with their origins. Consequently, their rituals incorporated a Victorian aesthetic, and their mediums began dressing in accordance with the envisioned European or European descent spirits they channeled. Contemporary depictions commonly show Eshus adorned in elegant capes, top hats, and wielding tridents, while holding cigars as distinctive elements of their attire and symbolism.

Contemporary statues of Eshus (on the left) differ from those of the early days of their cult in Umbanda (on the right), when they were more associated with roles related to 'hell.' The statues depict: Eshu Black Cape; Eshu Road Locker; Eshu Seven Forks; Juvenile Eshu.

Displayed here are contemporary and primitive versions of Pombagira statues. From left to right, they depict: Pombagira Mary Skull; Pombagira of the Cabaret; Pombagira Queen of Hell; Pombagira of the Souls.

Some Eshus have a skeletal appearance, while others exude a more jovial and seductive aura. Yet, there are also Eshus with an eerie presence, and these various appearances correspond to their specific fields of operation.

Statues of Eshus, portrayed as red or satanic-looking entities, continue to be prevalent in some temples. This is partly attributed to an early Christian association of the Orisha Eshu with the devil. However, it is important to note that some Eshu spirits may indeed manifest a frightening appearance, contingent upon their field of operation, such as in lower zones where they control revolted spirits. Conversely, Pombagiras typically manifest in the form of vibrant, vivacious women. A prevalent attire choice for them is a Victorian-style dress, often in shades of red, reminiscent of cabaret fashion. However, it is noteworthy that certain factions of Pombagiras may exhibit a mysteriously dark demeanor, while others are portrayed clad in rags. Some may even adopt the guise of a skeletal figure. These varied manifestations symbolize the diverse facets of their work, illustrating the multifaceted nature of Pombagiras in their engagements and interactions depending on where they operate.

Eshus and Pombagiras are often sought after for assistance in matters related to money, passions, and power. However, it is important to note that their aid is provided within the framework of the divine laws of cause and effect.

As for Juvenile Eshus and Pombagiras, they typically manifest as older children and preteens. They operate in domains similar to Eshus and Pombagiras, with Juvenile Eshus displaying a distinct inclination towards constructing and dismantling intentions, and Juvenile Pombagiras focusing on instilling interest. (Eshus primarily focus on will, while Pombagiras concentrate on desire).

Widely acknowledged as a sub-class of spirits stemming from that of Eshus, some temples classify the Juveniles separately. However, Umbanda theologians[23] generally perceive them as a bridge connecting individuals to Orisha Eshu. This parallels the belief regarding the class of Children, observed to enhance the connection with one's head Orisha.

In practice, Juvenile Eshus often mirror the names of the medium's main Eshu, fostering a personalized association. For example, if a medium's primary Eshu is "Eshu Road Locker," they may also work with a Juvenile Eshu named "Little Locker." Similarly, if a Pombagira is named Mary Rose Skull, the Juvenile Pombagira working with that medium would likely be referred to as "Little Mary Rosy Skull.

Some Umbandists believe that Juveniles may have never incarnated on Earth. Consequently, they often refer to them as "the

---

[23] Rubens Saraceni's book "Orixá Exu Mirim," published in Brazilian Portuguese by Madras in 2008, offers great details on the nature of these entities.

enchanted." In this line of thought, Juveniles are spirits adopting the persona of a young Eshu based on their accustomed density, polarity, and cheerful traits, akin to the Children of the Right polarity in Umbanda.

The cult of Juveniles closely resembles that of Eshus and Pombagiras, emphasizing prowess in matters of intention. Juveniles exhibit notable power, navigating realms where other spirits might encounter difficulties. They also demonstrate an ability to manipulate energies that may be challenging or toxic for other spirits. Regarding lower magic, Juveniles are considered highly proficient in swiftly dismantling the intentions that creates it.

As previously mentioned, the places where their energy is most abundant are crossroads—either urban or rural crossroads, including those in the shape of T or Y, with the latter associated with Pombagira. However, depending on their field of work, a specific Eshu or Pombagira may have their point of strength at cemeteries, the beach, and so on.

Offerings made to Eshus typically include gari (cassava flakes) or corn flour, usually mixed with yellow palm oil. This mixture may also be combined with whiskey or honey. Additionally, a glass of whisky or rum, along with a cigar or straw cigarette, is presented. For more complex petitions, offerings may include red carnations, red chilies as garnish, and other specific items tailored to the nature of the request.

In the case of Pombagiras, similar mixtures can be prepared, accompanied by a glass of champagne, cider, red wine, or red sweet liquor. Additionally, a red rose is crucial for the offering. Thin, natural cigarettes or flower incense may also be included.

For a simple offering at home, it is advisable to place the altars of Eshus or Pombagiras outside one's home. Their energy is densely rapid, and placing their altar outdoors prevents interference with other energies within the house. The altar can be set up on the floor in the garden or external balcony. A red and black, or just red, or just white candle can be lit, accompanied by a glass of either whisky or champagne.

It is worth mentioning that the Orisha that governs this class is Orisha Eshu, and it is the only class that Orisha governs individually.

Offerings in their cult parallel those for Eshus and Pombagiras, often including candies, cola drinks with whiskey or rum, and other traditional sweets. Elements, colors, and instruments align with those used by Eshus and Pombagiras, with the distinctive addition of toys. The crossroads holds particular significance as a point of strength in their worship, and their salutation, like that for Eshus and Pombagiras is "laroye" (pronounced *lah-roy-YAY)*.

Chants

(for Eshu Velvet)
In the moonlit night, where shadows play,
Eshu Velvet, in darkness, finds his way.

Iron gates and wooden locks, they cower,
In the graveyard's reign, Eshu Skeleton's power.

At midnight's hour, Eshu takes flight,
Invisible threads weave through the night.

No service is complete without his might,
Without Eshu, we cannot fight.

(for Gypsy Pombagira)
Walking on foot, to meet Pombagira
She read my palm, and showed me a mirror

Truth she said, no lies to spread.
Is she the one, the one in red?

(for Eshu Little Skull)
Eshu Little Skull, working with the bones,
Rise up from the grave, move that stone.

In your left hand, an ax held tight,
And a knife gleaming bright.
Stay on the track, man,
And don't look back.

Bohemians

The Bohemians, known as 'malandro' (derived from the Italian word *malandrino*, meaning scoundrel or rascal), earned this label because the elites of Rio de Janeiro, during the post-slavery period, deemed those leading a bohemian lifestyle as outcasts, vagabonds, and the like. Historically, the lower classes faced oppression, and in response, an anti-heroic figure emerged—one who outwitted or deceived the upper class to gain some advantage. Over time, this term was embraced by spiritualists and their mediums to promote the image of street-smart and charismatic individuals.

The Bohemians, in their initial manifestation, constituted a phalanx, or a subclass of spirits associated with rural or countryside groups engaged in various magical-religious activities, including Catimbó. Subsequently, this cultural phenomenon permeated other religious circles and eventually Umbanda centers in Rio de Janeiro and São Paulo, undergoing a transformation and adopting a more urban, bohemian, anti-heroic, streetwise, and somewhat provocative style. This transformation mirrors the characteristics of the local bohemians in Brazil's largest cities.

Having initially appeared in services dedicated to Eshus and Old Blacks, the Bohemians represent one of the newest classes within the Umbanda framework.

The Bohemians constitute a class of spirits recognized for their association with the *bon vivant* lifestyle. As urban spirits, they operate in environments where gambling, competition, and typical bohemian pursuits such as drinking, cabarets, music, dance, and street activities prevail. More significantly, they aim their aid at those who have been neglected, excluded, and marginalized, including victims of societal prejudice. Renowned for their street smarts and acumen in such surroundings, they assist incarnate individuals in navigating the adversities and perils associated with this lifestyle or life condition.

Having predominantly experienced past lives as either mischievous bohemians or those who suffered prejudice at its worst, they exhibit a perpetual sense of contentment despite life's challenges. In their current roles as agents of the 'Light,' they focus on preventing crimes and misfortunes inherent to the nightlife and rescuing those at the bottom of society. While audacious in their remarks, they adhere strictly to the truth and maintain a strong sense of justice. They inspire positivity and enable people to escape life's pains and adversities. Despite their presence in urban settings akin to Eshus and Pombagiras, the Bohemians specialize in aiding those engaged in gambling and bawdy activities typical of nocturnal bohemian life. With their streetwise demeanor, they help individuals abandon malevolent activities, fostering a perception of luck and steering them away from unnecessary risks.

Closely aligned with the classes of Eshus and Pombagiras, the Bohemians occasionally collaborate with them, occasionally forming a phalanx within the Class of Eshus. Some Bohemians also appear to be associated with the Class of Old Blacks, contingent on their specific work field. Typically jovial, and tinged with sarcasm and sassiness, these spirits, when channeled through a medium, emanate the aura of individuals commonly found in bars and cabarets.

This class is distinguishable by its members' impeccable white linen suits and white hats, which occasionally have red accents in honor of their patron, Ogun. They are often depicted with decks, dice, and other gambling paraphernalia. In the astral realm, some are observed wielding shaving blades, especially the female Bohemians, which they use to sever nefarious energy strands.

Their rituals primarily involve clearing pathways for individuals, dismantling magic, dissolving energies accumulated in nightlife settings or gatherings of large crowds, and restoring dignity to the neglected.

The points of strength for Bohemians—where offerings can be given and their energy more keenly felt—are at the base of urban hills, corners in bustling nightlife areas, crossroads, and cemeteries, depending on their field of work.

Offerings to the Bohemians closely resemble those made to Eshus and Pombagiras, although they are simpler and less focused on desires or self-esteem. They also appreciate sugarcane sweets, hand-rolled tobacco, and cold beer. Items such as decks, snooker balls, dice, and coins are also suitable offerings. If these offerings are not placed on the temple or home altar, they can be presented at crossroads or wherever their field of work is manifested.

Their salutation is simply "save the Bohemians!"

Universally influenced by Ogun, these spirits occasionally come under the sway of Eshu when operating on the Left polarity, and Oshala or even Obaluaye when working on the Right polarity.

Chant

Beware, oh beware,
Mister, don't mess with this dame,
If you tread lightly, s
he'll pave your way to fame,
But if you dare to scoff,
Mary Razor will unleash her flame,
She'll take you down,
and you'll never be the same.

Bohemian, Bohemian, Bohemian
Bohemian you didn't meet your end,
Bohemian, Bohemian, Bohemian,
Bohemian you didn't meet your end,
Bohemian, turned into smoke,
vanished around the bend.

Bohemian, turned into smoke,
vanished around the bend.
When I climb the hill, it's solely to meet your gaze,
Bohemian, I need to talk, I need help to find my way

Sailors

In the post-abolition era in Brazil, sailors were predominantly individuals from black and impoverished communities. Often conscripted by the government for wars or maritime endeavors, they faced the perilous prospect of venturing into the seas without a guarantee of a safe return to solid ground. Adrift for months, they resorted to prayers and rituals seeking protection and solace. Some began to venerate the "masters" of Catimbó, which encompassed seven realms, including the "Depths of the Sea."

In subsequent decades, within the context of Catimbó, these spirits began to manifest, although their past as sailors was not explicitly acknowledged. As Umbanda welcomes all spirits communicating messages of the Light and contributing to the advancement of others, this new group started to manifest within its services.

Originating in the spiritual realm predating Catimbó or Umbanda, the sailors from every part of Earth gradually gained prominence and evolved into a distinct class.

The Class of Sailor includes spirits who have experienced at least one life where they were connected to the sea, including roles such as sailors, fishermen, pirates (which is also a subclass), and marine military personnel. In most instances, these spirits perished at sea, yet were either rescued by sea spirits or now reside and operate alongside the denizens of the astral sea.

Sailors primarily focus on energetic cleansing, but they also address emotional imbalances in people's lives, particularly those related to feelings of isolation or abandonment. This emphasis reflects their past experiences of solitude while at sea.

During channeling sessions, Sailors often manifest with a demeanor resembling drunkenness or the swaying motion of boats and ships. This characteristic presentation is indicative of their association with maritime activities and the historical reputation of sailors for indulging in heavy drinking. However, as Sailors sway, they cleanse the emotional nodes of the individuals they treat within the temple. Their speech may mimic that of individuals under the influence of alcohol, yet Sailors typically maintain a cheerful disposition, conveying messages of love and faith.

Mediums channeling Sailors frequently wear attire reminiscent of sailors, often donning white and blue garments, navy-style hats, and occasionally holding smoking pipes.

The places where the energy of Sailors can be most strongly felt are, indubitably, the beach, seaports, and the sea.

As is customary for most classes, their salutation consists of "save" followed by the name of the class, hence "save the sailors!"

Offerings made to Sailors align with those traditionally associated with Yemanja. Rum serves as their preferred libation, and white roses stand as their favored flowers.

The sustenance of this spiritual class is overseen by the Orisha Yemanja, although on occasion, they may also be sustained by Oshun.

Chant

In the sacred waters,
I know where I stand,
A fisherman's soul, in Yemanja's land.
Beneath the waves, where secrets lie,
I know who I am, under the sea and sky.

Mr. Sailor, don't let me be adrift,
For life's rhythm echoes the sea's uplift.
A glass of rum, eyepatch, and hat,
A sailor hinted, life's good, just like that.

Witches

The Class of Witches, being the most recent auxiliary class to emerge in Umbanda, remains poorly understood. It is known that this class comprises spirits embodying the archetype of witches; however, they are customarily observed to include a variety of female spirits from other classes, such as Pombagiras, who align with witchcraft or have a pagan background, rather than purely being witches.

The first services where witches were observed was in those of Eshus and Pombagiras, where the Pombagiras would identify as having had previous lives as witches, and thus they operate today in like manner to their past within the class of Pombagira. Old Blacks also started to present spirits who would say they were 'Kimbandan' Old Blacks—meaning they would work with spells, and manipulate energies as such.

The Class of Witches is more prevalent in Kimbanda (or Quimbanda), a religion rooted in magic, enchantments, pacts, and other witchcraft-related beliefs. It serves as a platform for spirits who present themselves as Eshus and Pombagiras. However, in many instances, this self-identification involves spirits falsely claiming to be Eshus. In Kimbanda, only one Orisha, Eshu, is revered.

Despite commonly associated with Pombagiras, male spirits are also prevalent within this class, often manifesting either as members of the Class of Witches or the Class of Orient.

These spirits have typically lived pivotal lives as pagans connected to natural magic, sorcerers, practitioners of witchcraft, or were folk healers from various cultures. Some may have been individuals persecuted under allegations of practicing witchcraft. However, it is not uncommon for a spirit who has not had a life as a witch of any form to adopt this archetype after discovering and resonating with it in the spiritual realms.

In Umbanda, this class predominantly engages in rituals, energetic manipulation, and delving into the intricate mysteries of magic. Their expertise extends to healing practices as well as the unraveling of lower forms of enchantment and spiritual obsession. Additionally, they engage in the transmutation of energetic substances.

Displaying profound wisdom in the arts of magic, these spirits exude an air of mystery and seriousness, coupled with a friendly disposition. Some exhibit refined characteristics, indicative of their connection to European witchcraft, while others possess a more mystical or liturgical demeanor, revealing ties to ancient Egypt and the Levant.

In the astral planes, or to those with the ability to perceive them, many of these spirits appear in the typical attire of witches, wearing black or purple garments. However, their appearance does not resemble the stereotypical portrayal seen in childish films and literature. They often wield tools such as athames, crystals, tridents (in the case of Pombagiras), and other magical implements. It is believed that most male and female witches possess extraordinary beauty, adding an aura of mystery to their harmonious traits.

The places most associated with their energies, where offerings may be given, are those found in nature, such as the woods, beach, and lakes. However, the night and the phases of the moon play a crucial role in establishing a powerful point of strength.

Offerings to the Witches typically consist of items akin to those presented to their patron Orisha, Nana, such as red wine, grapes, red roses, and violet candles. Their favored herbs include belladonna, rosemary, and patchouli. A traditional salutation used for them is "Save the witches!"

Chant

In shadows deep, the whispers hitch,
You can shout, 'burn this witch',

From fire's dance, her power sours,
In the flames, her spirit towers.

You can shout, 'burn this witch',
As flames engulf, who will bewitch?

A cauldron roars, at crossroads grand,
Pombagira strong, in fiery stand.

Seven candles and pentagram spell,
Around a circle, where shadows dwell,

She'll triumph now, the fiery dame,
Born from flames, she'll win the game.

Gypsies

It is purported, albeit through various anecdotal accounts, that the introduction of Gypsies into Umbanda occurred during the latter half of the 20th century. This introduction occurred through a medium who initially intended to channel Mestizos during a specific spiritual service. However, instead of Mestizos, the medium seemingly channeled an entity identifying herself as a gypsy. The presiding priest at the center harbored suspicions, deeming it a case of a lower spirit masquerading as something else. Despite initial skepticism, the channeling of that spirit persisted through days, leading the medium to disassociate herself from the Umbanda temple.

She came to realize that the spirit she was channeling was not malevolent but rather well-intentioned, prompting her to embark on a journey to Europe in search of historical context and further elucidation regarding the gypsy spirit she had encountered. Upon her return to Brazil, the medium established her own Umbanda center, welcoming a class of spirits simply referred to as "gypsies" to channel, impart wisdom, and offer assistance. As more mediums connected with and channeled the Gypsies, her temple in Rio de Janeiro emerged as the pioneering institution to engage with this specific group of spirits.

The Gypsies symbolize a unique and highly esteemed group of spirits, embodying the nomadic Roma peoples from various parts of the world, primarily Europe, but also from India, Egypt, and the Middle East. While many of them may have had previous lives as gypsies, some are spirits who have joined this group based on their affinities and professions, centered around promoting happiness, romance, freedom, and material prosperity. This inclination often arises from their past experiences, where many were predetermined to marry someone even before their birth, depriving them of the freedom to choose love. Also, in the pursuit of prosperity, many embarked on journeys across lands and seas, only to encounter limited success. Consequently, the Class of Gypsies offer a fresh perspective and a glimmer of hope to those seeking assistance in these aspects. In contrast to the charitable principles of Umbanda, gypsies tend to charge for their services, such as in oracle readings. However, in Umbanda centers, no fees or any charge is ever demanded. Another notable contrast lies in material opulence. Despite being regarded as a considerably elevated group of spirits, the gypsies indulge in golden objects, lavish feasts, and wealth, which contradicts the principles of material detachment upheld by the religion. Nevertheless, it can be understood that, ostensibly, the gypsies are addressing their own missed earthly desires by reflecting them and thus helping others prosper in those areas.

According to Bairrão (2004), the Gypsies' mission in Umbanda is to prophesy about the future, as they bring messages along the lines of "there is a way out; there is a path; another time is coming; there is another place to go."

The Gypsies descend, in terms of spiritual agroupation, from the peoples of the Orient, which encompass a great variety of spirits from the Middle East, Egypt, India, Nepal, Tibet, China, Japan, and others. Undoubtedly, all of these groups existed before the formation of Umbanda, hence, they use Umbanda and other religious or spiritualist platforms to aid those who seek their help there.

In Umbanda, they not only make significant contributions within their own class but also influence other classes and the entire Umbanda community. As a result, many Eshus and Pombagiras, belonging to their respective classes, also incorporate the distinctive traits of the Gypsies, such as their use of oracles, magical instruments, and other esoteric symbolisms.

Gypsies radiate a cheerful dream-like demeanor, mysticism, and a deep connection with magic and natural forces that often intertwine with flamenco-style rhythms, the arts, and feast celebrations.

Characterized by their vibrant attire, women typically adorn themselves in flowing dresses or skirts that swirl gracefully while dancing, as the men wear attire that resembles classy pirates, exuding a mystical elegance. Their appearance is further accentuated by golden accessories such as coin tiaras, headscarves, rings, necklaces, earrings, and bracelets.

Operating in the realms of happiness, Gypsies assist individuals in overcoming material attachments and past resentments. Their nomadic nature and love for celebrations enable them to help others navigate difficult times, dissipating bad moods and reducing attachment to material losses. Moreover, they excel in promoting prosperity, passion, and self-esteem.

They work with incense, flowers, and fire—candles being extremely important in their services—as well as other materials such as fruits, honey, sugar, and crystals.

The open fields are the places where the energy of the Gypsies may be stronger.

Offerings to this class include an array of fruits, breads, cider, wine, nuts, colorful flowers, perfume, incense, and golden coins. Colorful ribbons also hold special significance in their rituals.

Their favorite colors for candles vary from spirit to spirit, as these would reflect their workfield and, to some extent, their own caravan —or clan—they pertained to in a previous life. Nonetheless, the most common colors are blue, red, green, yellow, and golden.

In Umbanda, Shango and Egunita, the syncretized Orisha with Sara Kali—the patroness of the Roma peoples—preside over this class, highlighting their profound connection with divine fire and prosperity. Ogun, due to his nomadic attributes, may also influence this class.

Chant

Come and swing your skirt, let the fabric twirl and flow,
Round and round, clapping hands, gypsies dance in the glow.

Come and swing your skirt, let the fabric twirl and flow,
Round and round, clapping hands, gypsies dance with a glow.

Your eyes enchant, a beauty so divine,
Clap, clap, castanets, my lovely Spanish shine.

Another common chant, though mostly attributed to Gypsy Pombagira:

She gave me an old dress,
a gift from the gypsy fair,

What's mine belongs to her,
what's hers, I do not wear.

Gypsy little, little fair, little fair, little fair
Gypsy little, under the moon's glare.

Orient

The Class of Orient emerged in the early years of the founding of Umbanda when Orisha Mallet, a spirit believed to have been an Asian Muslim in his previous life, began working in the new religion alongside Seven Crossroads and Father Tony. The term "Mallet" was used by enslaved Africans in Brazil to refer to those who were Muslims, who were embracing their Eastern philosophy and culture. The word "mallet" originates from the Yoruba term *imali*, meaning a "renegade who adopted Islam."

During the 1930s and 1940s, many spirits from the Orient, often identifying themselves as doctors, predominantly Hindus, joined Umbanda. In the first decades of the religion, various Eastern entities manifested, including monks from Tibet and Nepal, gurus and yogis from India, samurais from Japan, and esoteric masters from Egypt. Each of them brought their philosophical methods of healing, viewing Umbanda as a means for their work in the Western hemisphere.

Not only is their alleged place of birth a mark of their origins, but the Class of Orient primarily works with a technique known as condensation and healing, which comprises the condensation of subtle light to heal individuals on Earth. Considered the most subtle and perhaps the most elevated class in Umbanda, they can reach very subtle light unlike any other spirits who work in the religion. Thus, the Class of Orient focuses on the healing of the spirit, using extremely precise and complex techniques for curing the soul directly.

This class incorporates esoteric principles from Hinduism, Buddhism, alchemy, and Hermeticism, as well as mystical and pagan elements from the traditions of the gypsies, Tibetans, and ancient Egyptians. Within the Class of Orient, one can also find spirits such as Mestizos and Old Blacks, who serve as chiefs of segments and phalanxes within the class.

The Class of Orient consists of many phalanxes or sub-classes based on their field of activity. Phalanxes of Chinese, Egyptians, and Indians (Hindus) are common. Egyptians are typically associated with hermetic, Rosicrucian, and Freemasonry groups of spirits; Hindus encompass teachings of Yoga, Brahmanism, and other Vedic schools; the Japanese and Chinese may bring teachings of *chi* or *ki*, Reiki, acupuncture, and other ancient East Asian understandings. In essence, Orientals represent the Asian influence in Umbanda.

Despite some Umbanda temples not offering services or cultivating a connection with the Class of Orient, these spirits are still present within the services as Old Blacks or Mestizos, either portraying an image that would be understood and accepted by the center, or by simply not channeling, but giving all invisible support to other spirit workers. These spirits manifest in every other spiritualist order in the world, regardless of whether their characteristics are acknowledged or understood, where they promptly choose another appearance [for those who can see them] and name.

Spirits of Orient typically dress in their cultural manifestation, with monks wearing robes and gurus wearing turbans. However, in Umbanda services, it is rare for mediums to dress according to the spirits they channel, as that class is more related to healing the spirit than other classes where their attires are important in the cult.

Open fields, mountains, and gardens are places where the energy of the spirits from the Orient is more pronounced.

Offerings include fruit juices, white flowers, lavender, and incense of myrrh and sandalwood. The Class of Orient commonly utilizes crystals, such as clear quartz and citrine. They also use candles, but alcohol and cigars are extremely rare.

The favored colors are white, as they are influenced by Oshala, and pale pink and blue, as Ibeji is another Orisha who patrons them in Umbanda.

Chants

The rising sun crosses the portal
Our masters come to present

Healing lights of body and soul
The people of the Orient

Cowboys

Although most Cowboys came from religious cults of shamanic roots and those of the countryside of North and Northeast Brazil, the first Cowboys to appear in Umbanda were among the Class of Mestizos, where initially it was somewhat difficult to distinguish them from the Mestizo spirits.

The Class of Cowboys pertains to spirits associated with the rural lifestyle, predominantly consisting of individuals who have, in their previous lives, lived in the countryside, and cultivated the land engaging with its fauna and flora. Despite their name, these spirits are not exclusively linked to cowboys or the contemporary equine and cattle industries. Instead, they might have lived previous lives as farmers or immersed themselves in agricultural pursuits.

Operating within the realm of Faith, they serve as mediators in various situations, akin to their ability to harmonize natural elements with their way of life. Primarily, they work in spiritual cleanse and in escorting obsessor spirits upon the rituals.

In the practice of Umbanda, the Cowboys act within both the Right and Left vibrations, although the Right vibration is their predominant modus operandi.

In the astral plane, the Cowboys primarily focus on managing obsessor spirits that aim to undermine individuals' self-belief or extinguish hope. Their role involves redirecting these spirits and preventing malevolent energies from infiltrating various spheres. For their work, the Cowboys use whips and lasso. Those who utilize the whips work in the fields of punishing unhinged spirits, as well as in the opening of paths; these Cowboys are related to Shango, the Orisha of Justice. On the other hand, the Cowboys utilizing the lasso are known for escorting and relocating those troublesome spirits. These Cowboys are commonly related to Ogun, an Orisha of order.

Despite their outwardly rigid demeanor, the Cowboys exhibit remarkable kindness and gentleness in their actions, indicative of their generosity, pacifism, and humility. Most Cowboys, however, are extremely cheerful and loud, and they enjoy dancing.

When channeled through a medium, they adopt a distinctive accent reminiscent of a humble rural dweller. Through this channeling, they instill a sense of simplicity, aiding individuals in navigating the complexities and challenges of urban life.

In the spiritual realm, the Cowboys typically appear dressed in dark blue, brown, or sometimes yellow attire, reflecting the typical clothing of rural inhabitants.

The open fields, plantations, and the general countryside are places where their energy may be better felt, where offerings may be more readily accepted.

Offerings include oranges, limes, pineapples, grapes, lentils, rice, beans, citric fruit juices, wines, and rum, along with straw cigarettes. Their favored herbs include lemongrass, basil, and seeds like bull's eye. Candles for them are commonly brown or red.

This somewhat less popular class within Umbanda is overseen by the Orishas Logunan, although occasionally Ogun may assume this role, and even more rarely, Yansa may serve as their patrons. In the initial period of their cult, however, they were believed to be overseen by Oshossi, as that is the patron Orisha of the Mestizos.

Chants

I'm a cowboy true, oh yes, my Lord,
A cowboy from the land, where I explore

Known as Cowboy in every part,
But Captain's the nickname, a name with heart.

Legions and Peoples

The spirits within Umbanda are structured into classes, phalanxes, legions, and peoples, based on hierarchical arrangements and affinities. However, outside Umbandist studies, these classifications may not always be applicable.

Each class of spirits in Umbanda is associated with a specific Orisha, who oversees and governs all the spirits within their domain. For instance, Eshus, Old Blacks, Children, Mestizos, Sailors, and Gypsies are linked to particular Orishas.

Within each class, there are seven Legions, each led by a Missionary spirit. These Legions comprise spirits embodying the traits and teachings of their respective Leader spirit. For example, a Mestizo Seven Crossroads leads all other spirits named Mestizo Seven Crossroads, forming a Legion.

Each Legion further includes seven Phalanxes, each with its unique focus and attributes. For instance, within the Legions of Pombagiras, there are phalanxes such as Mary Padilla, Mary Trashy, Seven Skirts, Pombagira Girl, of the Beach, of Souls, and of the Woods.

"Peoples" is a term colloquially used to denote spirits from the same or different classes and legions operating in the same locations. Although they share the same environment, they may differ significantly in their methods, tasks, and the domains they serve. For instance, "Pombagira of the Cemetery" and "Old Black Father Graveyard" are both part of the cemetery peoples, operating within the cemetery's locales but belonging to distinct classes and roles.

Spirits identified as 'Pombagira of the Beach' belong to the Pombagira class and serve under the influence of Yemanja. This particular phalanx specializes in tasks related to the beach, reflecting their dedication to Yemanja in matters concerning deep emotions. While multiple spirits share this designation, one spirit holds the position of chief within the hierarchy. That is, a spirit who was the first one to be named 'Pombagira of the Beach' leads all other Pombagiras of the Beach. Similarly, spirits known as "Mestizo Seven Mountains" belong to the Mestizo class and operate under the influence of Shango. The phalanx of "Mestizo Seven Mountains" is a group associated with the mountains (representing Shango) and operates across the seven domains. This allows for the identification of the class (Mestizo), the operational domain (in the seven domains), and the governing Orisha (Shango). While many spirits share the name 'Mestizo Seven Mountains,' only one is recognized as the chief or leader of the legion.

For spirits named "Father Jacob," they belong to the Class of Old Blacks (Father) and under the tenets of Ogun (Jacob). Whereas the Phalanx named "Father Tony" represents spirits that, in addition to being Old Blacks, are specifically dedicated to working under the influence of Ogun, and occasionally Eshu.

As a final example, spirits named "Little Peter of the Woods" belong to the Class of Children and operate under the guidance of Oshossi. The phalanx known as "Little Peter of the Woods" comprises Little Peters (Children associated with Shango) engaged in matters related to the woods, indicating their connection with Oshossi.

As mentioned, spirits in Umbanda do not possess names such as Catherine or Robert, or any reference to their previous lives. Instead, their names are derived from their class, phalanx, and legion affiliations. In essence, the name is obtained when, invited by the chief of the legion, the spirit acquires that name for themselves. For instance, "Little Peter of the Woods" denotes their class (Little, indicating Children); the Orisha they serve, which is Shango—Peter, derived from the Greek word "Petros" and Latin "Petrus," meaning "rock," as rocks and stones are emblematic of Shango—and their area of expertise, in this instance, the woods, symbolizing Oshossi and representing knowledge and prosperity. However, "Little Peter" is under the leadership of the chief of the legion 'Little Peter,' who imparts his name to his followers.

Within the classes, the leaders holding high ranks in each phalanx are referred to as the leaders of the Legion, given that their pupils are integral members of that legion. Legions, in this context, represent distinct groups within a phalanx that operate under the guidance of a high-ranking spirit.

"Peoples," however, are not bound by hierarchical relations; instead, they are a collective term for spirits who, irrespective of class or phalanx, share a common area of operation. All spirits engaged in activities related to the woods, for instance, such as Little

Mary of the Woods or Eshu King of the Woods, are collectively known as the "Peoples of the Woods." Similarly, spirits associated with cemeteries, like Eshu Skull and Pombagira Seven Graves, are naturally recognized as the "Peoples of the Cemetery." This naming convention applies across various realms of activity, like Peoples of the Mud, Peoples of the Cabaret, Peoples of the Beach, Peoples of the Lyre, and so forth.

Peoples of the Mud: Spirits serving Nana Buruke, Orisha of mud and slime, representing the decantation of emotions.
Example: Eshu of the Mud

Peoples of the Cabaret: Spirits operating in the nightlife; dealing with its dangers. Primarily Eshus, Pombagiras, and Bohemians.
Example: Pombagira of the Cabaret

Peoples of the Beach/Sea: Spirits working under the vibrations of Yemanja, particularly at sea, beaches, and coasts. All spirit classes have entities associated with the sea.
Example: Mestiza Jurema of the Beach

Peoples of the Cemetery: Entities who assist recently deceased people in detaching from earthly attachments.
Example: Eshu Skull

Peoples of the Lyre: Spirits associated with the arts, especially music, expression, and healing.
Example: Eshu 7 of the Lyre

Peoples of the Darkness: Spirits connected to what some perceive as 'hell' and the astral planes of cemeteries. Primarily Quimbanda entities, rarely seen in Umbanda.
Example: Eshu Darkness

Peoples of Magic: Spirits skilled in manipulating and dismantling energies. Primarily Pombagiras, Eshus, and Old Blacks.
Example: Old Black Conjurer

Peoples of Commerce: Spirits dedicated to cleansing and maintaining the energy flow in shops, businesses, and busy areas. Primarily Eshus, Pombagiras, and Bohemians.
Example: Eshu Draws Money

Peoples of Rubbish: Spirits who deal with the emotions of those burdened by low self-esteem and clinging to negativity. Primarily Pombagiras and Eshus.
Example: Pombagira Trashy Mary

Peoples of Fire: Spirits working with fire, often associated with Shango and Divine Justice.
Example: Eshu Spark Fire

Peoples of the Orient: Elevated spirits identified with Gypsy, Egyptian, Yogi, Monk, and Eastern philosophical traditions.
Example: Gypsy Ramon

Peoples of the Streets: Spirits who govern the crossroads, or the paths between the physical and spiritual realms. Primarily Eshus, Pombagiras, and Bohemians.
Example: Mary Razor

Peoples of the Woods: Spirits aligned with Oshossi and the energy of the woodlands. All spirit classes have entities associated with the woods.
Example: Old Black of Jurema

Bellow is a table containing the most well known phalanxes; an example of a class to which that phalanx belongs, and what that phalanx is commonly known as when referred to as 'Peoples.'

Phalanx	Class	People
Eshu Road Locker	Eshus	Peoples of the Streets
Pombagira Queen of Hell	Pombagiras	Peoples of Hell
Eshu Seven Graves	Eshus	People of the Cemetery
Old Black Conjurer	Old Blacks	People of Magic
Gypsy Ramon	Gypsies	People of the Orient
Pombagira Trashy Mary	Pombagiras	People of Rubbish
Little Joe of the Woods	Children	Peoples of the Woods
Eshu of the Mud	Eshus	Peoples of the Mud
Eshu Draws Money	Eshus	Peoples of Commerce
Mestizo Seven Arrows	Mestizos	Peoples of the Woods
Eshu 7 of the Lyre	Eshus	Peoples of the Lyre
Old Black Graveyard	Old Blacks	Peoples of the Cemetery
Mestizo Seven Crossroads	Mestizos	Peoples of the Road
Little Mary of the Beach	Children	Peoples of the Beach
Calm Tide	Sailors	Peoples of the Sea
Seven Waves	Sailors, Eshus	Peoples of the Sea
Lasso	Cowboys	Peoples of the Field

Obsessors, Dragons, and Cocoons

In Umbanda services, treatments for spiritual obsessions are commonplace. These obsessions usually manifest when a disembodied spirit fixates on the incarnated consultant. They are frequently fueled by unresolved grievances from past lives or by sorcery performed by others, prompting malevolent spirits to seek harm against the incarnated victim. Furthermore, obsessions can arise when the incarnated individual draws a suffering spirit due to mental and energetic affinity or addictions. In such instances, the suffering spirit feeds on the emanated energies generated by the incarnated individual.

These maladjusted spirits are commonly referred to as *kiumbas*, denoting their apparent lack of enlightenment. Some kiumbas, depending on their affiliation in the spiritual plane, are also associated with Kimbanda (Quimbanda). If so, they purportedly present themselves as Eshus and Pombagiras, offering their services in exchange for fulfilling specific requests. In this context, they claim neutrality regarding moral alignment, suggesting their capability to perform benevolent or malevolent deeds based on the petitioner's desires and what they can gain from them. Contrary to this portrayal, Umbanda maintains a distinct perspective on these entities, asserting that they are not genuine Eshus and Pombagiras but rather disembodied spirits manipulating and deceiving believers under the guise of such practices. According to channeled communications from Eshus and Pombagiras, these spirits are not aligned with their class, which exclusively serves the forces of 'Light' and the 'Most High' through the guidance of the Orishas. Despite the proclaimed neutrality of kiumbas, there is a belief that over time, some will reincarnate for another chance to redeem themselves, while others may transition into becoming dedicated workers for genuine Eshus and Pombagiras.

As there are hierarchies dedicated to the spiritual progress of Earth, there also exist hordes of spirits motivated by a thirst for control, a desire for revenge, harm, and avoidance of reincarnation. Their objective is not only to divert incarnate individuals from progressing but also to plunder their energy, thereby acquiring more means and power to interfere in earthly affairs. Among these spirits, believed to operate as leaders of lower astral mafias, are the Dark Wizards, occasionally interchangeably referred to as 'Dragons.'

Characterized by their exceptional intelligence, these spirits have, over centuries or millennia, evaded reincarnation, subsisting on semi-physical energies stolen from incarnated spirits. Accumulating knowledge and energy, these malignant entities exercise control over numerous other spirits who become their subordinates. Although all these spirits were once incarnate humans, their inclination toward control, animosity, and opposition to the Divine often manifest in intimidating and frightening appearances. This is also true for the regions they inhabit.

Dark Wizards command legions of spirits, predominantly comprised of those who, in life, committed crimes, were generally psychopaths, or engaged in other nefarious activities. In the afterlife, these spirits find themselves in lower zones where malevolent spirits forcibly recruit them. This recruitment aligns with the laws of cause and effect, as well as laws of affinity.

As the world collectively emanates more compassion, they find themselves with fewer means to continue controlling their own astral zones and avoiding spiritual ascension—a process governed by divine law. Therefore, sooner or later, these spirits decide to evolve, typically beginning the process in an astral hospital before undergoing reincarnation, whether on Earth or in another realm. However, this change in mindset is never an internal calling; instead, it usually arises from their observation that their subordinates are being drawn to treatment and reincarnation, indicating a decrease in their numbers.

Dark Wizards seldom engage directly in battles or visit the surface on the astral plane, as they cannot do so given their vibratory condition. Instead, they delegate tasks to their legions, instructing them to obsessively control individuals to hinder their spiritual evolution and to steal their semi-physical energy. They employ various forms of manipulation, such as influencing culture through music, video, and literature to disseminate malicious messages and emphasize mundane and addictive sensual content, which is also observed in eating habits and drug addictions. They also exert influence in politics, although this is a more intricate arena due to the karmic history of nations being a sensitive issue. Nevertheless, they tend to influence societies that, in one way or another, contribute to the rise of governing powers.

Traditionally, both ordinary obsessors and their leaders are commonly referred to as obsessors or kiumbas. However, the rich Umbandist and Spiritist literature, exemplified in works by Ranieri (1989) and Pinheiro (2013), among others, has introduced a broader range of nomenclatures into Umbanda. This infusion appears to draw from the wellsprings of Spiritism, particularly in relation to the spirits' realm.

As observed by the mediums and priests who conduct "disobsession" sessions at Umbanda centers, it has been noted that malignant spirits participating in low magic—where incarnate individuals procure their services to harm others—or in cases where a high-ranking obsessor aims to induce depression or illness in someone, may employ various tools. These tools include what can be understood as chips installed on individuals' astral bodies; ropes and chains aimed at hindering someone's progress; veils, blindfolds, toxic liquids, and other spiritual apparatuses. However, one of the most common instruments they employ is an item usually referred to as a "cocoon."

A cocoon derives its name from its ovoid shape, and it typically consists of a spirit—commonly someone who, during their life, pursued nefarious paths and upon physical death had their astral vehicle completely annihilated due to a constant and absolute thought of sadness, revenge, or fear. In such instances, they no slowly become unable to manifest a form in the astral realm. These spirits are almost certainly incapable of communication or voluntary movement. The cocoons, or ovoid spirits, are said to portray opaque grey spheres approximately the size of a basketball.

Fixed in their regrettable thoughts, they emanate a potent vibration of these emotions, which sinister spirits then use to place them near an incarnate person, such as within someone's home, thereby inundating them with those thoughts.

During disobsession services, the Umbanda spirits channeling through the mediums are usually able to perceive these cocoons, and they subsequently detach them from the individual undergoing treatment. These cocoons are not only removed from the individual's home or surroundings but are also treated.

In the spiritual realms, benevolent spirits may assist them in acquiring a new astral body, typically necessitating reincarnation onto the physical plane. Their initial incarnation following cocoonhood, however, is typically brief and depicts a malformed infant.

According to Umbanda tenets, God is pure love, and the divine hierarchies ceaselessly work to assist all beings. Nonetheless, malevolent hierarchies are permitted to exist due to the laws of affinity and cause and effect. The creation of problems by humanity necessitates encountering karmic lessons, observable in the lives of a significant portion of both the incarnate and disincarnate worlds. Along these lines, Umbanda teachings assert that to reduce the influence of obsessors or Dark Wizards on humanity, people must choose to replace hostile and selfish thoughts and actions with more altruistic ones. In essence, both sides coexist, yet God and the forces of Light cannot choose for the people, respecting their human free will. Consequently, everyone is allowed to resonate with ideas and actions aligned with themselves, attracting consciousnesses that share a similar nature to their lives.

The Temple's Layout and its Tools

In the physical temple, a specific arrangement of objects and directional guidance is consistently followed. For instance, the main altar, where the primary source of energies is located along with imagery, candles, and other objects for the Orishas, is commonly used for initial salutations before the services. Within the temple's altar, only Orishas of the Right polarity are venerated. Orisha Eshu, however, is worshiped solely outside the temple walls. This also applies to spirits of the Left polarity, Eshus, and Pombagiras.

The mediums reserve a central space in the temple for channeling and receiving the audience for spiritual cleansing, while the attendees' seats during the services surround this main space. Besides the main indoor altar and the shrine of Eshu outside, various temples will also have an external area commonly called 'the Soul's Cross.' This place comprises an erected cross where candles and prayers are offered to those who have died. However, this place is primarily designed for the candles and prayers to Old Blacks who work in the domains of cemeteries, as well as to the Orishas Omulu and Obaluaye.

The Altar

The altar functions as an amplifier of waves emanated by the Universal Orishas. It also serves as an attractor, drawing thought-forms from the attendees and purifying and draining them with the assistance of Cosmic Orishas. The altar also continuously sustains an aura visible to clairvoyants. This part of the temple is where the vibrations of the Orishas are most potent, making it the optimal place to submit petitions for more effective responses.

The altar typically features images of the temple's patron Orisha, who is the head-Orisha of the priest who founded the house. This Orisha is also the patron Orisha of the priest's head-Entity, understood as the founding spirit of the temple.

Image 7: Altar at a Sacred Umbanda temple.

The altar usually follows a triangular structure, with the temple's main Orisha positioned at the top. The images of the priest's counter-Orisha and ancestral-Orisha are usually placed on the bottom-left and right of the top image, signifying that those three are the main Orishas revered in that temple. Four other Orishas are positioned in descending order, forming the triangle shape. Vases with water for the Orishas, symbolizing the source for emanated or purified energies, may be present as well.

A sacred stone is commonly buried beneath the altar, signifying the altar's fixation in that corner. By each statue, a candle for the respective Orisha, along with glasses of beverages, flowers, and other offerings, is placed. At the bottom of the triangle, below the shelves containing the Orisha representations, are the statues representing the phalanxes working in that temple, which essentially include entities pertaining to the Right polarity. Candles and offerings for those spirits are also placed there.

The shrine for Eshu and Pombagira, however, is located outside the walls of the Umbanda temple, often in the garden or near the temple's entrance. This separation is essential due to the diverging frequencies between Eshu and Pombagira, the other Right-polarity entities, and the Orishas' altar within the temple. The shrine of Eshu and Pombagira can be understood as headquarters for managing dense and heavy energies. It is a center of dissipation and movement that is closest to the physical world.

While other Orishas and entities operate primarily within the temple walls, the influence of Eshu and Pombagira extends beyond the temple boundary. Eshus and Pombagiras are the guardians of the entire premises and protect the sacred space from interfering obsessor spirits. They are uniquely capable of containing these entities.

The shrine is typically on the ground. Statues and offerings are placed directly on the floor. A "stone of Eshu" is buried below the shrine to fix its energy point. A copper wire is usually buried, connecting the temple's entrance to the shrine to filter dense energies. This separation of energies is also observed in the homes of Umbanda practitioners. The Right-polarity altar, usually for a single Orisha, should be kept separate from the Left-polarity space for Eshu and Pombagira. This typically means a small altar for the Right-polarity deity inside the home, while offerings and candles for Eshu and Pombagira are placed outside.

Tools of Umbanda

Umbanda rituals incorporate a diverse array of objects and tools, constituting an essential set of instruments utilized by the entities during services. These encompass cigars, cigarettes, pipes, beverages, candles, special chalk, statues, herbs, water vases, and even items such as capes and hats, which channel mediums may employ to facilitate the spirits' work.

All the instruments and tools employed in Umbanda, whether they appear overtly evident in the cult, such as candles, or take on a mystical guise, carry profound significance within the tradition. Their utility extends beyond mere symbolism, as each element serves a well-defined and purposeful role in the rituals.

Cigar, Cigarettes, and Pipes

The sight of mediums seemingly smoking during Umbanda services may raise questions, especially for those unfamiliar with the tradition. Despite appearances, the entities involved do not engage in earthly activities like smoking; rather, the symbolic use of pipes, cigars, and cigarettes holds a deeper meaning that transcends mere indulgence. Contrary to some beliefs, these "smoking tools" are not connected to any lingering earthly attachments of the entities. Instead, they serve as instruments for smudging, a potent cleansing practice intended to purify the environment, the mediums, and the public.

The key to understanding the ritual smoke lies in the concept of the etheric-double—a subtle energy body present between the physical and spiritual body, holding vital energy and connecting the two. When the spirit, who channels via the medium, blows the smoke infused with the medium's own etheric energy, dense negative "astral larvae" or "gunk" are cleansed and dissolved.

Tobacco is considered a potent vessel for cleansing power. Its etheric composition, enriched by minerals, water, and the sun's energy, makes it effective when combined with fire and air. Importantly, the smoke is not inhaled but mixed with the medium's breath, further amplifying its purifying effect. In some instances, mediums may excrete ectoplasm[24] during deep trance or focus. This semi-physical element, believed to be a blend of subtle organic compounds, adds another layer of energy to the smoke. The efficacy of cigars, cigarettes, and pipes lies in their use during exhalation, infusing them with the individual's intention and etheric energy.

While entities can perform their work without smoke, these traditional tools resonate with the public on a familiar level.

---

24 Ectoplasm is a semi-physical, gaseous, and semi-gelatinous substance that mediums excrete during trance, deep focus, panic, or delirium (Barreto, 2019). It is a combination of carbon dioxide, hydrogen, albumin, potassium, and glucose produced by the organic cells of the body. In contact with physical photons, it rapidly evaporates. In spiritualist hospitals, healers use this fluid, which the physical body produces and the astral body controls to some extent, as a vital source of energy to help materialize physical cells and tissues. Only a specific type of medium can externalize ectoplasm. Ectoplasm is invisible and can rarely be seen, except when observed as a translucent substance under low, red light.

Throughout history, smoke has been employed by shamans and folk healers worldwide for cleansing and protection, making it a readily understood and accepted practice in Umbanda rituals.

It is essential to note that other herbs like sage and rosemary are also utilized in these rituals, each offering unique cleansing properties and energetic signatures.

Beverages and Alcohol

Similarly to tobacco, alcoholic beverages are observed being consumed by the mediums during channeling in almost all Umbanda temples. An Umbanda service demands that the medium intermediates between dense energies and the spirit at work, making themselves prone to suffering the repercussions of contact with those  energies. The energies in question include the cleansed energies from the public, the removal of debris from the space, the dissolution of energetic threads, and even the dismantling of mental nodes and lower magical objects. Exposed to these energies, the medium must find a way to cleanse them from their energetic body.

These energies are semi-physical, meaning that while the spirit channeling may have the power to cleanse the spiritual side of them, the semi-physical aspect of these energies cannot be reached with a conductor such as alcohol and its semi-physical properties. The etheric properties of alcohol are substantially potent in terms of disinfection and serve to cleanse the medium's energetic field during the service. As a volatile element, alcohol enters the individual's body cells and, once processed, transfers to the medium's semi-physical aura, thereby disinfecting it.

This process of alcoholic influence within one's aura differs from the mere act of drinking alcohol recreationally. The energies that permeate the medium's aura during the service are categorically dense and, in most cases, nefarious. The alcohol, in those instances, is imbued by the entity to become a disinfectant for that ritualistic purpose. On the other hand, recreational drinking of alcohol results in harm to one's auric fields, as alcohol coerces it, without necessarily dissolving the negative stains within it.

Candles

One of the most widely utilized instruments within Umbanda is candles. In the realm of symbolism, the flame of the candle alludes to a mysterious energy that appears almost otherworldly, while the paraffin may symbolize the physical form of a person, where the wick represents the head. With roots dating back to early times and deeply ingrained in both Christian and pagan circles worldwide, candles hold more than symbolic significance or visual manifestation and serve as tools that collaborate with the bridging of physical and semi-physical elements in ritualistic practices.

Within Umbanda, the candle is regarded as a fundamental tool that facilitates the connection between the physical and spiritual realms. The act of lighting a candle is believed to transcend the ordinary into the ritualistic, as the flame, once ignited on the physical plane, is thought to be kindled simultaneously on the spiritual plane. Thus, its subtle radiation is assumed to bridge the two realms.

In ritual practice, including that of Umbanda, candle flames are deemed to emit a vibratory signature specific to the element of fire, holding semi-physical properties. Consequently, candles are employed to expedite processes, imbuing them with specific movement and altering the oscillation of etheric objects. When lit, the candle is expected to emanate intentions as vibrations. Furthermore, the color of the candle serves to distinguish the wave associated with the vibratory signature emitted by the flame. For instance, a violet candle aligns with the vibratory nature of Nana and the domain of Evolution. This choice of color is not only symbolic but also indicates how that instrument is perceived in the etheric plane.

Evoking an antenna in the altar or as an offering, Umbandists tend to pray to or speak to the candle before lighting it, as well as anointing it, although the latter is less common. Once lit, the candles must be allowed to burn until they are completely consumed, especially in controlled areas, for safety reasons. In rituals involving deities, candles typically require approximately 5 minutes of burning before they are extinguished.

As an offering, the candle is often the most prominent item, sometimes being the sole item presented.

Herbal Baths and Smudging

Herbs hold a prominent position in Umbanda, serving diverse functions ranging from their use in baths, burning for smudging, incorporation as whiskers in cleansing rituals, offering to deities, to their cultivation as plants that emit a vibratory signature aligned with their energetic properties. Additionally, they are associated with the

vibratory essence of each Orisha. Drawing inspiration from shamanic, Yoruba, and Celtic traditions, the extensive knowledge surrounding herbs establishes them as a fundamental component of the cult.

When utilized for their purported extra-physical powers, plants contribute their qualities as a whole, meaning that any part of the plant used will consistently yield similar, albeit not identical, results. While plants possess both physical and semi-physical auras, their they represent a broad magnetic field that transcends individual bodies, seamlessly connecting with other plants and soil.

In Umbanda, all plant parts are collectively referred to as 'herbs,' with leaves and petals typically favored for rituals.

In Umbanda, herbs[25] are categorized as hot, lukewarm, or cold. Hot plants possess purifying properties and act aggressively on the

---

[25] It is important to note that these classifications pertain to their extra-physical nature and may not align with their botanical or traditional value descriptions.

etheric-double of objects, spaces, and beings. They are used for energetic disinfection and deep cleansing. Examples include rue, camphor, tobacco, belladonna, and guinea pepper (*Schinus terebinthifolius*). Warm herbs balance and rebuild the auric field, donating the plant's qualities to one's energetic body. Examples encompass rosemary, sage, peppermint, basil, chamomile, fennel, uplift (*Croton gossypiifolius*), and road opener (*Croton heliotropiifolius*). Cold herbs serve specific purposes. For example, some attract energies, such as blackberry and cinnamon. Others provide vitality, like sunflower and coffee leaves. Still, others induce calmness, including lemongrass, wormwood, Melissa, and Valerian.

Mediums commonly prepare particular herbal baths before conducting services, a tradition from which the general public can also derive benefits. The process entails grinding the herbs into water, meditating over the mixture with the assistance of a candle, invoking a specific entity to activate its magical properties, taking a regular shower or bath, and then pouring the infused concoction over the body. Finally, the individual dresses after a gentle drying process. However, for herbs known as 'hot,' it is advisable to avoid pouring the mixture directly on the head, focusing instead on the shoulders down, to prevent potential harshness on the crown chakra, or *ori*.

Herbal baths are recommended for auras saturated with imbalanced emotions, while smudging is suggested for dissipating or energizing thought-forms. Smudging is often employed in the temple, either before or after services, serving the same purposes as herbal baths. Incensing, although practiced by Umbandists, involves burning herbs directly in thuribles or, when conducted by mediums or in offerings, cigars are used.

When used as whiskers, certain herbs are believed to possess the property of attracting nefarious dense energies to its leaves, provided an appropriate ritual has been performed to activate such mechanisms. Common herbs used in these rituals include rosemary, rue, and others, which are then discarded or burned following the cleansing.

As offerings, herbs serve to make particular semi-physical elements readily available to the spirit, although it is more common to see offerings of flowers or fruits, rather than herbs.

Bead Necklace

In addition to the widespread use of rosary beads in Catholic culture, Africans also brought their tradition of using bead necklaces to the New World. Sheales[26] (2012) comments that, in pre-colonized Africa, cowrie shells were considered a form of currency. As storing wealth on the body was considered the most effective method among the people, they utilized these shells in necklaces. In the African tradition, Orisha Eshu, known as the lord of commerce, contributed to the association of wearing cowrie shell necklaces with wealth.

While cowrie shells are not commonly found in Umbandist bead necklaces, they, along with Catholic rosaries, were initially introduced by the spirits of Old Blacks, the founding entities of Umbanda. This practice was also emphasized by new adherents of Umbanda with roots in other slave descent cult circles.

Primarily worn for their impact on energetic points, also called chakras, the bead necklace is to be understood as an amulet energetically magnetized by the entity or spirit worker of that entity it is attributed to. It serves to bring the vibratory emanation of the entity to the medium's or devotee's energetic body. For this reason, the necklace should always be worn in contact with the skin, never entirely over clothing.

The materials used in the making of necklaces must be, invariably, crystal, stone, porcelain, or glass. Those that include seeds and vegetable fibers are also common. Plastic is strictly avoided, as it is believed to block the energies or lack the proper qualities for the frequency of an entity to cling to. The clasp, where the two parts of

---

26 British Museum · Curator's comments: "Cowries throughout Africa are symbols of wealth and well-being and, in some parts of West Africa, were used as a form of currency."

the necklace close, is commonly made of a different material than the rest of the beads or, usually, of a different color.

The necklaces should be of the color associated with the operating entity. For instance, a necklace for Eshu would typically be black and red, alternating between one black and one red bead, or seven black and seven red beads. For Orisha Logunede, it might consist of milky blue and yellow or golden beads, and for Yemanja, it would comprise white and pale blue beads.

Bead necklaces are instruments that emanate energy but also serve as protection, with thinner necklaces being more related to protective uses.

They are worn during services at the temple, and it is rarely necessary to wear them outside the place of worship. However, some mediums continue to wear them outside the temple for reasons of continuous energetic protection.

Crystals and Sacred Stones

All stones or crystals are associated with different Orishas. Several cultures, which have identified or fabricated a plurality of gods and heavenly deities to represent the frequencies of creation in a practical manner, have found that 'frequency' serves as a form of identification of a non-physical nature. These cultures permit devotion to be conducted through personified entities rather than adopting an inconceivable, and yet hardly known scientific approach, such as 'frequency' or 'vibration.

In Umbanda, the use of crystals, as observed in the New Age movement, is not necessarily prevalent. However, stones of power that represent and serve as conduits to the vibration of an Orisha are common within certain types of Umbanda. Both Esoteric Umbanda and Sacred Umbanda incorporate crystals into their practices, although many Umbandists of other traditions also include them in their individual spirituality, such as in home altars.

Crystals manifest various divine frequencies. Despite not being characterized as prototypes of spirits, elementary particles of matter do have a spiritual origin, traceable back to one of the facets of God on Earth – the Orishas. Physical molecules have non-physical counterparts on subtle planes.

According to Umbandist teachings, all crystals are related to Faith and, thus, to Oshala, signifying that the holographic particles of that crystal resonate with or were generated by the Divine frequency of Faith, which eventually manifested in the material plane. Nevertheless, all other rocks are believed to relate to Shango.

Clear crystals generally consist of particles generated by frequencies associated with faith, while other crystals receive the influence of different Divine traits. For instance, rose quartz, a type of macrocrystalline or coarse-grained quartz, symbolizes love. This Divine composition empowers rose quartz with the ability to propagate faith through love, meaning it propagates the vibration of Oshala in manner akin to Oshun.

Each crystal relates to its own kind of friendly resources, including sunlight, moonlight, fire, specific herbs, smoke, water, sounds, and other minerals. This correspondence is based on equivalent Divine frequencies that formed or sustain such elements. Crystals naturally belong to the mineral kingdom, conferring physical life through experiences that do not necessitate active interactions with the environment. Despite primarily externalizing mineral vibration, each variety of crystal may also manifest other elements based on its formation and molecular composition.

Crystals inevitably exert influence over the auras of other crystals, plants, animals, and humans. However, the extra-physical functions of crystals are limited to the etheric barriers of bodies. In other words, only the physical and semi-physical aura of individuals may be affected by crystalline electromagnetic fields. Crystals, therefore, cannot influence an individual's spiritual aura or activate mediumistic or parapsychic abilities, as these are inclinations of consciousness, not of the semi-physical ether. Despite the intrinsic characteristics of parapsychic abilities, which pertain to the soul, crystals may only aid in cleansing or slightly influencing one's outer auric field but cannot 'activate' them. However, in Umbanda, crystals seem to serve a more ritualistic purpose, acting as points of magnetism that spirits use to root or link and emit their vibration.

Such sacred stones are usually referred to as *ota*, which are stones typically buried beneath certain altars and believed to fixate the entity's energy in that specific point. These stones are typically gathered by the priest of the temple at the natural point of strength of that entity. For instance, a sacred stone of Oshun would be respectfully collected at the waterfalls; one of Ogun would certainly be collected near a train rail; that of Yemanja at the beach; that of Nana at a lake or swamp; for Shango on the top of a mountain or hill; for Oshala, any stone found in an open field; one of Ibeji in the gardens; for Eshu at any crossroads; for Omulu and Obaluaye at a graveyard or deserted land; for Yansa in the fields, especially those with bamboo trees; for Oshossi, a stone kindly collected in the deep woodlands; for Logunede, a stone found in the waterfalls or woods; for Oshumare at the waterfalls; for Oba at the margins of a wild river, and so on.

Ritual Chalk and Sketched Points

A specific type of chalk, crafted from a blend of chalk and herbs, although it is also commonly found made solely from chalk material, serves as a ritualistic tool in Umbanda. This tool is utilized to draw circles, sigils, and various symbols on the floor or on a wooden board placed on the floor. Its purpose is to represent and establish a connection with the spirit participating in the service.

Before its use, the chalk tool is usually imbued with the characteristics of a specific class or polarity of spirits. This involves a blessing from a spirit belonging to that class, whereby they magnetically trace circles with the vibratory signature typical of their group. That is, if an Eshu, channeling through a medium, 'blesses' the piece of chalk, that piece of chalk may not be used for any other class of spirits or Orisha, other than Eshus and Orisha Eshu. Consequently, various pieces of chalk, each linked to different domains, can be found in Umbanda centers.

The circles and sigils created with this chalk are referred to as "sketched points." These points serve as centers of force and portals that spirits utilize during the services. Typically, these portals are promptly closed after the service concludes.

The sigils, or circles, are traced by the spirit during channeling, implying that the medium, before the service, is not responsible for their creation. Circles usually consist not only of a circular line but also include symbols that identify the spirit. For example, a circle containing a large trident might represent an Eshu; a large arrow would represent a Mestizo; a big cross would denote an Old Black; a large lolly would signify a Child, and so on. The number of particular symbols within a circle, such as seven little crosses, for instance, corresponds to the seven domains in which that spirit operates. For example, seven little crosses would indicate that the spirit works in the seven domains as a worker of Omulu, where the cross signifies the domain of Omulu, associated with cemeteries.

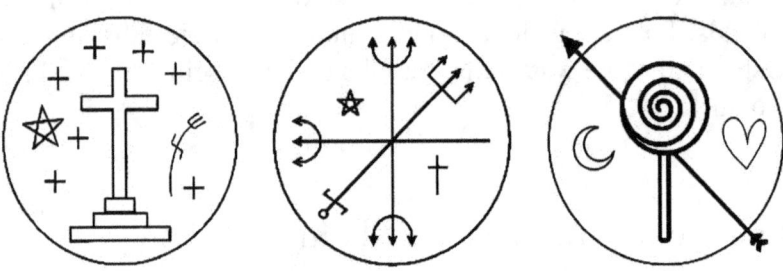

Examples of sketched points: Old Black Conjurer; Eshu Shadows; Golden Arrow Kid

During services, it is common to observe personal objects being placed within the circle for the spirit to magnetize or work on. Additionally, mediums often deposit public petitions within the circle. In the astral realm, the spirit is understood to receive these written messages through the sketched portal, mirroring it in the physical world. Some centers will employ daggers if a spirit requests it during channeling. The daggers are usually affixed onto a wooden board, which is assumed to firmly anchor the spirit's energies effectively.

Other symbols indicating the field of operation are also present in the sigils. For example, tridents are indicative of whether the sigil pertains to an Eshu or Pombagira (tridents with angled corners denote Eshu, while those with rounded corners are attributed to Pombagira). Roses indicate that the spirit is a Pombagira associated with the phalanx of 'Mary' (not the mother of Jesus, but rather Mary as in the Pombagiras who operate under the frequency of Oshun, syncretized as Virgin Mary). Additional symbols, lines, and shapes found in sigils further specify their class, phalanx, or field of operation.

Symbols based on their field of operation	
rose, trident, skull	Pombagiras
trident, skull	Eshus
herb / leaf	Herb workers; of Ossain
fire / flame	Eshus, Gypsies
triangle	Old Blacks; Orient
anchor	Sailors

The symbols based on the Orishas they serve	
sun	Oshala
waves, stars, anchors	Yemanja
lightning, wind, chalice	Yansa
heart, moon	Oshun
cross	Omulu; Obaluaye
bow and arrow	Oshossi
key, branch	Nana
sword	Ogun
axes	Shango
snake, rainbow	Oshumare
lollies, candy, doll	Ibeji
trident	Eshu

Occasional Items

On occasion, a vase containing water is observed adjacent to an offering or positioned near the altar of an Orisha. These vases symbolize the human form, specifically the individual's energetic body.

A simple bell is occasionally utilized to signal the commencement and conclusion of spirit channeling by mediums.

Although uncommon in Umbanda rituals, gunpowder finds application in ceremonies aimed at dispelling curses and spells. It serves to disperse the energy underlying the spell, given it has been imbued by an entity.

Mediumship and channeling

The majority of individuals associated with an Umbanda center, particularly those fulfilling roles as temple workers, possess mediumistic abilities. In essence, Umbanda, akin to Spiritism, constitutes a faith wherein mediums[27] serve as conduits for spiritual communication and assistance. Consequently, most of those tasked with conducting services are either established mediums or individuals in the process of developing their mediumship skills. The latter group undergoes categorical studying, training, and supervision under the guidance of the resident priest of the house. Once deemed ready, such mediums are able to engage in channeling spirits for public services.

During a service, the mediums are aware of the entities by their sides—entities set to channel in that service. They chant to maintain focus and achieve a lower brainwave frequency, in states believed to allow for auric expansion, creating the possibility for the spirit to link up.

---

27 As proposed in the 2019 book "Supernatural Science: Theory and Magic" by David Barreto, spirits may imprint mediumship characteristics in their genes before reincarnating, particularly when they choose or are advised to develop such abilities during their physical life. According to the author, spirits opt to reincarnate as mediums driven by a karmic debt or a mission. The purpose of mediumship, in these terms, is to assist others and address the medium's own past transgressions in the realms of the paranormal, mediumship, and faith. From a spiritual perspective, spirits deliberately choose, and are guided to choose, compatible physical bodies aligned with their inherent nature and future lessons. Family selection before birth is grounded in shared experiences, contributing to the formation of "group karma." The chosen parents' genes reveal the traits intended for the spirit's reincarnated life, resulting in an optimal matching between spirits and physical bodies.

The densest aura field of a discarnate spirit is somewhat similar, in terms of mass and frequency, to the astral aura of an incarnated human. If the auras of both individuals come into contact by mutual agreement, they can form a common aura, enabling one to influence the other. Therefore, the thoughts and commands present in the spirit's aura field are absorbed by the astral aura of the medium, subsequently perceived by their semi-physical aura, and then captured by their chakras, which function as energy transformers. Following this, the chakras convert the semi-physical information into electrical signals for the neurons, ultimately influencing the medium's behavior.

For a complete channeling—bearing in mind there are different levels, ranging from spiritual influence to full channeling—the energy vortices of the medium must interconnect with the spirit's. This connection allows the spirit to control specific body parts for externalizing other forms of communication or behavior. The interconnection of the medium's chakras with the spirit's is facilitated by magnetism, or what can be understood as a sort of magnetic pairing. When the chakras of both parties interconnect, the spirit gains direct access to the body regions that the chakra is responsible for. If the spirits couple their auras with only the top three main chakras of the medium, they can access the medium's mind and speech organs but lack control over their bodies. In instances where the spirits couple their respective auras but can only pair their lower chakras with the medium's (due to the medium's lack of concentration), the spirit can influence the medium's movements and manners, though comprehensive ideas may not be fully understood.

In channeling, the medium invariably retains total control, as the entity cannot impose power on the medium's will. Consequently, all channeling is executed by the medium, with the spirit merely suggesting ideas, speech, and movement. Ultimately, mediums listen to and sense the entity, replicating their words and behavior. Overall, the medium's actions and activities are influenced but not controlled by the third party. For more on the mechanisms of mediumship, refer to Barreto's 2019 book, "The Supernatural Science."

What may be misconstrued as a form of spiritual possession is not representative of the occurrences within Umbanda temples. For that reason, it is essential to differentiate between spiritual channeling and spiritual possession. In the practice of channeling, the entity couples their aura with the medium's astral aura, creating a unified field. Additionally, the spirit remains beside the medium at all times and does not enter the medium's body. In contrast, spiritual possessions are characterized by malevolent entities purportedly linking their chakras to the victim's, exerting control over their senses, including synaptic activity, and therefore influencing their behavior and emotions. In most possession instances, the spirit is so intertwined with the victim that an abrupt removal from the victim's aura could lead to physical death.

The Medium's Spiritual Guide

The Umbanda center is overseen not only by its medium priest or priestess but also by other mediums responsible for channeling spirits during services. Typically, these mediums channel various spirits regardless of their class or polarity of work. However, each medium has what they refer to as their 'head entity': the spirit that primarily guides them in their religious works and private lives. This guidance encompasses advice, protection, and instructions on how to proceed during channeling services, as the spirits are there not merely to visit but to perform tasks, such as cleansing, healing, and more.

While everyone has spirit guides, who may not necessarily be actively involved in their lives, the continuous presence of the spirit guide is crucially necessary for the medium or spiritualist worker. The medium's primary spirit guide, whether a Pombagira, Mestizo, Old Black, or others, serves as the main entity that accompanies the mediums in their services. It is common for mediums to have more than one spirit guide, although a specific one usually takes the lead in most situations. For those not affiliated with Umbanda, the same principle applies. Any individual has their spiritual guides, albeit in the case of a clairvoyant, they may appear in a more local or familiar form and name. For example, an Old Black or Pombagira guiding an Umbandist medium might manifest as a nurse to someone of a pure

Catholic background, or as a Renaissance philosopher to someone more inclined toward scientific or agnostic beliefs. Nevertheless, the spirit worker may not necessarily play an active role in cases where the individual is not a medium.

Umbanda asserts that each inhabitant of the world has a spirit guide, which is distinct from the 'guardian angel,' another spirit that accompanies everyone. The guardian angel is perceived as a benevolent spirit providing advice and mentoring for spiritual progress. In contrast to the Abrahamic concept of a perfect being, the guardian angel is understood to be a human spirit who is familiar with and willing to assist the person in their current incarnation. One's 'angel' also plays a role in planning the individual's paths of reincarnation.

Chants

To facilitate the medium's channeling of a spirit or to facilitate their coming under its channeled influence, several methods are employed. During the service, mediums may engage in chanting accompanied by percussion, utilizing a predetermined rhythm. This practice is believed to induce their brains to adapt to the sound patterns, leading to altered states where their brainwave frequency changes to one typically associated with channeling.

It is probable that chants developed through a fusion of church hymns, Afro-drumming circles, and shamanic rhythms. In the initial years of formal Umbanda, percussion was notably absent. However, with the incorporation of additional Afrocentric elements, including a broader spectrum of Orishas, worker spirits, and, significantly, practices derived from the traditions of Macumba circles, percussion chants emerged as an indispensable component.

As crucial as the lyrics are, keeping the mediums or devotees immersed in thoughts regarding that entity or collective of spirits, the rhythm of each chant follows a specific and well-defined structure. Music, or more precisely sound, has the capacity to influence the mental and emotional states of individuals. As demonstrated by Will and Berg (2007), sound can also influence brain waves and cognitive responses through brainwave synchronization and auditory stimuli.

In a parallel scenario, music serves as a tool to enhance focus both before and during the channeling process. It not only induces a shift in brainwaves but also assists in maintaining the individual's attention on the character of the music, often aligning with a spirit resonating with the theme of the music (Barreto, 2019). In the case of Umbanda chants, the rhythm associated with Yemanja, for instance, represents a mild and usually mid-paced interval, resonating with the characteristic vibratory nature of her domain. Conversely, Ogun's chants reveal a faster rhythm, with the tempo reflecting the velocity at which his vibration operates. For this reason, in almost all Umbanda centers, percussion plays a vital role, with specific percussionists maintaining the rhythms throughout the entire service.

The chants of Umbanda, which are recited during services but also sung at home for appreciation or the pleasure of listening, constitute the music associated with every Orisha and every class and legion of spirits. These chants serve as worship pieces wherein the entity and their qualities are exalted and recalled. The lyrics are crafted in a poetic manner, allowing it to be easily understood. Chants, having been conveyed through channeling, are no longer being composed or transmitted. This is because the chants for all Orishas, classes, and nearly all legions have already been introduced and cataloged.

Chants for each spirit within certain classes commonly share the same tempo and rhythm, with only the lyrics and melody varying. For example, in the chant for the spirit of the phalanx Gypsy Pombagira, three characteristics can be assessed: lyrics, tempo, and melody.

"Walking on foot, to meet Pombagira
She read my palm, and showed me a mirror

Truth she said, no lies to spread
Is she the one, the one in red?"

Lyrics:
In the lyrics, a simple message is conveyed poetically through the imagery of a gypsy lady on the road who tells fortunes. The message provides essential information about the spirit:

'walking on foot' refers to the road, indicating where Pombagira operates; under the tutelary of Eshu or Ogun.

'She read my palm' alludes to her phalanx of Gypsy Pombagira.

'Is she the one, the one in red?' suggests her identity as Pombagira related to self-steam and desire, since they typically wear red.

Tempo:
The pace is measured in BPM (beats per minute), and for Eshus and Pombagiras, it tends to be fast and very fast, described in music theory as *allegro* and *presto*, respectively. Chants for Pombagira would commonly be played and sung at a tempo ranging from 168 to 200 BPM.

Melody:
The melody, often overlooked, reveals whether the spirit is inclined to extroversion or introspection, or if it is a spirit of fierce action or calculated attitude. The melody is the most memorable and identifiable part of each chant, and it provides more information than the lyrics alone, based on emotional expression, contours, scale, and mode.

The Services

Services in Umbanda centers are predominantly held in the evening rather than the morning. These sessions, typically open to the public, offer them the opportunity for consultations or energetic cleanses conducted by channeling spirits. However, certain days of the week are designated for private services, during which the mediums work on their own personal spirituality, while trainee mediums practice their ability to channel spirits. This practice is essential for both the mediums and the spirits they channel. Mastery of mediumship is crucial to avoid potential pitfalls, such as mistaking spiritual influence for imagination or excessive animism. Animism, derived from the Latin word *animus* meaning "soul," refers to mental phenomena or behaviors produced by an individual without external interference. Thus, mediums undergo rigorous training to distinguish the impression of spirits from their own thoughts, in order to accurately portray them, avoiding preconceived ideas.

In both open and private services, the space is ceremoniously cleansed by the priest and other members. This involves smudging the area and preparing it for the specific vibrations of spirits expected to manifest during the service. Additionally, candles, beverages, and various tools are prepared for the spirits who will channel during the service.

An altar is meticulously arranged to accommodate candles and various objects. However, before services commence, it is customary to make offerings to the Eshus and Pombagiras of the house. In the outer part of the temple, even a modest offering such as a candle is placed for the guardian Eshu. More elaborate offerings are made, particularly on days dedicated to services for the Left polarity. Some centers opt to offer directly to Orisha Eshu, the patron of Eshus and Pombagiras.

Offering to Eshu, whether to the Orisha or the spirit, is of utmost importance as they are regarded as guardians who seal the sacred place before any spiritual work begins. Additionally, Eshu is perceived as the force that moves energy; hence, its movement is considered essential for optimal results in a service.

Following the offerings to Eshu, attendees start to arrive. As they gather around the main space of the center, the mediums, under the guidance of the priest, conduct a prayer that reveres, in most cases, God, Jesus, the Orishas, and the classes of spirits slated to channel that evening. Subsequently, they engage in chanting specific to the class of spirits they are about to channel. In cases where the service is not centered on channeling but is instead a worship day for a particular Orisha, the chants persist throughout the entire session.

As the service officially commences, chants, typically accompanied by percussion, are sung by the mediums and the attending public, if familiar with them. The mediums, immersed in deep focus, begin to channel the spirits designated for that service. Generally, the medium [channeled spirit] manifests by vocalizing their distinctive greetings; for instance, Eshus and Pombagiras often laugh loudly, Mestizos may hooray, Old Blacks usually bless in a quiet voice, and Children may exhibit playful behavior, such as jumping.

Through the medium, the spirits appear to assume control over the movements, behavior, and word, thereby engaging in various activities, such as requesting a drink or cigar, having their candles lit, and tracing their sketched points or circles. Simultaneously, they work on astral tasks like cleansing the premises, manipulating energies, isolating obsessor spirits, and connecting the energy wires of the attendees to their tools, addressing issues specific to that service.

When the entities are prepared to provide energetic cleansing and magnetization, they typically inquire if individuals wish to express or ask about anything, signifying a consultation. During the cleansing, which is performed beforehand the possible consultation, the entity may blow cigar smoke on the person's body, use herbs to whisk them, or perform the cleanse using the medium's hand movements.

During the consultation, the spirits attentively listen to the individual, who often inquires about issues for which they seek solutions. The entity typically provides advice, explaining the situation and suggesting actions for resolving the problems. Frequently, this advice emphasizes the connection between occurrences and the individual's thoughts, emotions, and actions. In certain instances, the spirit may request the person to write something on a piece of paper, which is then magnetized and placed over their sketched portal. After the service, these petitions are said to be collected and worked on in the spiritual realms. Alternatively, the spirit may magnetize a candle, handing it to the individual with instructions to light it at a specific day and time either at home or elsewhere. On-site rituals may also occur, involving the magnetization of objects, cleansing with alcoholic drinks, or imbuing items with herbal energy. These consultations, which typically lasts for approximately 10 minutes, conclude with the individual being invited to sit back, while the spirit attends to another person from the public. It is crucial to emphasize once again that absolutely nothing during the service is ever charged.

The spirits channeling usually receive assistance from a non-channeling member of the center, who may not be a medium but is dedicated to aiding the mediums and spirits by handling objects, guiding the public, and performing other tasks during the services.

Once the public is energetically cleansed, the spirits continue channeling, guiding other spirits, manipulating energies, and completing their tasks before departing. From the perspective of the public, however, it may seem like the spirits are merely dancing to the rhythm of the chanting or focused on their sketched points.

At a specific time, typically within a few hours of service, the main spirit channeling, often the one channeling the priest of the temple, announces that the spirits are ready to depart. The percussionists are then invited to play a farewell rhythm. Shortly after, all the entities appear to have departed. The mediums then offer salutations to the entities, Orishas, Jesus, and God once again, signaling the conclusion of the service for both the mediums and the public, who then leave.

Festivities

Every Orisha has a designated day of the year for worship, typically aligning with the feast days of the saints with whom they are syncretized. For instance, Oshossi's day, celebrated on January 20th, coincides with Saint Sebastian's day, Oshossi's syncretized figure. Temples often treat the day festively, involving the active participation of the public. On that day, Umbanda centers dedicate themselves to Oshossi, featuring the class of Mestizos channeling to amplify Oshossi's ashe.

This festive spirit is particularly renowned on Ibeji's day, dedicated to the infant Orishas and the Children of Umbanda. During their celebration, the public is invited, receiving bags of sweets, pieces of cake, and toys, echoing the tradition observed nationwide on the syncretic figures' day, Cosma and Damian, as well as on the national Children's day.

Devotees honor the Orisha on these days through offerings, prayers, and celebrations, whether at temples, at home, or in natural settings. In the woods, beach, fields, riverbanks, and so on, practitioners may present fruits, beverages, candles, and other offerings to the Orishas, absorbing their emanations in their highest form.

Devotees at home may also choose those specific days to reverence that Orisha, offering the year's sole tribute. Many opt to present offerings to each Orisha just once a year, aligning with their specific days.

These celebrations hold profound significance in Umbanda, serving as reminders of each Orisha's unique essence and emphasizing the interconnectedness of every manifestation of the divine within the larger whole.

Offerings

Offerings presented to the spirits or Orishas in Umbanda serve the purpose of aiding in a request or fortifying the relationship between the individual and the entity.

As previously noted, there exists a prevalent misconception that the spirits, to whom these offerings are dedicated, eat and drink the presented items. In reality, the entity or spirit manipulates the etheric-double of the elements offered, provided that these foods and objects resonate with the frequency in which they operate.

When an offering is given, various elements may contribute to its vibratory signature, such as chants, symbols, or prayers, enabling the spirit to readily access that etheric-double through holographic portals built by varying vibrations. Through chanting and prayer, the etheric-double of the elements is volatilized, and the chanter imbues the offering with their intention of presenting it to a deity.

The etheric-double, defined as the semi-physical energy that permeates all material beings and objects, is abundant and robust in humans and animals, less so in plants, even less in minerals, and nearly absent in artificial objects such as plastic.

During a ritual, when specific foods or objects are presented to a spirit, the aura of the offerer and that of the offering are drawn together. Throughout this process, the offerer imprints their mental and emotional signature, via vibratory emanations, on the offering's aura.

As the offerer extends their aura onto the offering, the energetic signature of the deity to whom the offerer is dedicating it is imprinted upon the offering. This process allows the etheric-double of the offering to loosen and become more readily absorbed by that entity. When the devotee's aura and the etheric-doubles are within the same auric field, the etheric-double of the offering is separated from its physical counterpart and is absorbed by the entity through a mental command.

This process resembles luminous smoke or radiant steam that emanates from the offering. If the petition is accepted, the spirit in charge of the offering will shape that energy and often transform it into a thought-form after absorbing its semi-physical emanation.

It is understood that the spirit will only proceed with the ritual if their superiors approve it. Benign entities will typically base their decisions on the laws of cause and effect to determine whether a desire should be fulfilled or not. On the other hand, if an offering is given to a malignant entity, they may proceed with the ritual anyway, but the outcomes may quickly dissolve, as universal laws do not solely depend on spirits or deities to exist; these laws[28], as observed in Umbanda, work ceaselessly for all.

Thought-forms play a crucial role in the concept of 'probable future,' where future occurrences unfold in holographic form before manifesting as physical reality. The thought-form created by the entity, which constitutes the majority of procedures upon receiving an offering, is intricately linked to the offerer, becoming their own. The entity contributes its magnetism to facilitate the development of the thought-form into an actual probable future, ultimately bringing it to reality by linking it to the offerer. However, this does not guarantee its effective occurrence, as it depends on factors such as the individual maintaining the artifacts' magnetism. In other words, if the offerer changes their mind or strongly thinks or feels something that contradicts the thought-form, the initial thought-form will lose its magnetism and dissolve.

Not all offerings serve solely to produce thought-forms; they may also act as a source of semi-physical energy required by an entity to operate in the physical realm. Upon harnessing these energies, entities can manipulate them to imbue a tool, create or magnetize an object, strengthen one's aura, and perform other actions, bridging the spiritual and earthly realms. In the context of Umbanda, it is recognized that even though spirits possess considerable capabilities, when individuals request tangible outcomes in the physical realm, they require semi-physical elements to bring those requests to

---

28 Due to affinity, the harmful work with offerings may progress. For example, if a malignant desire to affect another discovers that the victim was a malignant sorcerer in the past, the works proceed to harm them, aligning perfectly with the laws of cause and effect.

fruition. Moreover, semi-physical elements provide the offered spirits with additional energy to undertake more challenging tasks, if needed.

The rhythm of the chants, the color of the candle, and the herbs used in the incense can all reflect energetically similar qualities to the essence of a particular spirit, at least in terms of the emanations they convey. For example, when making an offering to Oshun, it is ideal to include components that emit vibratory qualities akin to those associated with Oshun's domain. This means that the elements included in the offering should stem from sources with frequencies analogous to the realm of love, which is synonymous with Oshun's essence. In the case of Oshun, the elements offered may include, but are not limited to, melons, apples, and other juicy fruits, sweet beverages, fragrant incense, yellow flowers, as well as makeup, perfumes, mirrors, and delicate decorations. In this way, a spirit working in the vibration of Oshun can use the etheric-double of liquids, sugars, natural pigments, and objects as material to produce thought-forms associated with the desired request to the Orisha. It is recognized that presenting an offering to a deity that diverges from their essence is likely to hinder its acceptance. Therefore, if an offering intended for Oshun includes whiskey, chilies, or black candles, it may contradict the vibratory nature of the Orisha, which is closely associated with love or beauty, symbolized by water, sweetness, and colors like pink or yellow. In contrast, whiskey, chilies, and black candles do not align with these vibrations. Consequently, sourcing the appropriate elements for any ritual offering is crucial.

In order to determine the frequency of such an element and its vibration, it is important to understand its physiological, botanical, and chemical components. Generally, the color of an element indicates the frequency of its etheric-double. Reds are associated with agility, vitality, conquering, and sexual energy; thus, red fruits and drinks, as well as red objects, almost certainly connote one or more of these qualities, making them suitable offerings to Orishas such as Ogun, Shango, Eshu, and spirits such as Eshus and Pombagiras. In this manner, the color red is mostly associated with spiritual entities that play a role in self-esteem, desire, and karma, as it utilizes organic pigments and reflected light as color to produce extraphysical objects. Nevertheless, the quantity of water present in the elements also reveals the temperament of the spirit, that is, their field of work.

Image 8: Offering to Pombagira

Red fruits high in water, like watermelons and apples, will rather assuredly be related to entities dedicated to love matters and relationships. If their pulp is red but not their peel, the fruit is more suitable for lack of desire petitions; if the peel is red but not the pulp, this fruit is more suitable for wishes regarding situations that lack or need emotional interest. Red fruits with a low water content, such as chili peppers and pomegranates, are typically associated with physical vitality and enthusiasm.

Orange-colored foods and objects, for instance, are invariably associated with movement and enthusiasm. Orange is the second-fastest color in this case; yellow, on the other hand, relates to self-esteem, wealth, happiness, and beauty; green invokes work, studies, health, and growth; blue relates to mental clarity and a lengthy perspective; and violet is linked to purification and change. Despite red light being considered to travel more slowly[29], while violet light is considered the fastest, humans perceive the opposite with their extra-physical senses, experiencing red as faster and violet as slower. This discrepancy arises from human's low capacity to perceive violet light, whereas they are more attuned to red light due to its closer alignment with their physiological composition. Thus, what is perceived to be a slow frequency from violet is actually one's inability to sense it.

The pigments and water content of the offering should be the best indicators of its etheric attributes; this correlation is based on the travel speed of the element's etheric photons.

---

[29] In the context of refraction, where light passes through a medium like glass or water, the speed of light varies for each color due to their different wavelengths. This phenomenon is known as dispersion, where different colors are bent by different amounts. Shorter wavelengths, such as those of violet light, are refracted more (or slowed down less) compared to longer wavelengths, such as those of red light. Therefore, within the context of refraction, violet light is typically considered to be refracted the most quickly, while red light is refracted more slowly.

The same principle holds true for beverages: the more alcoholic they are, the longer their oscillation will be. Therefore, alcohol may be used in offerings to deities who work in the cleansing of places and auras or in protecting or guarding specific places and people. The nature of the beverage's components, such as malt, vegetables, barley, fruits, or herbs, may also determine its corresponding use. In like manner, juices and water relate to entities that work with emotions, relationships, family cases, self-esteem, and harmony between individuals. Therefore, Orishas such as Yemanja, and Oshun, and spirits such as those of the classes and phalanxes of Sailors, Mermaids, and Mestizos are the best receivers of such offerings. The sweeter the beverage, the more it is related to love, as fructose and its chemical subdivisions also collaborate with joy, passion, and euphoria.

Image 9: A ritual offering to the spirits of Children

The shapes and forms of the elements displayed in an offering also play a crucial role when sourcing for a specific deity. Pointy leaves and sharp-edged fruits, commonly used in offerings to Eshu and Ogun, indicate great movement. Entities associated with the emanation of peace, like Yemanja and Oshala, as well as their spirit workers, are often presented with round fruits and round leaves.

Furthermore, the tactile nature of the element can provide insights into the associated entity. Velvety elements, characteristic of Orisha Oshala and Old Blacks, are linked to the color white, conveying peace, faith, and ascension. On the other hand, hard shells and thick, dry leaves, as found in the cult of Omulu, are associated with the healing of traumas. Thorns and needles, as seen in offerings to Obaluaye, symbolize emotional traumas and the initiation and ending of cycles.

Overall, it is crucial to consider the entire composition of foods and objects in the offering based on the nature of the intended entity and the desired outcome of the ritual.

Another specific point is that when an offering is given to an Orisha, it is not the Orisha who collects it, but a spirit who operates in the frequency of that Orisha. The Orisha, in this context, is to be understood as an intelligent movement of forces, and not as a being or as a spirit who needs offerings.

Unlike many religions where offerings are integrated into rituals, in Umbanda, placing an offering is deemed essential to initiate the flow of energy. While similar mechanisms may apply to offerings in other religions, Umbandists are distinctly aware that their offerings are not intended to appease or merely please an entity. Instead, the offerings are viewed as instruments that empower spirits to carry out their work in other realms.

Offerings in Umbanda range from simple candles to elaborate banquets and can be made regularly or in response to specific requests. For regular offerings, adepts often adhere to fixed days and times for rituals. For example, there might be a large offering to Yemanja on a specific day each year, while a candle and sparkling wine are offered to a Pombagira every Monday.

A significant annual offering comprises a variety of elements such as fruits, flowers, beverages, objects, candles, incense, and more. This offering fulfills the devotee's yearly commitment to the associated Orisha. While not explicitly mandated, devotees uphold this tradition, considering it a substantial offering that will imbue them with the vibratory blessings of the Orisha throughout the year. Similarly, a weekly ritual involving a candle offered to a specific spirit is practiced with the intention of enhancing the spirit's capabilities. This ritual aims to foster a close connection between the spirit and the devotee, allowing the entity to consistently impart protection and positive vibrations.

The initial procedure, whether conducted in the temple or at a home altar, involves the devotee lighting a candle for their designated guardian angel. This guardian angel, as per Umbandist tenets, is considered a kindred spirit with a vested interest in the spiritual progress of the individual. Often referred to as a spiritual mentor, this spirit may have shared past lives with the incarnate person, choosing to mentor their protege after attaining a higher level of awareness in their spiritual journey. As the devotee lights a candle for their guardian angel, typically accompanied by a glass of water, a prayer is recited. This prayer seeks the mentor's participation in the rituals by safeguarding the space and elevating its frequency, thereby aiming at keeping less empathetic spirits at bay.

Subsequently, when making an offering to an Orisha, it is customary to begin with an offering to a spirit of Eshu, or more rarely, to Orisha Eshu. This practice is rooted in the belief that both Orisha Eshu and its spirit workers are intermediaries who convey messages to the Orishas. In this context, it is understood that due to their proximity to the physical plane, the entities of Left polarity may be the only ones fully capable of accessing the entirety of physical offerings.

The size and complexity of the offering to Eshu, be it the Orisha or a spirit worker, align with that of the main offering. For example, if the primary offering is an elaborate feast for Shango, the offering to Eshu or Orisha Eshu might consist of a *padê* (pronounced pah-day), a simple dish comprising cassava flakes mixed with palm oil and commonly adorned with 7 red chilies. This offering should be accompanied by a glass of whisky or rum and a cigar. Similarly, if the offering to Shango involves just a glass of dark beer and a red candle, the offering to Orisha Eshu or an Eshu spirit typically includes only a black and red candle and may also feature a cigar or a glass of rum or whisky.

The offerings are meticulously prepared and presented on the altar. In the case of offerings to Eshu or Pombagira, they are arranged on their respective altars or at a crossroads. While offering outside the temple or home may not be common due to public hygiene habits and urban laws, offerings to Eshus and Pombagiras are invariably conducted in external spaces.

The time lapse between offerings to the guardian angel, Eshu, and an Orisha is generally negligible. Once an offering is presented to an entity, the devotee can promptly proceed with offerings to another.

The act of giving an offering begins with the individual assembling it by the altar, crossroads, or another appropriate location. As a preliminary step, they light the candles. If cigars are employed, the individual may draw on the cigar and, without inhaling the smoke, blow it over the entire offerings. At this point, they may invoke the entity by uttering their name, accompanied by their typical salutation and clapping. The devotee initiates a conversation with the entity, which may be articulated aloud or maintained in silence. Upon completion, they may clap a designated number of times, signifying the conclusion of the offering.

Image 10: Elaborate offerings for the Orishas. The first column features offerings to Yemanja, Shango, and Ibeji, while the second column is dedicated to Ogun, Oshossi, and Yansa.

Glossary

A

Ashe: divine energy; analogous to prana.
Astral: that which relates or belongs to the astral plane; the spiritual plane where spirits without a physical body dwell.
Astral plane: a level or dimension of existence beyond the physical universe.

B

Bohemians: (Umbanda) spirits of those who look like and act as the hedonists of urban areas of the 19th century.

C

Caboclo: (Umbanda) how 'mestizos' or 'amerindian' spirits are referred to in Portuguese.
Cabula: a cult that was one of the precursors of Umbanda; religious circles that included Afro-Brazilian, Catholic, and indigenous elements.
Calundu: slave gatherings for rhythmic drumming, dance, and ritual trance.
Candomblé: an exclusively Afro-based religion emerged in Brazil, where the cult of many Orishas is put as one.
Chakra: a vortex of energy; a center of etheric or astral mass located in diverse parts of the body.
Channeling: (spiritual) the communication of a spirit via the physical body of a medium individual.
Class: (spiritual) an extensive group of spirits who use the same archetypal traits for their spiritual work.
Clairvoyant: an individual who can see beyond the physical plane.

Counter-Orisha: the Orisha who is present in someone's life to balance the excessed influence of the head-Orisha.
Cowboys: (Umbanda) spirits who portray the appearance and behavior of those typical of the countryside.

D

Domain: (spiritual) a frequency in which a certain divine expression is found; all that relates to a specific Orisha.
Deity: a god or high-ranking spirit believed to be of great importance.

E

Ectoplasm: a semi-physical substance that some individuals excrete during trance, deep focus, panic, or delirium.
Enchanted: (Umbanda) spirits who may have never incarnated on planet Earth.
Enlightenment: the process or state of achieving spiritual advancement.
Entity: any spirit or higher-ranking individual who is of respectable position.
Erê: a spirit who portrays an appearance and behavior of children.
Etheric: the fluid, wave, or particle that is too subtle to be considered only physical but too dense to be considered fully spiritual.
Etheric-double: the energetic counterpart of a physical body.
Extraphysical: that which exists beyond its physical particles.

F

Folk-healer: a person of modest demeanor who employs prayers, amulets, and other religious artifacts to provide assistance to the local community.

H

Head-Orisha: the Orisha who governs the individual's life journey; the most important Orisha in someone's life.

I

Incarnate: to enter a physical body to experience life in the physical plane.
Incarnated: the spirit who has a physical body and thus dwells in the physical plane.
Incarnation: the process or condition of entering or having physical life.

J

Juvenile Eshu and Pombagira: spirits who portray the appearance and behavior of preteens, who work in the fields where Eshus and Pombagiras do.

K

Kardecist: related to Allan Kardec, the founder of Spiritism; that who follows Kardec's philosophy.
Karma: the experience an individual or group of people undergo as a result of their past actions; a planned consequence based on the law of 'cause and effect.'

L

Laroye: a salutation used by the devotees to Orisha Eshu and the spirits of Eshu, Pombagiras, Juvenile Eshus and Pombagiras.

M

Macumba: generic terms for circles of religious expressions where practitioners may get into trance on the rhythm of percussion; a musical instrument used in primitive African-Brazilian circles.
Magnetization: (spiritual) imbue with or emanate etheric or spiritual fluids onto something or someone.
Mediumistic: relating to mediums or the channeling of spirits.
Mesmerism: the practice of inducing a trance or altered state of consciousness in individuals through focused attention, often associated with healing or therapeutic purposes; to project or guide healing energy onto others.

Mestizo: spirits who work in Umbanda maintaining an appearance of native peoples of Brazil.

O

Obsessor: a spirit who haunts, harms, or energetically drains an incarnated person.
Old Black: wise and kind spirits who portray an appearance and behavior of former enslaved and elderly people to convey humility and forgiveness.
Ori: derived from Yoruba, signifies the "head," denoting the crown chakra or the pivotal point of the incarnated soul where the essence of the Orisha is located.
Orisha: deities who are understood as the expression of God on Earth; forces of nature.

P

Padê: the common offering to Eshu and its spirit workers, such as Eshus and Pombagiras; a mix of cassava flakes or corn grits mixed up with palm oil, rum, or honey.
Pass: (spiritual) the act of projecting healing fluids, usually performed in Spiritist and Umbandists centers.
Phalanx: (Umbanda) a group of spirits working under a specific leader, typically in a designated field or area.
Physical Plane: a level or dimension of existence known as the physical universe.
Prana: vital life force or energy that permeates the universe.
Proto-Yoruboid: the reconstructed common ancestor or proto-language from which the Yoruboid languages are believed to have descended.
Psychic: an individual who has any paranormal ability, such as clairvoyance or lucid astral travel.
Psychography: the production of written material by spirits via the use of a medium's hand and arm; automatic (or spiritual) writing.

R

Reincarnate: to be born again in the physical plane.
Reincarnated: the spirit who has a physical body and thus dwells in the physical plane.

Reincarnation: the experience or condition of being reincarnated.
Reiki: a technique where an individual draws subtle healing energy and guides it to whoever and wherever it is needed.

S

Séance: a gathering or session conducted to communicate with spirits.
Sigil: a magic or esoteric symbol.
Sketched points: (spiritual) the circle and symbols drawn by the spirits during channeling that serve as temporary portals.
Spiritism: a doctrine based on the immortality of the spirit, reincarnation, and altruism, that emerged in France and is popular in Brazil, from which Umbanda drew its foundations.
Spiritist: that which or who relates to Spiritism.
Spiritualism: a school of thought and movement that states that life continues after death and that spirits may communicate with the living.
Syncretism: the blending of two or more religious beliefs into one; how a deity is observed as though pertaining to other cults.

T

Tent: how Umbanda temples used to be called in its first years.
Throne: (see Domain)

Y

Yoruba: that which relates to the Yoruba people, from West Africa, and their religion, language, and cultural traits.

Bibliography

Akintoye, A. (2010). *A History of the Yoruba People*. Dakar: Amalion Publishing.

Aubrée, M., and Laplantine, F. (1990). *La Table, le Livre et les Esprits: Naissance, évolution et actualité du mouvement social spirite entre la France et le Brésil*. Paris: Lattès.

Bairrão, J. F. (2004). "Espiritualidade brasileira e clínica psicológica." In V. Angerami-Camon (Org.), *Espiritualidade e Prática Clínica* (pp. 193-214). São Paulo: Thompson.

Barreto, D. (2019). *The Supernatural Science: Theory and Magic*. London.

Bastide, R. (1978). *The African Religions of Brazil*. London and Baltimore: The Johns Hopkins University Press. (Originally published in 1960 as *Les Religions Afro-Bresiliennes: Contribution à une Sociologie des Interpénétrations de Civilisations*. Paris: Presses Universitaires de France.)

Beniste, J. (2006). *Mitos Yorubás: O Outro Lado do Conhecimento*. Rio de Janeiro: Bertrand.

Brandon, G. (2009) 'World View and Divinity', in Molefi Kete Asante & Ama Mazama (eds.), *Encyclopedia of the African Religion*. Thousand Oaks: Sage Publications.

Braude, A. (2001). *Radical Spirits: Spiritualism and Women's Rights in Nineteenth-Century America* (2nd ed.). Bloomington: Indiana University Press.

Brock, W. (2008). *William Crookes (1832–1919) and the Commercialization of Science*. Aldershot: Ashgate.

Cadwallader, M. E. (1917). *Hydesville in History*. Chicago: Progressive Thinker Publishing House.

Carroll, B. E. (1997). *Spiritualism in Antebellum America*. Bloomington and Indianapolis: Indiana University Press.

Cossard, G. O. (2006). *O Mistério dos Orixás* (2nd ed.). Rio de Janeiro: Pallas.

Cuchet, G. (2012). *Les Voix d'Outre-Tombe: Tables Tournantes, Spiritisme et Société*. Paris: Seuil.

Davenport, R. B. (2013). *The Death-Blow to Spiritualism: Being the True Story of the Fox Sisters, as Revealed by Authority of Margaret Fox Kane and Catherine Fox*. Charleston: Repressed Publishing LLC. (Originally published in 1888).

Doyle, A. C. (1926). *The History of Spiritualism*. New York: Arno Press.

Duncan, J. (1987). Translator's *Preface* to Kardec's *The Gospel According to Spiritism*. London: Headquarters Publishing.

Faraday, M. (1853). "Experimental Investigation of Table-Moving." *Journal of the Franklin Institute*, 56(5), 328-333. Amsterdam: Elsevier.

Hessen, J. (2016). *Os Primórdios do Espiritismo: A História do Espiritismo No Brasil*. São Paulo: Autores Espíritas Clássicos.

Kloppenburg, B. (1991). *Espiritismo: Orientação Para os Católicos*. São Paulo: Loyola. (Original work published in 1964 by Vozes).

Lachapelle, S. (2011). *Investigating The Supernatural: From Spiritism And Occultism To Psychical Research And Metapsychics In France, 1853-1931*. Baltimore: The Johns Hopkins University Press.

Lawrence, E. A. (1994). The Centaur: Its History and Meaning in Human Culture. *Journal of Popular Culture*, 27(4), 57. Oxford: Blackwell Publishing.

Maior, M. S. (2013). *Kardec - A Biografia*. Rio de Janeiro and São Paulo: Record.

Olumide, L. (1948). *The Religion of the Yorubas*. Lagos: C. M. S. Bookshop.

Pinheiro, R. (2013). *Os Guardiões* (from the trilogy *Filhos da Luz*). Belo Horizonte: Casa dos Espíritos.

Prandi, R. (2000). *Mitologia dos Orixás. São Paulo:* Companhia das Letras.

Ranieri, R. A. (1989). *O Abismo*. São Paulo: Editora da Fraternidade.

Reis, S. M. (2011). *Universo Umbandista*. Joinville: Clube de Autores.

Rivail, H. L. (1828). *Plan Proposition pour l'Amélioration de l'Éducation Publique: Couronné par l'Académie Royale d'Arras*. Paris: Dentu.

Rivers and Civilizations: What's the Link? (2007) Debating the Documents." College Entrance Examination Board. Culver City: MindSparks.

Saraceni, R. (1993). *O Livro das Energias*. São Paulo: New Transcendentalis.

Sheales, F. (2012) *Asante Gold Regalia in the British Museum collection*. BM, London.

Silva W. W. (1956). *Umbanda de Todos Nós*. Rio de Janeiro: Esperanto.

Smith, C. (2004). *Latin American Religion in Motion*. London: Routledge. (Originally published in 1999 by Routledge).

Smith, F. (2013). *Vedic Meru and Nile Pyramid: African Ifa to RigVeda-Pachisi to Tarot to Llull to Cartan-Dirac-Riesz-E8 Physics*. viXra, 1305.0060.

Stuart N. R. (2006). *The Fox Sisters: Spiritualism's Unlikely Founders* (originally published in 2005), viewed at: https://www.historynet.com/the-fox-sisters-spiritualisms-unlikely-founders/ [Accessed 23rd June 2021].

Vartier, J. (1971). *Allan Kardec: La Naissance du Spiritisme*. Vanves: Hachette. p. 114.

Verger, P. (2019). *Lendas Africanas dos Orixás* (Posthumous). Salvador: Solisluna.

Weisberg, B. (2005). *Talking to the Dead: Kate and Maggie Fox and the Rise of Spiritualism*. San Francisco: HarperOne. (Originally published in 2001).

Will, U. and Berg, E. (2007) 'Brain wave synchronization and entrainment to periodic acoustic stimuli.' *Neurosci Lett.*, 424(1), pp. 55-60. doi: [10.1016/j.neulet.2007.07.036. Epub]. PMID: 17709189. [Accessed 23rd June 2021].

Xavier, F. C. (1938). *Brasil: Coração do Mundo, Pátria do Evangelho*. (by Spirit Humberto de Campos). Rio de Janeiro: Federação Espírita Brasileira.

Further Readings

Johnson, K. Phd., and Tunde Oyinade, R. Phd. (2004). *Monotheism in Traditional Yoruba Religion, The Concept of God: The People of Yoruba, Thinking About Religion.* Vol. 3. Fayetteville: Fayetteville State University.

Johnson, S. (1921). *History of the Yorubas: From the Earliest of Times to the Beginning of the British Protectorate.* London: G. Routledge & Sons. Original from: Indiana University.

Mathias, J. (2017), 'Seeing is Believing: Spiritualism in the Victorian Era-Part 2', *Curious Histories,* viewed at: https://oldoperatingtheatre.com/seeing-is-believing-spiritualism-in-the-victorian-era-part-2/ [accessed on 8th February 2024].

Nery, N., & Cysneiros, I. (2004). *Fundamentos de Umbanda: Revelação Religiosa.* São Paulo: Cristális (originally published in 1978).

Stoll, H.W. (1852). *Handbook of the Religion and Mythology of the Greeks,* translated by R.B. Paul.

Credits

Image 1:
Description: The Fox Sisters.
Date: 1884
Source: 'Nineteenth century miracles, or, Spirits and their work in every country of the earth: a complete historical compendium of the great movement known as 'modern spiritualism,' New York: Published by William Britten: Lovell & Co, 1884.
Author: Emma Hardinge Britten.
License: Public domain.
Reference: The Fox sisters, by Emma Hardinge Britten (Published by William Britten: Lovell & Co, 1884).

Image 2:
Description: Parisian salon with people practicing three variations of table-turning using a ring, a table, and a hat.
Date: 14 May 1853
Source: Journal "L'Illustration" from 14 May 1853.
Author: Ange Louis Janet (1815–1872).
License: Public domain.
Reference: "Histoire de la semaine, L'Illustration," Paris, 14 May 1853.

Image 3:
Description: Brazilian stamp commemorating the centenary of the codification of Spiritism.
License: Public domain
Date: 1957.
Source: Brazilian Government.
License: Public domain.
Reference: "Selo de comemoração do centenário da codificação espírita."

Image 4:
Description: Gabriel Malagrida (1689-1761), an Italian Jesuit missionary in the colony of Brazil and influential figure in the political life of the Lisbon Royal Court.
Date: Circa 1760s-70s
Source/Photographer: Biblioteca Nacional de Portugal
Reference: "Padre Jesuíta Gabriel Malagrida."

Image 5:
Description: Zelio de Moraes.
Date: 1939.
Author: Arquivo TENSP.
License: Public domain.

Image 6:
Description: Statue of Yemanja – The queen of the sea.
Date: 27 December 2010.
Source: Leandro Neumann Ciuffo
Note: Some people were digitally erased from the photo.
Source: http://www.lciuffo.com/
viewed at
https://www.flickr.com/photos/leandrociuffo/5297404821/in/photostream/
Reference: "A rainha do mar. Praia do Meio, Natal, RN, Brazil."

Image 7:
Description: Altar at Umbanda Sagrada Templo do Sol de Aruanda.
Date: February 2020.
Source: Terreiro de Umbanda Sagrada - Templo do Sol de Aruanda.
Location: São Paulo, Brazil.

Image 8:
Description: Full offering to Pombagira. Consisting of red candle, gari, roses, golden coins, cigarette, and sparkling wine.
Source: viewed at https://www.youtube.com/@UmbandaOnline [accessed on 25th March 2024].

Image 9:
Description: Offering to Children spirits.
Source: Terreiro de Umbanda Sagrada Templo do Sol de Aruanda
Date: June 2020.
Location: São Paulo, Brazil.

Image 10:
Description: Offering dishes to the Orishas Yemanja (white pudding and peaches; Ogun (baked yam with bamboo sticks and palm oil); Shango (fried okra with onions and palm oil); Oshossi (corn and coconut slices); Ibeji (fruits); and Yansa (pineapples and flowers).
Source: viewed at https://oferendadeorixa.com.br [accessed on 25th March 2024].

Other Works by the Author

The Supernatural Science
Theory and Magic

A must-read book that explores the hierarchies of spirits, mediumship, psychic abilities, witchcraft spells, reincarnation, and even ghosts through the lens of scientific thinking.

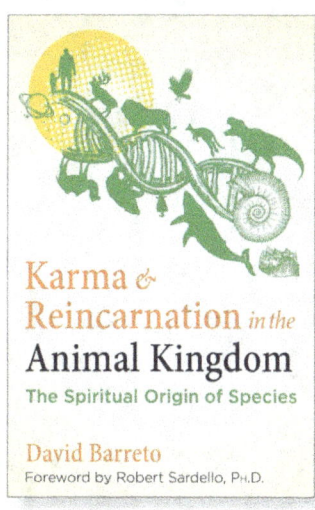

Karma and Reincarnation in the Animal Kingdom
The Spiritual Origin of Species

A comprehensive study of the spiritual genesis, reincarnation processes, and the physiology of animals' spiritual bodies.
This work also delves into the spiritual consequences of meat consumption and uncovers hidden truths surrounding religious slaughter.

The books are available at the best retailers and on
www.davidbarreto.net

www.ingramcontent.com/pod-product-compliance
Lightning Source LLC
Chambersburg PA
CBHW052017070526
44584CB00016B/1789